MIXING IT UP

Mixing It Up

Taking on the Media Bullies and Other Reflections

ISHMAEL REED

DA CAPO PRESS
A Member of the Perseus Books Group

A number of essays have appeared in a previous form under a different title. For more information, please see page 305.

Set in 11 point Minion by the Perseus Books Group

Library of Congress Cataloging-in-Publication Data

Reed, Ishmael, 1938–
    Mixing it up : taking on the media bullies and other reflections / Ishmael Reed. — 1st Da Capo Press ed.
        p.   cm.
    ISBN 978-1-56858-339-6 (alk. paper)
    1. United States—Race relations. 2. Racism—United States. 3. Mass media and race relations—United States. 4. African Americans in mass media. 5. African Americans—Press coverage. I. Title.
E184.A1R4265 2008
305.008973—dc22   2008007681

First Da Capo Press edition 2008
ISBN-13 978-1-568-58339-6

Published by Da Capo Press
A Member of the Perseus Books Group
www.dacapopress.com

Da Capo Press books are available at special discounts for bulk purchases in the United States by corporations, institutions, and other organizations. For more information, please contact the Special Markets Department at the Perseus Books Group, 2300 Chestnut Street, Suite 200, Philadelphia, PA 19103, or call (800) 810-4145, extension 5000, or e-mail special.markets@perseusbooks.com.

1 2 3 4 5 6 7 8 9

*In memory of Jerry Pope, educator
and Gary Webb, journalist*

Whoever controls the media,
the images, controls the culture.
—ALLEN GINSBERG

Contents

Introduction

Since the publication of *Another Day at the Front*, I've written a number of essays, some of which have been published in the *New York Times* (where my first op-ed appeared in 1973), *Playboy* (which my mother requested I not send her in the mail, claiming that at ninety and as an author of her own published book, *Black Girl from Tannery Flats*, she had enough attention from her neighbors), *Le Monde*, and *Green Magazine*, which is devoted to professional golf. A Spanish magazine called *Matador* also ran an essay included in this collection. Others appeared in the *San Francisco Chronicle* and TIME magazine. Some have been published in anthologies.

Essay collections allow me to gather my public reflections in one place, as well as respond to critics, some of whom, like John H. McWhorter, through the efforts of the Manhattan Institute, have access to millions of readers and listeners. I don't expect NPR, one of the many outlets available to the well-funded Manhattan Institute, to invite me on to rebut his trivialization of my views, but unlike the black underclass, which has taken a pounding from media bullies over the past thirty years, I have an opportunity to talk back, and now, for the first time, with the advent of bloggerspace, so do they.

A writer for the Anglo-Irish *National Review*, Mark Goldblatt, referred to me as "reliably silly." When I reached him and asked

him to elaborate, he wrote a letter claiming that in comparison to
me he was an insect. When he was assigned to review *Airing Dirty
Laundry* for the same Irish American magazine that was thrilled
by Charles Murray's *The Bell Curve*, he refused to do so he wrote,
as a favor to me. I wish he had presented my views. I could have
reminded some of those *National Review* Italian, Irish, and Jewish
American readers and contributors—the new Aryans—how they
started out. They didn't arrive here on *Carnival Cruise*. At one
time, the Anglos were hostile to Italian, Irish, and Jewish immigrants and considered them to be "genetically damaged."

Those West Coast Italian immigrants who were political prisoners during World War II and the Italian American citizens whose
movements were restricted during that time would be awed by the
current leader of white supremacy, Rudolph Giuliani, an Italian
American whose political philosophy is guided by the Manhattan
Institute. Some firefighters say that he wasn't the hero of 9/11 and
that the drastic reduction in New York crime began under Mayor
David Dinkens. But mainstream journalists, who are adverse to
homework and do the bidding of people like Rudolph Murdoch,
enabled him as they enabled George W. Bush. One hopeful sign in
2008 was the voters' rejection of Giuliani's using racial code words
as part of his campaign appeal. He constantly bragged of his crime
fighting and welfare reform accomplishments.

Goldblatt said the issues I was concerned with are no longer
relevant. Which issues do editors at *National Review* (*NR*) find interesting? Well, I saw John Derbyshire, a writer for *NR* who became a naturalized citizen, recently take questions on C-Span's
Washington Journal. When asked his opinion as to why African
Americans haven't progressed as far as whites economically, he
said that the answer might be found in genetics and biology. In-
credulous, I sent him an e-mail asking whether he truly believed
his comment. His answer came back, "Yes, though not likely *all*."
He made that statement without the host challenging him, which
calls into question Philip Roth's idea that if you say boo to blacks

you'll lose your job and your wife will perish from a heart attack. So from this answer, I assumed that scientific racism is the new issue of interest to the intellectual establishment. The issues I write about, particularly the continued obstacle to African American progress posed by American institutions and the 24/7 slandering of African Americans by the segregated media, have been placed on "the back burner," which is how one commentator put it. He said that issues of the LGBT (lesbian, gay, bisexual, and transgender) communities are, using his image, on the front burner. Even those who are hostile to blacks—Rudolph Giuliani, Gray Davis, Jerry Brown, and San Francisco Mayor Gavin Newsom (who, according to the San Francisco *Bay View* newspaper, wants San Francisco to become a "white city")—are favorable to gay rights.

One thing about *National Review*, I have to give them credit. They sent a member of their staff to toss off a flippant comment about my ideas. *Commentary* outsourced the job. One critic noted that "seventeen of the researchers whose work is referenced by the book *[The Bell Curve]* are also contributors to *Mankind Quarterly*, a magazine with a slant towards racial eugenics." Yet *Commentary* provided Charles Murray with space to answer his critics.

Commentary founder Norman Podhoretz was an adviser to the Giuliani campaign. In an article entitled "His Toughness Problem—and Ours," writer Ian Buruma summarizes the Podhoretz and neocon position on blacks. "The most articulate analysis of the obsession with power and violence was written by Podhoretz in 1963 in his famous essay 'My Negro Problem—and Ours.' Despite what the title might suggest, it is actually an argument against racism and in favor of miscegenation. When Podhoretz grew up in Brooklyn, the common assumption was that Jews were rich and Negroes were persecuted. This was not how things looked to Podhoretz on the playground of his local public school, where poor Jewish boys were regularly beaten up by Negroes: 'There is a fight, they win, and we retreat, half whimpering, half with bravado. My first experience of cowardice.'

"Negroes, he goes on, 'made one feel inadequate. But most important of all, they were *tough*, beautifully, enviably tough, not giving a damn for anyone or anything. . . . This is what I envied and feared in the Negro.'

"And then there were the effete snobs, 'the writers and intellectuals and artists who romanticize the Negroes, and pander to them,' and 'all the white liberals who permit the Negroes to blackmail them into adopting a double standard of moral judgment.'"

Podhoretz ally John McWhorter says that the only complaint remaining among African Americans is racial profiling, which he downplayed when assigned to do a hatchet job on me in *Commentary*, founded by a man whose son-in-law lied to Congress and belongs to a coterie of intellectuals who persuaded the president to invade Iraq, perhaps the biggest foreign policy debacle in history; he recently advocated the bombing of Iran. Ralph Ellison was right when he accused *Commentary* of advocating segregation. White supremacy, too. McWhorter spent much of his *Commentary* time nitpicking at typos in my book, yet Jonathan Yardley of the *Washington Post* found such sloppy composition in one of McWhorter's books scolding people about their bad language that Yardley ended his review with advice to McWhorter: "Physician, heal thyself." Yardley criticized McWhorter's *Doing Our Own Thing: The Degradation of Language and Music and Why We Should, Like, Care.* "The issue," Yardley wrote, "as McWhorter sees it, is not, as it may reasonably appear, the difference between 'bad' grammar and 'proper' grammar, which is just as well since McWhorter's own prose often takes a decidedly ungrammatical turn. He obviously is a very smart guy, but a lot of the time he writes like a dumb one. Over and over again he begins sentences and/or paragraphs with 'and' mostly in usages where 'and' is unnecessary and unjustified: 'And for that reason,' 'and it's true that.' He has an exceedingly dim understanding of the singular and plural: 'the student . . . has a three-by-five card in their hand,' 'the person would hardly find themselves,' 'the young person who tries their hand,' 'nuances of vocabulary is one thing.' Sometimes he commits unforgettable howlers: 'she felt more linguistically corsetted than him,' 'in today's America, it would be quizzical.'"

"Sometimes you just have to pause and take a deep breath before trying to figure out what on earth he's trying to say: 'W.E.B. Du Bois dwelled casually in terms quite similar to Bernstein's, and often more nakedly judgmental.'"

McWhorter is the go-to star for those who believe the answer to why blacks haven't made more progress lies in their character and genes. Loads of cash are behind McWhorter, who works with the new ubermenschen. You know, the kind of people who were reluctant to introduce their mothers and dads to their college mates for fear of their parents lapsing into a brogue or Yiddish. Or trailing off into Ebonics. I asked Moshe Dann, an Israeli Zionist with whom I have been corresponding, his opinion of Jewish Americans like Abigail Thernstrom who hang out with those who advocate scientific racism. He answered tersely, "Racial theories are proposed by racists. I'm not one of them."

The Manhattan Institute has such access to the media that it has succeeded in influencing "the national dialogue about race," while hundreds of black scholars—intellectuals who have studied the issue over a lifetime and, in their scholarship, transcend the predictable fabrications about the issue from the right—seldom receive airtime.

When Gwen Ifill of *Washington Week in Review* and Eugene Washington of the *Washington Post* questioned Tim Russert of *Meet the Press* about his cooperation with Don Imus, Russert pulled a note and read from it. It was a quote from McWhorter opining that Don Imus's remark about women members of the Rutgers basketball team being "nappy headed hos" wasn't worthy of discussion. He constantly gets his facts wrong. He told a passive C-Span interviewer that the impact on African American labor in the face of immigration from Mexico was "negligible" and pointed to invisible "studies." A number of studies, including one from Harvard, conclude that cheap Mexican labor has had a devastating effect on both white and black labor.

When I called McWhorter "the black front man for the eugenics movement," the Manhattan Institute apparently felt it necessary to arrange a debate between him and me. During the debate, aired on Michael Eric Dyson's show in Philadelphia, he couldn't identify William Casey, former CIA head and the founder of the Manhattan Institute where McWhorter is a senior fellow, and claimed he didn't know that it harbors race science thinkers like Meyer Levin. The policies of the Manhattan Institute influenced Mayor Rudolph Giuliani and contributed to the ethnic cleansing of Harlem, an issue I address in "The Last Days of Black Harlem."

He also claimed that the Manhattan Institute had cut ties to Charles Murray. Not so. Media critic Norman Solomon wrote, "Shortly after *The Bell Curve* was published [in late 1994], the Institute sponsored a luncheon to honor Murray and the book, in which he proposes a genetic explanation for the 15-point difference in IQ between blacks and whites that is the basis for his dismissing affirmative action policies as futile."

Solomon went into detail about the institute's funders: "Along with ongoing subsidies from a number of large conservative foundations, the Manhattan Institute has gained funding from such corporate sources as the Chase Manhattan Bank, Citicorp, Time Warner, Procter & Gamble, and State Farm Insurance, as well as the Lilly Endowment and philanthropic arms of American Express, Bristol-Myers Squibb, CIGNA, and Merrill Lynch. Boosted by major firms, the Manhattan Institute budget reached $5 million a year by the early 1990s." Besides, the Manhattan Institute sponsored Charles Murray in a debate about black IQ on November 28, 2007, at the Harvard Club. Murray's coauthor, Richard Herrnstein, another Aryan, taught at Harvard.

Instead of his claim that I was jealous of McWhorter's having a slot on *All Things Considered*, a open invitation to write for *Commentary* and the *New Republic*, an unearned appearance on *Face the Nation* where he was reduced to gibberish by Marian Wright Edelman, he should congratulate me, an inner-city dweller living far from the media capital, for being able to position myself to debate a highly paid opinion salesman for an institute heavily funded by some Fortune 500 companies. I don't even live in the media center of Manhattan, but I'm able to enter into debates with media stars like John McWhorter from my humble inner-city dwelling in Oakland, California.

Finally, an exasperated McWhorter said that I, being "much older" than he, was upset because he supplies regular commentary on *All Things Considered.* (NPR fired Tavis Smiley and Ed Gordon but kept McWhorter. Of course, I had a commentary on *All Things Considered* during the Bush I administration but wasn't invited to do additional commentaries after I predicted that the Willie Horton campaign, masterminded by the late Lee Atwater, would backfire on both Atwater and Bush I.) He also became upset when I referred to his mother's criticism of his book *Losing the Race.* He said that she was mentally incapacitated and that I shouldn't have gone there, yet he is the one who publicized her disapproval.

Why didn't McWhorter study the history of the institute before he was lured away from his job at the University of California by Abigail Thernstrom, and why has he ignored "the tangle of pathologies" that exist in her ethnic group? Shouldn't Thernstrom and her husband, Stephen, who have profited from bashing the morals and aptitude of African Americans, reveal whether their daughter was a virgin when she married in her forties?

Author Norman Solomon discusses the institute's history in *The Manhattan Institute: Launch Pad for Conservative Authors* (1998): "The Manhattan Institute was founded in 1978 by William Casey [another Aryan, no doubt], who later became President Reagan's CIA director. Since then, the Institute's track record with authors has been notable. Funneling money from very conservative foundations, the Institute has sponsored many books by writers opposed to safety-net social programs and affirmative action. During the

1980s, the Institute's authors included George Gilder *(Wealth and Poverty)*, Linda Chavez *(Out of the Barrio)* and Charles Murray *(Losing Ground)*. Murray's *Losing Ground*—a denunciation of social programs for the poor—catapulted him to media stardom in 1984." The *Philadelphia Inquirer* (October 13, 1997) recalled that *Losing Ground* "provided much of the intellectual groundwork for welfare reform." As Murray wrote in the book's preface, the decision by Manhattan Institute officials to subsidize the book project was crucial: "Without them, the book would not have been written."

While some of the institute's fellows are Irish and Jewish Americans, who in a former time were considered genetically damaged, Robert Lederman (ARTISTpres@aol.com), a Jewish American, is among the institute's strongest critics. "You won't find swastikas or paintings of Hitler decorating the walls at the Manhattan Institute nor will its staff be seen wearing Nazi uniforms. Their stable of well paid academics, writers and intellectuals are masters of using politically correct terminology to advance and express racist ideas. They are often the most effective guest speakers on television programs and at university conferences on social issues. While the ideas they advance may superficially appear to be about improving quality of life, cutting government waste, improving education and perfecting police strategy the common thread is that every policy is aimed at targeting minorities, immigrants and the poor while benefiting the corporations and wealthy individuals with whom they are aligned and by whom they are funded.

"These ideas are very similar to those espoused by Adolf Hitler with one notable exception. There is no anti-Semitism involved. The despised groups in this contemporary NYC branch of Eugenics are African Americans and Latinos."

The new ubermenschen done gone uptown from their downtrodden digs in Brooklyn, and John wants to be uptown with them and he wants to get up there on the backs of people like me because as he put it, I don't get to do commentaries on *All Things Considered*. He even got to participate in CNN's town hall meeting about race, when CNN is one of the biggest perpetrators of racism. Their holding a town hall meeting about race and pretending to be a neutral observer is like the wolf trying to pass itself off as Little Red Riding Hood's authentic grandmother. They assigned one correspondent, Jeff Koinage, to Africa, where he got into trouble for reporting that people in Zimbabwe eat rats. When I pointed to Koinage's journalistic habits—he and some other journalists exaggerated the false reports of widespread looting and raping during the Katrina calamity—his African American colleague, Michel Martin, in a reply to me, defended him. But the African press, which is not beholden to white conservative bosses, quoted my early warnings about the guy. A former airline attendant, Koinage was fired from CNN allegedly after some embarrassing e-mails from him to a lover were blogged. CNN tries to boost its ratings by daily presenting black men as sexual predators and prowling around for black male celebrities involved in scandal to feed to a large part of their viewership, people who thrive on the downfall of famous black men. When O. J. was arrested for his actions at a Las Vegas hotel, there must have been rejoicing in CNN newsrooms, since the O. J. trial rescued the network and the president of CNN unleashed his group of snarling Barbie faces to ridicule the fallen athlete.

Carol Costello is one. Whether Isiah Thomas, the New York Knicks coach, inspired a December 16, 2006, brawl that took place between the New York Knicks and the Denver Nuggets is open to question, but Costello knew. There she was the next day wondering why Isiah wasn't blamed. The producers at CNN and MSNBC use white women to take down the brothers because the feminist movement has propagandized over the years that gender trumps race in oppression poker so they can make racist statements without criticism; in their minds, racism is a black male problem. Nothing like watching Lisa Bloom and other designated hitters vent their hatred as they take down Kobe, Tyson, O. J., and others. When Michael Vick was indicted for dog fighting, Kyra Phillips, another CNN anchor assigned to attack black men, asked whether his participation in such a heinous activity was cultural. Susan Roesgen showed great rudeness during an interview with Mayor Ray Nagin. Roesgen is a general assignment correspondent for CNN based in New Orleans who was made a star after she criticized Ray Nagin for calling New Orleans a "chocolate city," demonstrating to CNN producers that she had the mettle to be tough with black men. She would never assault a white male politician with the kind of rudeness she threw at Mayor Nagin. John McWhorter is right at home in the media atmosphere where ratings are raised from the berating of blacks.

Not satisfied with dumping on me in *Commentary* (whose neocon editors expected me to get into a print battle royal with their rookie for the entertainment of their liberal readership like the one they staged between Richard Wright and James Baldwin, Richard Wright and Ralph Ellison, etc.), the *City Journal*, the house organ of the Manhattan Institute, distorted my views. What did former labor secretary Raymond J. Donovan say when he was cleared after his name was dragged through the mud? Where do I and others who have been slammed by McWhorter go to get our reputations back? Well, I have my own outlets. A magazine. I publish books by authors that many other publishers would be afraid to touch. I can take care of myself, and now I'd like to see members of the underclass strike back by using their minds to respond to the far Reich's intelligentsia whose salacious, often nasty and sarcastic comments about their character have filled up thousands of column inches, phony television town hall meetings, forums, all designed to hurt and bully those whose opinions are smothered by a media that humiliates those who can't fight back.

Orlando Patterson told President Ford that unlike African Americans who are mired in "an atavistic cocoon," he came to the United States because he desired cosmopolitanism. Who is mired in an "atavistic cocoon"? Those who live in all-white towns or insist on a white power curriculum, driving some of the brightest Latino and black students from education, or the African American suburban homeowners who brave the wrath of suburban mobs to join Patterson's cosmopolitanism. Maybe Patterson has Bensonhurst or Howard Beach in mind as centers of cosmopolitanism. Why are West Indians like Orlando Patterson and those of West Indian ancestry like Juan Williams so hard on traditional African Americans? Yet Patterson uses his guest column in the *Times* to post a tourist ad for Jamaica, where one travel agency advises white Americans that they will find a place where things are "the way they use to be." Why doesn't the *Times* give some space to the great Trinidad-born writer Elizabeth Nunez, who credits the civil rights movement for the gains Caribbean Americans have made. Op-ed managers invite only a few African Americans like Patterson to weigh in on discussions involving race, op-ed writers with whom these editors are comfortable; they deprive their readership of access to a variety of opinions.

Would Patterson be teaching in Cambridge, where a black person is seldom seen on the street, the center of American cosmopolitanism no doubt, were it not for the civil rights movement and those enveloped in an "atavistic cocoon"? And his friend Nathan Glazer, who has made a living at bullying blacks: did the civil rights movement make it possible for him to live in neighborhoods that once had covenants restricting people of Glazer's background? Patterson and Glazer are bullies. Their kind gathered steam when Ronald Reagan came to office criticizing invisible welfare queens when he was one of the most inattentive presidents in history. One man said he spent a whole afternoon with Reagan and not once did the phone ring.

One of the tasks of this book is to challenge media bullies and encourage members of the underclass to do the same. If a high school and college dropout who spent years living in the projects can do it, so can they. But keep in mind that African Americans wouldn't be the first group to be assaulted by a media controlled by their enemies.

Randall L. Bytwerk's book, *Julius Streicher: Nazi Editor of the Notorious Anti-Semitic Der Stürmer*, includes the following remarkable passage: "Ironically, many early *Stürmer* readers seem to have been Jewish. After the war Streicher claimed Jews had given him valuable financial support by purchasing the paper." His statement is supported by an advertising circular from a Jewish newspaper in Nuremberg around 1925: "It is of great concern to the Licht Verlag that the Stürmer is very frequently read even in Jewish circles."

I know how those Jews felt. Each day I read newspapers and watch television shows that depict African Americans the same way *Der Stürmer* characterized hated minorities in Germany. But you have to get your news from somewhere. I know some will object to this comparison. Although multinationals may have a patent on the genes of some island natives, no one, as far as I know, has a patent on history. History has yet to be auctioned on eBay. Complaints from African Americans about the refusal of the American media to view blacks with as much variety as they do whites have been made for over one hundred years. In Charles Chesnutt's novels, *The Marrow of Tradition* and *The Colonel's Dream*, the villains are newspapermen. Inflammatory coverage by one leads to a lynching and the other, a race riot. Very little has changed.

Bytwerk reports that one of *Der Stürmer's* correspondents was Jewish. We're also familiar with that arrangement: African Americans cooperating with institutions that defame blacks.

Look at the kind of roles Hollywood has assigned to black actors from *Birth of a Nation* until now. Contemporary white script writers for Hollywood and television have created sinister images of black men that arguably surpass those of D. W. Griffith's. A neoliberal movie like *Crash*, with a pathological white cop as the hero, is much more subtle in its racist underpinnings than *Birth of a Nation*. Blacks aren't the only ones who give ammunition to their enemies. Richard Goldstein writes about "attack queers," homophobic homosexuals who design homophobic initiatives on behalf of the Republican party. There are blacks who work for news outfits which view the degrading of African Americans as a marketing strategy. I'm sure these black opinion makers and syndicated columnists hold their noses as they submit copy to or serve as anchors and reporters for a media whose coverage of blacks is aimed at a market that enjoys viewing blacks as less than cerebral beings. That uses the scandals associated with individual black celebrities as a way of humiliating the general population of blacks. That sees improving the status of whites while lowering that of blacks as a way to woo advertisers and audiences.

That's why it's going to be O. J. and Michael Jackson forever and that's why some blacks applauded when O. J.'s acquittal in the criminal trial was announced: many whites saw them and O. J. as being interchangeable and so his acquittal was theirs. Those who don't share or even seek to understand the experience of blacks dismiss such displays as exercises in racial chauvinism, when black Hispanics and Asians as a rule have little trouble with living alongside those who are different from them; statistics show that it is whites who prefer living among themselves. Some estimates have it at 83 percent. Orlando Patterson's cosmopolitans. Who be the ethnic chauvinists? Who are the chauvinists?

As I write this, it's Michael Vick and Barry Bonds who are being lynched in the media's public square as an example and warning to the rest of us. Uninterrupted coverage about Michael Vick and his dogs is meant to embarrass blacks and entertain whites. Some enterprising merchant even came up with a dog chew product made in the image of Michael Vick, a product I would nominate for the Jim Crow Museum at Ferris State University. I don't wish any harm on animals, but during the period that the talking heads were expressing "outrage" about the treatment of pit bulls, the threat made by President Bush to veto legislation that would extend health insurance to children was largely neglected. Where is the outrage from CNN's Kyra Phillips, who was outraged by Michael Vick and Hedi Collins, who was "mad" at Marion Jones, at Governor Arnold Schwarzenegger? A *San Francisco Chronicle* photo shows the governor with his comic book grin lumbering into the state Capitol to veto a bill that would appropriate $55 million to house the mentally ill, while giving his yacht-owning friends a $55 million write-off for yacht ownership. Do the talking heads Phillips and Collins care more about pit bulls than children? Why aren't they upset with President Bush, who vetoed a bill that would have extended health insurance coverage to millions of children?

Maybe this is why many blacks refused to abide the media stampede that found Clarence Thomas, O. J. Simpson, Mike Tyson, Kobe Bryant, and Michael Vick guilty before they had their day in court. With a history full of examples of lynching, African Americans are reluctant to endorse trial by television. In *Lynching for Profit* (1927), the great American satirist George S. Schulyer foresaw a day when the virtual lynching of black men would become a big business.

Why would anyone object to my characterization of kangaroo court television as engaging in media lynching? It was Mark Geragos who described the media pundits who judge defendants guilty before court arguments begin as "cheerleaders for the prosecution." O. J. Simpson was held liable by an all-white civil jury. According to the late Johnnie Cochran, 60 percent of jury members believed the ex-football star was guilty before they were chosen. One tearful white juror said she voted to hold Simpson liable for the deaths of two people because Denise Brown resembled Nicole Simpson. Why is it a surprise that some blacks and whites found such a jury composition unsettling? Moreover, the plaintiffs' lawyers challenged every prospective black juror. I'm sorry, but blacks have had a difficult history with all-white juries. All-white juries rank with bloodhounds and the Confederate flag in African American history.

I was also deemed odd for presenting an unpopular viewpoint about Mike Tyson's conviction. After the trial, some of the jurors said that they would have voted for an acquittal had they known Washington and her lawyer were after money, a motive that had been concealed from them. Writer Richard Kostelanetz also had some questions about Tyson's accuser in a trial where the prosecutor chose the judge, a feminist. Commenting on feminist Barbara Kopple's two-hour documentary on Tyson, he wrote, "While the Kopple film was even-handed in some respects, it white-washed Ms. Washington, for instance featuring interviews with her Caucasian high school classmates saying, among other flatteries, that Miss Black Rhode Island wanted to attend Brown University (my alma mater, fool that she be) without revealing that she matriculated instead at Providence College, by common consent a less striking choice. The film did not reveal that Ms. Washington waited twenty-four hours before reporting the 'crime.' It did not deal with the question, obvious to most, of her previous sexual experience or the possibility, since suggested, of a similar earlier ex-post-facto rape charge. An avowed feminist, Ms. Kopple apparently believes that women are allowed fibs not available to men. *People* magazine alleged that she lied about her age, her education, and the identity of her child's father, all in a few dozen words." After Tyson's imprisonment it was revealed that Desiree Washington had alleged that a man named Wayne Walker raped her in 1989 and that her family had withheld discussions they had with attorneys about book and movie rights about her story. I'm also not the only one who believes that Clarence Thomas was subjected to a media lynching. Even Nina Totenberg, *The Bell Curve* enthusiast and part of a group that runs NPR, the person who outed Anita Hill as the source of a disparaging report about Clarence Thomas, said she didn't know whether to believe Thomas or Hill. For the Thomas hearing, NBC hired feminist last stander Catherine MacKinnon as the prosecutor, a commentator who like Kopple and Hill believes that women don't lie. For her part, Anita Hill also exhibited the kind of double standard accorded white and black men by feminists. She, who showcased Clarence Thomas's genitals for the world to gawk at, told a talk show interviewer that the "explicit details" of Clinton's relationship with Monica Lewinsky should not be revealed.

Recently a writer for the *African American Review*, edited by a black feminist who admitted to me that she doesn't read what is printed in her magazine, accused me of relying on facts. Well, you can't have it both ways. Accuse black intellectuals of resorting to rhetoric and then criticize them for relying on facts. Maybe I'm not "paranoid," as her queer studies reviewer and Marxist Andrew Strombeck suggested; it could be that I pay more attention to trials involving black men because those whom the media refer to as "the general public" see them and me as the same. Also, unlike members of the black punditry elite, I have the freedom to be eccentric, to say things that others are prevented from saying or wouldn't dare say. While one local black journalist was fired for wearing cornrows, I have the liberty to wear any hairstyle I desire (except when I visit my mother in Buffalo). Andrew Strombeck said that a character in my novel *Reckless Eyeballing*, a powerful white feminist who promotes black male hating cultural products, was based on my "paranoia."

Toni Morrison in an interview with Cecil Brown in the *Massachusetts Review* and Michele Wallace in the *Village Voice* have also written about the power of an influential white feminist over trends in black literature. How long do you think Andrew Strombeck, the author of the article "The Conspiracy of Masculinity in Ishmael Reed" would last in academia were he to call Morrison and Wallace "paranoid?" What kind of reception would he receive at a women's studies conference were he to read a paper calling Morrison and Wallace "paranoid"? In preparation for a play I've written entitled *Body Parts*, I researched the attitudes toward African Americans held by the psychiatric profession (a pretty bad history). White psychiatrists often misdiagnose blacks as paranoid because they are ignorant of their everyday life experiences. So do white feminists have influence over how black men are represented in fiction? bell hooks says that white feminists told her that if she wanted to succeed, she had to write for them. She also said that they discourage any conversation about race, believing that white middle-class women, as Gloria Steinem has written, share the social predicament of blacks. White middle-class feminists took the late Shirley Chisholm's remark that she had more problems as a woman than as a black to mean that racism is a black male problem. Gloria Steinem and others abandoned Chisholm's presidential campaign to support the male candidate, leaving a tearful Chisholm betrayed. With such daffy thinking on the left, which increased when the white middle-class feminist movement gained influence, it's no wonder that tough-minded think tank wonks heavily financed by the corporations are able to expose the fragile foundation of their thought.

Even an excellent and decent journalist like the late Ed Bradley had to work for people who portrayed black Americans, especially males, in the manner that Julius Streicher portrayed members of his ethnic group in *Der Stürmer*. *Sixty Minutes* did Muhammad Ali and Michael Jordan all right, but black men are typically portrayed as sexual predators or criminals. Michael Berkowitz in his book *The Crime of My Very Existence: Nazism and the Myth of Jewish Criminality* demonstrates how the association in the Nazi media of Jewish men with crime created the atmosphere that led to the Holocaust. Perhaps the most notorious piece, narrated by Lesley Stahl, referred to a black as a "wild man," shades of Ota Benga, who was harassing passersby in the West 50s, New York. The man was suffering from mental illness.

On a *Sixty Minutes* broadcast, Stahl used a sledgehammer to flatten the black woman who alleged being raped by Duke University lacrosse players, introducing the woman's sexual and psychiatric history, even to the extent of identifying her medication. White and black feminists, who defended Kobe Bryant's accuser even when exposed by the *Los Angeles Times* as a liar, expressed no outrage. The white middle-class defendants in the lacrosse case were able to ruin the career of District Attorney Mike Nifong, the man who brought the case against them, prompting one talking head to say that prosecutorial misconduct is rare. What? Tucker Carlson, one of those who bait blacks for ratings, battered an unsuspecting Marc Morial, head of the Urban League, for the organization's plans to rehabilitate incarcerated black prisoners. Carlson attacked Morial for suggesting that the American criminal justice is racist. Morial seemed puzzled by this bizarre twisting of his remarks, because he never suggested that the criminal justice system is racist. Is it? (In a subsequent program, Carlson lied when he accused the NAACP of defending dog fighting.) Prosecutors lie all the time and even the Bush administration admits to the existence of racial profiling.

Police plant evidence as they probably did in the O. J. case, and black kids get arrested for acts that would be considered pranks if committed by white kids. Moreover, the police use traffic stops to ensnare blacks and Latinos disproportionately, a method for boosting the economies of rural communities by creating the need for more prisons. In this case, blacks and Hispanics become the fish that are harvested by a wide net. After Morial's appearance, I, thinking that Carlson would welcome some challenges to his rant against the Urban League president, sent him an e-mail about his view that the criminal justice system is absent of racism and other points he made during his staged berating of Morial. I wrote, "Richard Nixon saw affirmative action as a national security issue. That there should be qualified people around in case there was an emergency. Even Ben Wattenberg, who says that white women aren't reproducing fast enough, congratulated black young army people for being able to deflect Scud missiles. And Gen. Powell received affirmative action, but nobody complains about affirmative action used when black bodies are on the line. Most recipients of affirmative action are white women, some kind of 'racial preference program,' right?

"Even the Bush administration admits there is racism in the criminal justice system. They issued a report about the existence of racial profiling. According to Senator Herb Kohl, black teens are five times as likely to be arrested for committing the same crimes as white kids. The Sentencing Project, which you can google, details racial disparities in the justice system. Of course, everyone condemns violent crime, but most blacks are in jail for nonviolent crimes—drugs. There exist harsher sentences for crack cocaine crimes than for white powder, which is what whites do, according to myth. Most of those who do crack are white; they just don't get sentenced for it. Tucker, I know that part of your ratings appeal is your being tough on blacks, so hard to do, right, but why don't you do your homework? Better still, broadcast your program from an apartment in the ghetto for a few months. I actually live in one in Oakland. It might challenge some of your prejudices (making judgments without the facts) about what goes on here. Ishmael Reed"

Unlike John Derbyshire, Andrew Sullivan, and Rich Lowry, whom I have challenged in the past, Carlson, a smarty-pants demagogue and media bully, didn't respond to my e-mail. One of my white critics has labeled me a "crank" for writing letters that challenge media misstatements, but until blacks develop organizations like the Anti-Defamation League and the American Jewish Congress, which keep a lookout on how Jews are portrayed, and until the newsrooms "look like America," and until there exists a core of independent black syndicated columnists, not just parrots, letters are all that we have.

Carlson and other talking heads rallied around the lacrosse defendants, who, of course, acted like angels during their encounter with the black strippers. They cast the district attorney Mike Nifong as the lone aberrant prosecutor in a criminal justice system in which, according to another talking head, a white woman, 99 percent of prosecutors are fair. Of his study of 124 exonerations of death row inmates in America from 1973 to 2007, Richard Moran, writing in the *New York Times* (August 2, 2007), said that "about two-thirds of their so-called wrongful convictions resulted not from good-faith mistakes or errors but from intentional, willful, malicious prosecutions by criminal justice personnel." Ninety-nine percent of prosecutors are fair? The *Chicago Tribune* (January 10–14, 1999) ran a series of scathing articles exposing the role of prosecutors in contributing to the number of wrongful convictions in the

United States in general, but especially in Illinois. On December 4, 2007, the *San Francisco Chronicle* published the results of a study conducted by the Justice Policy Institute, which concluded that 97 percent of large-population counties have racial disparities between the number of black people and white people sent to prison on drug convictions. The Washington, D.C., think tank said that "whites and African Americans use illicit drugs at similar rates. But black people account for more than 50 percent of sentenced drug offenders, though they make up only 13 percent of the nation's population."

The CBS executives who attended Bradley's funeral were sobbing and joining a funeral procession led by a jazz band, and waving white handkerchiefs. But if they really wanted to honor Bradley's memory, they wouldn't end their exposure of one prosecutor in the lacrosse case, which involved clean-cut, privileged middle-class white kids who acted with the utmost decorum on the night of their encounter with two black strippers. They would conduct an investigation of prosecutorial misconduct nationwide and how it affects the incarceration rates among poor people, and they would show blacks in as much a variety of roles as whites. Blacks do more than play basketball, box, sing, and sell crack and rape people. It took a controversy about Don Imus to introduce the white public to the Rutgers basketball team, which included black women with straight A averages. It took a massacre at Virginia Tech to introduce the white public to Ryan Clark, a black murder victim who had several majors and a 4.0 GPA. The white network commentators seemed shocked by such young African Americans. That's because the media ignore these kids in favor of providing entertainment to their white consumers by presenting black kids in a negative light. Why don't you condemn rap music? Imus enablers asked their black guests. It was the white media that selected the rappers to represent African American young people. (The black columnists at the *Daily News* and the *New York Times* who condemn hip-hop are at odds with the newspapers' sales departments, which cater to a younger demographic by publishing lengthy features about hip-hop, no matter how mediocre the artist.) Why don't you condemn Jesse Jackson and Al Sharpton? Nobody would ever have heard of the two were it not for the white media. Jesse Jackson rose to prominence after he appeared on the cover of *Time*. Blacks lack the power in the old media to make any aspect of black life become mainstream.

Writing in the *St. Petersburg Times* (December 11, 2006), Eric Deggans said, "It remains a sad irony that Bradley, widely known as a quiet mentor to black journalists across the country, never saw more than a few minorities rise into premier positions in his own newsroom." It was CBS that launched a *Survivor* show in which people of different ethnicities were pitted against one another, a glimpse at how the networks make money, pitting group against group and providing a one-sided view of black life and ignoring the achievements of blacks.

The formula for sending the shuttle into space and returning it was devised by a black woman. Two of the leading astronomers in observatories in Philadelphia and New York are black men. California has an African American poet laureate, Al Young, who has been just about ignored by the local papers, which attach black male faces to crime reports every day. The media almost seem to hide cerebral blacks. So that their white readership won't get their feelings hurt?

Even the most liberal of African Americans and Hispanics who are chosen by white media conservatives must call out their ethnic group from time to time, a tendency I address in "The Colored Mind Doubles." They can take blacks and Hispanics to the woodshed, but their owners deny them the opportunity to address "the tangle of pathologies" that exist in the white community as I do in "Showing White Students Some Love." After my essay "The Colored Mind Doubles," about how the views of some members of the pundit elite are no different from their conservative owners, one black journalist said I was trying to deprive him of his ability to criticize black thugs. Richard Prince reported, "Columnist Barry Saunders, writing in the *News & Observer* in Raleigh, N.C., said 'As much as I love Reed, I'd like to ask him if it's possible to criticize other blacks out of love or a genuine feeling that some of us deserve to be taken to the woodshed, that some of our injuries are indeed self-inflicted. When black writers criticize poor parenting among blacks or the glorification of pimps, thugs and drug dealers, are we all, as he contended, merely trying to 'maintain credibility with (our) employers'? "Naw, homes."

"All journalists have a right, even an obligation, to confront issues in all communities, to focus attention on them and to demand or offer solutions." It doesn't occur to Saunders that his editors would be less enthusiastic were he to criticize brown, red, white, and yellow thugs. Though some conservatives like *Times* education writer Samuel Freedman and Fox News political commentator Juan Williams view Asian Americans, in an attempt to embarrass blacks, as "the model minority," the Asian Gang Force considers Asian gangs a threat to national security. Even NBC, which is not friendly to blacks, issued a report which concluded that Asian gangs are more of a threat than the Crips and the Bloods. Even the *New York Times*, which typically portrays blacks as criminals and welfare recipients, in its New York Report and National Report sections, traced the origin of China white distribution, a potent form of heroin, to New York's Chinatown, which one Chinese American writer described as "crime infested." Juan Williams should come to California where the largest Asian American group, Filipino Americans, are saddled with a "tangle of pathologies," so much so that they are referred to with the n-word by some members of other Asian American groups. Another problem for which black and white pundits scold the so-called black underclass is teenage pregnancy. Yet the November 22, 2006, *New York Times* reported the findings of the National Center for Health Statistics, which showed a steep decline in such births. A later report (*New York Times*, December 6, 2007) showed that there were more illegitimate births among Hispanic women per thousand than blacks, yet one station commented on "racial disparities" in the report. Hispanics can be members of any race, or so the urban myth goes. Shouldn't the athletes, entertainers, and various designated Head Negroes In Charge and pundits who make such observations read facts that might challenge their stereotypes about black life?

Shouldn't they be more scrupulous about making comments that influence public policy and play into the hands of a neo-Nazi agenda lurking underneath the tricky rhetoric of the far Reich, like a rattlesnake in the picnic basket.

The report said, "But while such births [born to single mothers] have long been associated with teenage mothers, the number among 10- to 17-year-olds actually dropped last year—as did the group's overall birthrate, to the lowest level on record."

In July 2007 the National Center for Health Statistics came to a similar conclusion, having already issued a report in 2003 that indicated a sharp decline in black teenage births, the issue that the right and the black tough-lovers in Cambridge whip to death.

Why didn't Juan Williams mention these facts during his appearance on C-Span? Why don't people like Juan Williams congratulate the underclass when they do something right? The newspaper did not identify white single mothers as contributing to a rise of out-of-wedlock births among women in their twenties, because it is the policy of the media to hide the tangle of pathologies that occur in the white community or to minimize them, like two white conservative writers for the *Times*—men who criticize what they regard as the mores of the black community. Do you think that a publisher would award Williams a contract to write about the rising rate of out-of-wedlock births among whites? Think that Fox News would send him to interview Mary Cheney, the vice president's daughter; get her views on the subject. Think that Shelby Steele would sell books or be honored with a $200,000 award by the Bradley Foundation, the financer of "scientific racism," were he to write about white women as the main recipients of affirmative action? Black intellectual delivery persons for their white conservative bosses will also neglect to mention that the gap between white and black graduation rates are closing. (The Bradley Foundation also finances the Pacific Legal Foundation, which argued on behalf of plaintiffs in the recent Supreme Court case that struck down plans for school integration in Seattle and Louisville. These people aren't interested in a color-blind society; they want to prevent what they regard as the genetic contamination of white kids.)

Samuel Freedman, whose *Times* education column is meant to entertain whites by embarrassing blacks, spent one hot minute at McClymonds High School in Oakland and then returned to New York to issue a dismal report about the school. I was the commencement speaker at graduation the year before his hit-and-run attack. Due to the hard work of its principal and faculty, 70 percent of McClymonds students passed the state exit exam. There have been other successes that the media have ignored, too.

Though 95 percent of the op-eds I submit are published, one that was rejected dealt with Haki Madhubuti's Afrocentric charter schools, which have been so successful that the Chicago board of education has invited Madhubuti and his colleagues to improve the test scores of other schools. I guess when it comes to blacks, the media policy is that good news is no news. What those who support chauvinistic Eurocentric curriculum can't seem to answer is why some African and Afrocentric schools have succeeded where the public school system has failed. Even the *Wall Street Journal* acknowledges this achievement.* The students under the charge of Haki Madhubuti (founder of Third World Press) and his associates are among those who have succeeded. Madhubuti described his role with the schools as "running interference with the board of

---

*Joe Davidson, "Private Schools for Black Pupils Are Flourishing," *Wall Street Journal*, April 15, 1987.

education and providing as much 'cultural substance' to our schools as possible."

Madhubuti's four schools—the Institute of Positive Education (1969), New Concept School (1972), Betty Shabazz International Charter School (1998), and the DuSable Leadership Academy (2005)—expose a thousand students to a curriculum that he describes as essentially "African Centric." By the age of two and a half, he says, his students are exposed to African and African American culture in a way that is not "didactic."

"We teach both the students and the teachers to learn and how to love to learn." He credits his partner since 1974, Safisha Madhubuti, with the success of his enterprises. Safisha has a doctorate from the University of Chicago and two of the principals of his schools have earned doctorates as well.

I asked him why his schools have been so successful in educating black children, especially boys, while others have failed miserably. He said, "We are not afraid of our children. We love our children."

When black op-ed writers like Juan Williams take after welfare mothers and those Mayor Jerry Brown refers to as "the dysfunctional," I wonder if they do so in order to maintain relations with their employers and demonstrate their objectivity. Do they perform this task like the prisoner that Andrew Young described? Former Ambassador Young said that when he was imprisoned for his civil rights activities, the white guards ordered a black prisoner to beat him. The prisoner submitted to the demand but cried while beating Young.

Juan Williams was given a generous amount of time on C-Span to push some inaccuracies about the social conditions of various ethnic groups. At one point, he compared the successes of Hispanics with the failures of blacks. Here are some Hispanics he missed during a interview conducted by Reverend Michael Eric Dyson on C-Span. According to the U.S. Centers for Disease Control and Prevention in a June report, Hispanic teens have a higher rate of risky behavior than blacks and whites. The categories listed were attempted suicide, drug use, and neglecting to use a condom during sex. Hispanics also have a lower high school graduation rate than blacks. The dropout rate among Hispanics is twice that of blacks. No one summed up Williams's arguments against the civil rights movement better than Professor Ron Walters. "He is like many other critics who attack civil rights leaders for not emphasizing personal responsibility" and "exhibit their distance from the black community—never been in the black church or they don't listen really to the Rev. [Al] Sharpton," because those leaders "have been critical . . . of certain aspects of African American behavior," Walters said. The book could have been "written to support a right-wing establishment point of view or it's just sloppy. In the context of this book, I would raise a question of journalistic accuracy." Why doesn't Walters get as much airtime as Williams?

The two-part commentary of mine that appeared on the *CounterPunch* website also drew the resentment of some of the columnists I mentioned by name as well as their colleagues. They accused me of trying to censor them, but unlike Woodrow Wilson, Abraham Lincoln, Andrew Jackson, and John Adams, I've demonstrated in a lifetime of publishing that I am open to views opposed to the ones I hold. My essays call for a plethora of views that I know exist among black intellectuals. No one has challenged my conclusion that there are no black syndicated columnists who are as left as black syndicated columnists are right, middle, or conservative. In fact, a study by FAIR shows that black opinion representatives in the media tilt toward the right. People who are unknown among blacks receive more time than black elected officials because they fit the opinions of a media that was thrilled by Charles Murray's *The Bell Curve*, which used Nazi science to claim that blacks have a lower IQ than whites.

One of the bitter pills blacks have to swallow is that David Brooks, Andrew Sullivan, and Charles Murray believe they are brighter than blacks. The tests don't identify a genius like Huey Newton, who scored 79 on a high school IQ test yet became one of the most influential American intellectuals of the twentieth century. Since Charles Murray's southern Scotch Irish countrymen have been accused of interbreeding by generations of comedians, does he plan to do an IQ study of this group? Or has he broken away from his less fortunate underclass relatives, the kind of people you see on Jerry Springer's show. Has he broken away as upwardly mobile Italian Americans broke away from the Sicilian underclass to whom they imputed "a culture of poverty," according to American Book Award winner Thomas J. Ferraro author of *Feeling Italian: The Art of Ethnicity in America*, or the way German Jews disowned Russian Jews. In his book *World of Our Fathers* Irving Howe wrote about how the uptown German Jews regarded newly arriving Jewish immigrants. "An uptown weekly, the *Jewish Messenger*, announced that the new immigrants 'must be Americanized in spite of themselves, in the mode prescribed by their friends and benefactors.'"

The *Messenger* found these plebian Jews slovenly in dress, loud in manners, and vulgar in discourse, which sounds very much like complaints leveled against the black underclass by the black academic punditry and by athletes and entertainers like Bill Cosby and Charles Barkley. (Bill Cosby can be excused because he and his spouse, Camille, have contributed millions of dollars to black institutions, a generosity that I mention in my essay "Black Philanthropy." The others, however, are blowing smoke and competing with each other to get television time. I hope that my friend Cosby acquaints himself with the facts.)

Unlike the other elites, this new black elite can't blend in with the "mainstream" population as successfully as the other ethnic strivers. Remove themselves from Orlando Patterson's "atavistic cocoon." They live in a society that judges people by primitive notions. The darker a person's complexion, the smaller his brain size or something like that. When I used to visit my late Park Avenue lawyer, the security people manning the desk would always direct me to the floor where deliveries were made. New biographies of

General Colin Powell and novelist Ralph Ellison reveal that even they, who had risen to the pinnacle of American success, were subject to indignities and slights. Ralph Ellison had to read that he was being retired by New York University in the press. Prior to that, he entered his suite at the university to find his furniture removed without notice. While teaching at Rutgers, he had to share his office with a graduate student. This was the reward he received for protecting the New York literary establishment from a rising generation of young black writers (except for a group of sycophants who took up so much of his time flattering him that he was unable to finish his second novel). This is a man who accused young writers of engaging in propaganda when the end of his novel is one long anti-Stalinist tirade. No wonder former Trotskyite Irving Howe and his friends Saul Bellow and Alfred Kazin awarded him the National Book Award. Before black queen maker Gloria Steinem, there was black king maker Irving Howe.

Given the admission in the Powell book that he was treated with disdain by the Bush administration, why would anyone object to Harry Belafonte's description of Powell as a house Negro, someone who resides in the Big House but can't sit down with the master's family for dinner. Always out of the loop. In his biography, *Soldier: The Life of Colin Powell*, Karen De Young states that when the Bush administration wanted to humiliate Powell, they assigned Condi Rice to carry out the task. Hillary Clinton was closer to the truth than she ever could have imagined when she called the Bush II White House a plantation.

If Powell and Ellison are treated in this way, you can imagine what black men go through. Finally, Powell's reputation was destroyed when he appeared before the United Nations to deliver a speech about Iraq's weapons of mass destruction. They didn't exist, and his rival, Vice President Dick "Five Deferments" Cheney, probably engineered this whole effort as a way of cutting this proud black man down to size. Powell was used.

Some black intellectuals like John McWhorter, Shelby Steele, and former affirmative action recipient Ward Connerly allow themselves to be used as pawns by race science organizations. They fit in with the neo-Nazi agenda by positing the backwardness of African Americans, but African Americans wouldn't be the first group in history to be subjected to collective punishment and humiliation by their adversaries. The Jews have been treated as such since Roman times. In the United States, white groups from northern Europe have achieved anonymity. And so after Timothy McVeigh, an Irish American, bombed the federal building in Oklahoma, Irish American males weren't subjected to racial profiling, while Italian Americans, a group from southern Europe, many of whom reside across the pond from Africa, are still stigmatized with the Mafia label. *Look* magazine went out of business after accusing the late mayor of San Francisco Joe Alioto of having Mafia ties. Alioto sued. His response was, how can I be with the Mafia, my family is from Florence. You can still ridicule Italian Americans in campaign ads, which was the case in a 2006 race for the New Jersey senate. It showed a man talking like a character from *The Sopranos*, assuring a man on the other end of the phone that the democratic candidate, Menendez, was good for the mob. Chris Matthews and Don Imus were correct when they attributed Harold Ford's loss in a U.S. Senate race to an ad signifying him as a threat to white women. The woman opponent of a newly elected black governor tried to do a Willie Horton on him. Writes blogger Skeptical Brotha, "Not satisfied with casting aspersions on Deval Patrick's character for defending a capital defendant on appeal, she has attempted to assassinate his character for defending a Hispanic defendant in a rape case involving—you guessed it, a white woman. In case the voters of the Commonwealth were too stupid to pick up on it in the last ad, they will not be safe if that negro becomes governor. Kerry sure is subtle. She's about as subtle as an AK–47.

"The subtext is crystal clear. The women of Massachusetts are in danger of being ravished by colored men if a strong white woman isn't elected Governor. We cannot let weak-minded Deval let rapists go free. The fact that Patrick paid for the post trial DNA test that proved his former client's guilt, or the all white lynch mob impaneled as a jury are left unexplored.

"Kerry Healey thinks the fear of black and brown crime is the wedge issue she can ride to the corner office on Beacon Hill. Poor Kerry, there are not enough trembling, weak-minded, scared of their own shadow suburbanites to make her dreams come true. On November 7th, all Kerry Healey will have are dashed hopes and a permanent scarlet R on her chest that means RACIST."

It didn't work in Massachusetts, and Deval was elected governor.

I've been in a disagreement with the writers of two products promoted by HBO television. All three are white—David Simon, Richard Price, and George Pelecanos. Their creations, *The Corner* and *The Wire*, present a tawdry, one-dimensional portrait of African Americans which recalls the stereotypes about minorities disseminated by the German media in the 1930s and 1940s: human garbage. David Simon, judging from a comment made by Amy Alexander, who worked with the writer at the *Baltimore Sun*, believes that he owns Ebonics, black speech, and black culture. She says that he got pushed out when another white reporter was assigned to cover the Baltimore ghetto. Yet Simon accuses me of opposing *The Wire* because it is written by a "white man," which is how he describes himself. Simon believes the black ghetto, a multibillion-dollar resource for books, movies, documentaries, and so on, is his territory, exclusively. I covered my dispute with Simon in my last book of essays, *Airing Dirty Laundry*. Since Simon has revived our dispute in the pages of *Jewish Week* in 2007, let me recap. When Simon went on tour in 1997, he was accompanied by a young black ghetto dweller. The purpose of his presence was to promote *The Corner*, a piece of black pathology merchandise meant to entertain white audiences. When he appeared on

Pacifica radio station KPFA-FM in Berkeley, I called Simon and accused him of exploiting the youngster. Later I compared it to P. T. Barnum's displaying Indians in his circus. Simon said that I was being "defensive," which is how white writers react when you accuse them of presenting a skewed vision of black life. Of course, some of them are members of ethnic groups whose "tangle of pathologies" are rarely mentioned by the press. Like the columnist for the *New York Times*, whose typical image of a black man is that of a criminal or welfare recipient, downplayed amphetamine use among rural whites, although it has led to the abandonment of thousands of white children. (But unlike black children who live in "pathological" situations, the faces of the white children who were shown on the front page of the *Times* were concealed. CNN reached one of its low points during the last week in January when it showed the face of a nine-year-old black kid who had been placed under house arrest for "conning his way onto two airlines." Later in the same hour, they showed a white teenager pummeling a classmate. Her face was concealed. In my opinion, the only difference between Jon Klein of CNN and Julius Streicher of *Der Stürmer* is that Streicher was hanged at Nuremburg.)

Later Simon appeared with the young black man on Amy Goodman's show. He had some laughs over the young man's lifestyle, which included affairs with more than one woman, in a country where all white men are monogamous or celibate.

A few months after my call-in, I got a call from the *New York Times*. The reporter said Simon had told her I opposed his writing a series about black life because he was a white man. I told her I wasn't against a white writer writing about black life. The problem with Simon's version of black life was that it was riddled with clichés. Later I heard his cowriter, George Pelecanos, being interviewed by Richard Lewinsky on KPFA radio. Pelecanos promoted the same stereotypes about black life heard on right-wing radio. He believes that fathers deserting their children is a peculiarly black male phenomenon in a country where the divorce rate is about 50 percent and only a third of divorced men pay child support. After years of singling out the black family as father absent, even Sam Roberts, reviewing current census figures, had to write that married heterosexual couples are in the minority. Fatherless homes can't be blamed on black Americans, since they are only 12 percent of the population!

In 2004 in Aix-en-Provence, I appeared on a panel with Richard Price, a *Wire* writer. I enjoy some of Price's work, but somewhere along the line he decided to become a screenwriter focusing on black life. I'm annoyed with the results. Though Price says that he gets his material from "research forays into the ghetto," *Times* critic Virginia Heffernan called Price, Pelecanos, and Simon the "lords" of urban writing, presumably over black writers who actually lived there or, in the case of Chester Himes, engaged in a criminal life for a time. I'm sure Heffernan hasn't read Iceberg Slim and other Holloway House authors, including Odie Hawkins, Joe Nazel, D. Goines, Leo Guild, Charles Goodman, J. Neyland, R. Stewart, Cole Riley, G. Fogelson, and M. Ruuth. (One of the mysteries of American culture is why blacks who are responsible for creating American art forms cannot rise to royal status in these fields. There's a white king of rock and roll, a white king of jazz, a white king of hip-hop, and now three white lords of urban fiction. In the December issue of *Atlantic Monthly*, where *The Bell Curve* was excerpted, the one hundred most influential Americans in U.S. history were chosen. Elvis Presley was chosen for music, instead of Chuck Berry and James Brown from whom he "borrowed," and Bob Dylan was chosen over musicians like Duke Ellington, Miles Davis, Charlie Parker. Yet white cultural nationalists are always complaining about black cultural nationalism.)

Heffernan isn't the only Simon fan at the *Times*. A lengthy story that began on the front page of the *New York Times* (August 9, 2006) featured individuals who inspired the two Simon projects, Donnie Andrews, a former stickup man with a .44 Magnum who robbed drug dealers and was sentenced to life in prison for murdering one of them, and Fran Boyd, a heroin addict who shoplifted "to get from fix to fix." Andrews inspired the character Omar Little, a ruthless thug who stalks dealers on the HBO series *The Wire.* Boyd was the protagonist of *The Corner.* The two have been rehabilitated and were featured in the style section of the *Times* on August 19, getting married with a beaming Simon standing next to them. (I wonder what share of Simon's multimillion dollar ghetto profits went to those who inspired him?)

How did the *Times* treat heroin addiction epidemic among white Philadelphia suburbanites? In a two-hundred-word article that was consigned to the back pages:

> The typical person whose death is related to heroin in the Philadelphia area is likely to be white, employed and living in a middle-class suburb, the *Philadelphia Inquirer* reported today. Heroin-related deaths in the suburbs have skyrocketed since 1990.

I said that Price was associating with bad company—Pelecanos and Simon. He didn't seem to grasp the import of my remarks. The other members of the U.S. delegation, New Yorkers, defended him and one writer accused me of denying white writers the right to write about black life. She mentioned James Baldwin's short story "Sonny's Blues." While black writers have read a variety of white writers, white intellectuals and academics seem to have read only two or three black writers.

In fact I have published white writers on black life and I belong to an organization that has awarded prizes to white writers for works about black life. But unlike the trio who write for *The Wire,* these white writers' black characters have depth. They've resisted the temptation to paint African American men with a broad brush. Another member of the delegation, a top white male writer, scolded me for bringing up Price, Pelecanos, and Simon's products before this French audience. He said it was a local issue. There was a full-page ad for *The Wire* that day in the international edition of the *Herald Tribune* that was available at the conference site. These sleazy portraits of black life encircle the globe. Later I suggested that this writer (whom I respect enormously) watch the 2006 season opening episode of *The Wire*, all about how black kids are trained to sell drugs, even though former drug czar Joseph A. Califano says that most of those selling drugs are white. He says kids buy drugs from their friends. Yet the idea that the typical drug dealer is black, like the media myth that affirmative action is a black preference program and that whites don't do crack, is an idea that is difficult to dislodge. In an op-ed published in the *New York Times* (January 3, 2007), Mike Males, senior researcher at the Center on Juvenile and Criminal Justice wrote, "Few experts would have suspected that the biggest contributors to California's drug abuse, death and injury toll are educated, middle-aged women living in the Central Valley and rural areas, while the fastest-declining, lowest-risk populations are urban black and Latino teenagers. Yet the index found exactly that. These are the sorts of trends we need to understand if we are to design effective policies."

After watching that episode, Price's friend sent me an e-mail describing the writers as would-be white Negroes putting Amos and Andy lines into the mouths of blacks. But he justified Price's participation in the show as a way of paying some debts. HBO answered David Simon's black critics by exhibiting ignorant, grinning hip-hoppers at a party the network held for the opening episode of *The Wire*.

Simon's interview in *Jewish Week* indicated that my 1997 call was still on his mind in 2006. He said that his success had been mixed with unhappiness because of critics like Ishmael Reed. I wrote and told *Jewish Week* that Simon and writers like him might try to do a fresh series. Something new. Maybe about the family life of a suburban gun dealer who is flooding inner-city neighborhoods like mine with illegal weapons. Issues that are not included in blame-the-victim coverage of the underclass. Suburban gun dealers and absentee owners who rent out their property to crimi-

nal operations, placing at risk not only those who dwell in underclass neighborhoods but black middle-class neighborhoods as
well, are rarely mentioned in the media. When is HBO going to do
a series about these groups? When are they going to investigate the
forces behind Proposition 209, which ended affirmative action in
California, instead of relying on Tucker Carlson's take?

Ward Connerly's organization received money from the Pioneer Fund, which has had Nazi ties according to Stefan Kuhl,
author of *The Nazi Connection: Eugenics, American Racism, and
German National Socialism*. And it helped finance Charles Murray's research. Is it a coincidence that Juan Williams's views about
the black underclass (a euphemism for untermenschen) comport
with those of his boss at Fox News, Roger Ailes, the mastermind
behind the notorious Willie Horton ad? For example, did Williams
denounce Jesse Jackson, who has risked his life countless times on
behalf of the civil rights movement and received daily death
threats while campaigning for president, because Ailes's style man-
ual calls for Jackson to be ridiculed? Juan Williams is given enormous media exposure, but corrections to his Fox News talking
points appear in a newspaper with fewer outlets. Obviously those
who hammer the so-called underclass cannot debate their critics
on equal grounds.

Instead of giving their critics equal time, the media, which have
had a long-term love-in with Shelby Steele and Ward Connerly
(Rudolph Murdoch contributed cash to Proposition 209, which
ended affirmative action in California) and now John McWhorter,
protect them. But I have shown that with persistence, patience,
and tenacity, from time to time one's message can get through.

NBC anchorman Brian Wilson had to respond when I challenged his assertion at Salon.com that Clinton's black female lawyer, Cheryl Mills, who represented him during the impeachment
trial, was playing the race card. The ABC News ombudsman and
the CNN vice president also had to respond to my criticisms of
their regularly associating drug use with black faces, when the

drug problem in white America is staggering. Calling out the media titans sends a signal to young black men who feel beset by institutions that down them. Maybe this is why black male authors rarely appear on television networks or why the daily newspapers don't treat blacks as cerebral beings. When a mostly self-taught, degree-less intellectual from the projects like me can debate representatives of powerful interests like the Manhattan Institute, ABC News, NBC, CNN, and the creator of *The Wire*, what ideas does this put into the heads of the thousands of underclass intellectuals across the nation, who, like Malcolm X, use the prison library or, like Elijah Muhammad, attended school as far as the fourth grade, yet read over one hundred books at the Library of Congress. The fact that only 8 percent of poor people are able to attend college does not prevent them from arming themselves for intellectual combat. I am living proof that the lack of a degree doesn't deprive one of a rich intellectual life. When I wanted to learn Japanese, I hired a tutor, which cost me $25, cigarette money for many, one hour per week, for ten years. I studied Yoruba the same way.

I got tired of reading long, abstruse articles about jazz poetry and jazz prose, mostly bullshit, and I decided to play jazz. I began when I was sixty years old. First I studied with Susan Musarella at Berkley's Jazz School; I have continued my lessons with Mary Watkins. Both are superior jazz musicians who, if they were men, would have the reputations commensurate with their abilities. I have produced my first CD in which I perform jazz piano with Carla Blank on violin, David Murray on tenor, Roger Glenn on flute, and Chris Planas on flute (Ishmael Reed Quintet available at CD Baby.com). While my New York and Cambridge critics were eating French food and drinking whiskey at the Century and Harvard Clubs and generally enjoying a movable feast and having a joke about my "half-baked" ideas and inveighing hypocritically against my alleged misogynist ideas, I have been building institutions in the West and woodshedding, I have been building an aesthetic workhouse and have been involved in serving the community in which I live. People at the bottom of the ladder who take abuse from the elite and the self-satisfied can do the same and do it without a doctorate or even a bachelor's degree.

With the rise of cyberspace and phone cameras (which have been very effective in reporting cases of police brutality), maybe members of the underclass can now respond to one-sided attacks from think tanks and the media, some of which is delivered by hypocrites like the Viagra-happy drug addict Rush Limbaugh. (Is Juan Williams really in a position to criticize people about their personal behavior?) You can't depend on Juan Williams, Clarence Page, Cynthia Tucker, and Bob Herbert to do the job. Herbert is too busy outing the out-of-wedlock children of black congressman Kweisi Mfume. He participated in a forum sponsored by the *New York Times* about oppression of women worldwide. The forum consisted of three black women and Bob Herbert. The moderator was a white woman. The panel's makeup implied that the oppression of women, worldwide, is attributable to black male behavior, ignoring the 20 million or so women worldwide involved in sexual slavery, the underage children in Southeast Asia who are sexually exploited by Western tourists, the abuse of white women by white men in the United States (half of Native American rape victims are attacked by white men), the shelters full of Arab American women who've been brutalized by men, the killing of thousands of unwanted Chinese infant girls. While the *New York Times* called Ike Turner an "ogre" for his treatment of Tina Turner (Tina Turner said that the movie *What's Love Got to Do with It*, in which she is rescued from the evil clutches of Ike Turner by feminist Phil Spector, was "unfair" to Ike. The white men who own the media and comment on everybody's misogyny but their own said that Ike Turner's name had become synonymous with domestic abuse, while Paul McCartney, whose ex-wife claimed he beat her during their marriage, was honored by the queen. I wrote an e-mail to Herbert pointing this out. He never answered. You can't depend on the designated "head Negroes" from academia to do it. They're too busy trying to determine whether badly written nineteenth-century novels were authored by white or black women, or scrutinizing Richard Wright's manuscripts for evidence of misogyny, or engaged in a trace-your-genealogy-back-to-Africa scam. The effectiveness of new media engines like cyber-space as a weapon in the hands of those who have been on the receiving end of what amounts to a propaganda hit can be seen in the response of welfare mothers to an attack on them by Oprah Winfrey, Queen of Television. Oprah might be the choice of millions of women for president, but among some welfare mothers she is, in the words of Pat Gowens, editor of *Mother Warriors Voice*, someone who "reinforces the U.S. war on the poor and unequivocally supports white male supremacy." She writes about what happened to welfare mothers who were invited to appear on Oprah's show after threatening to picket the TV megastar:

> For 30 minutes before the show, Oprah's cheerleader worked the audience into a frenzy of hatred against moms on welfare. When the show started, Welfare Warriors member Linda, an Italian American mom with 3 children, was sandwiched between two women who attacked and pitied her. The African American mom on her right claimed to have overcome her 'sick dependence on welfare' and bragged about cheating on welfare and allegedly living like a queen. The white woman on her left was not a mom but had once received food stamps. Both women aggressively condemned Linda for receiving welfare. Throughout the show Oprah alternated between attacking Linda and allowing panel and audience members to attack her. Poor Linda had been prepared to discuss the economic realities of mother work, the failures of both the U.S. workforce and the child support system, and the Welfare Warriors' mission to create a Government Guaranteed Child Support program (Family Allowance) like those in Europe. But instead Linda was forced to defend her entire life, while Oprah repeatedly demanded, How long have you been on welfare?

Like a fool I stood in the audience with a mike (turned off) around my neck. Oprah only approached me after audience people insisted that I be allowed to speak. She stuck the mike in my face and I began to describe how welfare reform was endangering children and impoverishing families. After about thirty seconds, Oprah cut me off. "But this woman says she wants to work," she said, and turned away to a woman in the audience. (My one sentence was edited out of the show when it aired!)

Later we complained to Oprah and her producer about the false promises they had used to lure us onto the show. (We had engaged in extensive negotiations prior to agreeing to appear. We said yes only after they agreed to discuss welfare reform, not our personal lives.) The producer shoved an Oprah cup (our pay) into our hands and pushed us out the door, angrily denying their treachery.

The limousine ride home was sad and silent. No wining and dining this time—Oprah was done with us—just an empty limo. Linda was crying and said she felt like she had been raped. But the worst part came later.

By the time we arrived home, we had received calls from moms on both coasts warning us about the promos Oprah was using to advertise her show: "They call themselves welfare warriors and they refuse to work. See Oprah at 4:00."

In 1982 *The Nation* magazine, in one of two hit jobs on me (the other appeared in the *New York Post*) sponsored by feminist deep ender Elizabeth Pochoda, referred to "Ishmael Reed's literary army." Many of the writers we championed in those days—Asian, African, Hispanic, and Native Americans—have become Pulitzer Prize winners, National Book Award winners, MacArthur recipients, American Book Awards winners, and PEN Oakland winners and at least one recipient of a President's Medal for Literature. Consequently we can report to *The Nation*, where 98 percent of the books reviewed are still authored by white males, as are the majority of contributors, in this day and age, even though the editor is a "progressive feminist," that the army won.

Members of "Ishmael Reed's literary army," who were little known when the *Nation* article was written, sit on the boards of prestigious literary organizations as distinguished faculty members and are authors of works that have become part of the canon.

There is one area where African Americans still take a beating: in the media. Perhaps it is time for a new intellectual army? Black and Latino men and women need a media army of academy-trained as well as outside intellectuals, men and women who are on unemployment and welfare, as well as those who view their doctorates as an excuse for pulling what they call "rank" on us or viewing themselves as members of an exclusive "club." Men and women who are homeless as a result of a propaganda effort that led to curtailed housing subsidies. Using the time between getting their lives together, they can use the public library's Internet facilities, scan what the right-wing and mainstream newspapers and cable shows are saying about them, create blogs, write letters, call in to shows like the *Washington Journal,* where their enemies are given three hours at a time. We need project dwellers to form Internet cafés and chat rooms to take on think tanks, which, even though they have millions of dollars behind them, are staffed by intellectual cowards and bullies. We need an underclass media army to respond to the white and black elite columnists who are always on their case. An army that will fight back against media bullies. An army like those welfare mothers who used the Internet tool to mix it up with the Oprah machine. An army to take on Ku Klux feminists, since many blacks in academia and the pundit classes are too scared to do it.

A blogger who calls himself Spocko shows what just one informed individual can do to combat media bigotry. He was offended by what he regarded as hate speech emanating from San Francisco Bay Area ABC affiliate radio station KSFO. KSFO features right-wing talk show hosts who endorse torture and mock the tortured, call for the public hangings of *New York Times* editor Bill Keller and other journalists, and demand that callers mock Islam. They also mock their own advertisers, calling Chevrolet shitty and recommending that Sears Diehard battery be attached to an African American's testicles.

Spocko began sending letters to advertisers on KSFO, including AT&T, Bank of America, Visa, and MasterCard, pointing out the station's content and directing them to his blog to hear proof via his audio files.

"The Walt Disney Company sent a cease-and-desist letter to the blogger and media critic 'Spocko,' effectively closing down his website, Spocko's Brain, after the online muckraker instigated a letter-writing campaign that caused national advertisers including Visa and MasterCard to flee the Bay Area ABC-affiliate radio station KSFO," Tom Siebert reported on Media Post.

Disney support for racist projects is nothing new. The 1932 *Mickey Mouse Annual* is a collector's item that includes racial epithets. A fantastic piece of black history that reveals the racist attitudes of Walt Disney, this 1932 Mickey Mouse two-hundred-page annual was published in Great Britain by Dean with the consent of Walt Disney. Only a few copies got into circulation. It is a rare and racist example of early pie-eyed Mickey Mouse in full form. The word "nigger" is used several times. The opening poem entitled "A Black Outlook" features Mickey and Minnie pitted against "fierce niggers." Walt Disney was one of the original media bullies.

In the following chapters, I mix it up with the media bullies. Lewis Hyde, before a meeting of MacArthur Fellows, traced the history of idea ownership. At one time, ideas were owned by the Church and the Crown. Up until recently media ownership was in the hands of multinationals. With cyberspace, the ownership of knowledge belongs to the people. *Writin' Is Fightin'*!

Charles Chesnutt

C harles Chesnutt was born in Cleveland, Ohio, on June 20, 1858, and died there in 1932. He attended Howard School, a public school for black children built with Freedman's Bureau funds. He was forced to discontinue his studies when his father, Andrew Jackson Chesnutt, took up farming after his grocery business failed. The young Chesnutt was invited by Robert Harris, his mentor and Howard's principal, to take a pupil-teacher job so as to spare a bright student from farmwork. Later Chesnutt became Howard's principal.

Chesnutt's life spanned a number of crucial periods in American history, from the Civil War to Reconstruction, the Confederate restoration. They call it the southern redemption since Andrew Johnson gave clemency to former Confederate officers. The Hayes-Tilden Compromise of 1876 gave power to southern Democrats and former Confederates, and John Hope Franklin refers to former Confederates regaining their seats in Congress. Moreover, organizations like the Klan (ex-Confederate officers) terrorized blacks who wished to exercise the franchise. (Southern redemption is too polite; that's why I call it the Confederate restoration.) World War I gave way to the rise of Franklin Roosevelt and the New Deal. Rather than becoming a neutral observer, Chesnutt, following the lead of his father, who was an elected official, actively participated in the events of his time as community leader, essayist, and organizer.

In 1881, he became a leader in the Fayetteville, North Carolina, A.M.E. Zion Church, serving as choirmaster and organist. In 1901, he chaired the Committee on Colored Troops for the 35th National Encampment of the Grand Army of the Republic, and in 1905 he became a member of the Committee of Twelve, a group that advised Booker T. Washington. It was organized to promote "the advancement of the interests of the Negro race." In a letter to Washington, Chesnutt congratulated the group for its role in defeating Maryland's disenfranchisement laws.

In 1913 he persuaded the mayor of Cleveland, Newton Baker, to oppose a bill prohibiting interracial marriage. His advocacy might have been attributable to the white-skinned Chesnutts, like millions of African Americans, having European ancestors. Some have even referred to him as "a voluntary Negro," which, in the 1880s, was like entering a combat zone instead of seeking a deferment.

In 1914 he helped establish Playhouse Settlement in Cleveland, which later became one of the premier African American theaters, Karamu House. In 1922 Chesnutt signed a protest against the American occupation of Haiti and in 1923 Harvard University's attempt to exclude black students from its freshman dormitories and dining halls.

In addition to his activism, Charles Chesnutt became a major American writer of his period; had he been white, he would have been canonized long before now. He was a prolific writer, publishing between 1885 and 1931 sixty-one short stories, one biography, thirty-one speeches, articles, and essays, and three novels: *The House Behind the Cedars*, *The Marrow of Tradition*, and *The Colonel's Dream*. The publication of his short story "The Goophered Grapevine" in the *Atlantic Monthly* (1887) was considered a breakthrough for a black writer. The editors were not aware of his race and have published few black writers since 1887.

Though not receiving as much acclaim as his contemporary, Mark Twain, whose seventieth birthday party he attended at New

York's Delmonico's, Chesnutt did everything that was required of him to become a leading writer of his time. He studied the classics and attuned his ear to a variety of American speech patterns, which enabled him to write about a wide range of characters convincingly, whether they were black or white, northern or southern, rich, poor, or middle-class.

His work as a Wall Street reporter for Dow Jones & Company also accounts for the sophisticated discussions of the southern economy in *The Colonel's Dream*. And in 1887 he passed the Ohio bar at the top of his class and subsequently started a court stenography business, a career path that contributed to the technical discussion of the legal contracts covered in the book.

Armed with these tools, he challenged the prevailing attitudes of his time, writing in a period when Americans, both in the North and the South, were undergoing a reconciliation after one of the bloodiest wars in world history, and when some influential opinion makers were remembering with affection the plantation, an institution that some current politicians, cabinet members, and northern intellectuals *still* pine for.

The Colonel's Dream is set in the post–Civil War South represented by a town called Clarendon, the birthplace of Colonel French, a former Confederate officer who has returned to the town after making his fortune in the North. The landed aristocracy has been stripped of its power and finds itself at the mercies of a new class of businessmen: "The mayor . . . had sprung from the same class as Fetters, that of the aspiring poor whites, who, freed from the moral incubus of slavery, had by force of numbers and ambition secured political control of the State and relegated not only Negroes, but the old master class, to political obscurity."

Unscrupulous overseers, former indentured servants, and former slave traders like William Fetters, "a mortgage shark, labor contractor and political boss," are now in charge and treat their former bosses in a manner that would have been considered insolent in antebellum times. The colonel is a member of this fallen aristocracy and discovers that members of his class lack the clout they once possessed.

Throughout the novel, those who once held his kind in awe abuse him with ridicule and sarcasm. When the colonel seeks the release of Bud Johnson, the novel's "bad nigger" who resists being "sold" to Fetters, Turner, Fetter's agent, the colonel's inferior in a former time, insults the colonel with vindictive relish: "Fetters has got this county where he wants it, an' I'll bet dollars to bird shot he ain't goin' to let no coon-flavoured No'the'n interloper come down here an' mix up with arrangements, even if he did hail from this town way back yonder. This here nigger problem is a South'en problem, and outsiders might's well keep their han's off." One reviewer, writing in the *Courier-Journal* of Louisville (September 16, 1905), agreed with the speaker, saying that after the colonel returned to the North, he hoped that he would remain there. Another reviewer, writing in the *Globe and Commercial Advertiser* of New York (September 9, 1905), perhaps embarrassed by some of Chesnutt's white characters, suggested that he stick to writing about blacks, a standard that wasn't applied to white writers like Mark Twain. The reviewer said, "Mr. Chesnutt has been more successful when taking for his principal characters the people of his own race," advice that is still given to black writers who, in the mind of white reviewers, dare to wander off the literary plantation, and advice never given to white writers, even those authors of fake ghetto books.

Chesnutt maintained that the end of slavery was beneficial, not only for the African captives but for the ersatz aristocracy that prospered from their labor. Of the loyal ex-slave, Peter, who was given to the colonel when he was a child and passed on to Phillip, the colonel's son, after the colonel returned to the South, the narrator says, "How easy the conclusion that the slave's lot had been more fortunate! But no, Peter had been better free. There were plenty of poor white men, and no one had suggested slavery as an improvement of their condition. Had Peter remained a slave, then the colonel would have remained a master, which was only another form of slavery. The colonel had been emancipated by the same token that made Peter free. Peter had returned home poor and broken, not because he had been free, but because nature first, and society next, in distributing their gifts, had been niggardly with old Peter."

This is one of the milder observations in this book about the treatment of African Americans; Chesnutt's indictment of the South during the backlash on Reconstruction is restrained but merciless.

But instead of resorting to invective, Chestnutt allows those responsible for southern backwardness to hang themselves through their words and actions. For example, as a black doctor, Miller, in *The Marrow of Tradition*, makes his way through the riot-torn streets, he is stopped by a white man: "Sorry to have had to trouble you, doctuh, but them's the o'ders. It ain't men like you that we're after, but the vicious and criminal class of niggers."

The narrator continues: "Miller smiled bitterly as he urged his horse forward. He was quite well aware that the virtuous citizen who had stopped him had only a few weeks before finished a term in the penitentiary, to which he had been sentenced for stealing. Miller knew that he could have bought all the man owned for fifty dollars, and his soul for as much more."

This passage shows why some black writers have alienated white readers. They have a tendency to expose hypocrisy. Moreover, they explode popular myths and comforting superstitions. John O'Killens skewered the racist and antidemocratic aspects of the Greatest Generation that fought for democracy abroad yet segregated blacks at home in his novel *And Then We Heard the Thunder*. John A. Williams revealed a fascist plan to intern African American leaders in his masterwork, *The Man Who Cried I Am*. Amiri Baraka's indictment of the capitalist system in poetry, essays, and plays has made him a nonperson among establishment reviewers. Kristin Hunter Lattany paid the price for her devastating portrait of the condition of black academics at white universities in her novel *Breaking Away*. It received hostile reviews and was not promoted.

Charles Chesnutt could be the predecessor of O'Killens, Williams, Baraka, and Hunter Lattany. His portrait of white supremacists who thwarted the ambitions of black citizens could be withering. After Colonel French defies southern custom by integrating a burial vault, a white mob that has already lynched a black man makes its objections known by digging up the corpse of the loyal ex-slave, Uncle Peter.

Members of the new master race leave a note alongside the coffin that they have deposited on the colonel's porch. "Kurnell French; Take notis. Berry yore ole nigger sonewhar else. He can't stay in Oak Semitary. The majority of white people of this town, who dident tend yore nigger funarl, woant have him there. Niggers by there selves, white peepul by there selves, and them that lives in our town must bide by our rules. By order of Cumitty."

A depiction of illiterate whites by a black writer was not likely to garner sales, nor was his treatment of miscegenation, the rabble-rousing white media, police brutality, and economic injustice. White workers at the colonel's mill object to having a black supervisor and smart over blacks earning the same wages as whites. Moreover, Chesnutt suggests that slavery didn't end with the Emancipation Proclamation. One character, a fading, "broken-down" belle, Miss Laura Treadwell, says of the convict labor system, by which blacks, including a harmless old uncle, were arrested on trumped up charges and "sold" to white businessmen, "Does slavery still exist?"

Some of the issues with which Chesnutt's colonel grappled continue to nag the nation. They are the new pictures set in old frames. (Long before Richard Nixon's southern strategy, Chesnutt has a character predict a time when the Republican party would become a white man's party!) Racial profiling, employment discrimination, a racist criminal justice system, disenfranchisement of African Americans, and a media many times more powerful than Clarendon's newspaper *Anglo Saxon* (or the *Morning Chronicle* in *The Marrow of Tradition*, whose inflammatory copy causes a race riot) that continues to portray African Americans in an un-favorable light and stir hateful passions against them in order to boost ratings.

New York Times reporter Peter Applebome (on *Good Morning America*, May 10, 1999) argues that much of this country has turned to the South politically, culturally, and for old-time reli-gion. If southern values are sweeping the United States, why should it come as a surprise that the editorial policies of Ches-nutt's fictional southern newspapers have been borrowed by present-day media. The relationship between blacks and the media is further strained by the absence of African Americans in many newsrooms. A 2003 report from the Newspaper Association of America put the number at 10 percent. This leaves black read-ers to the mercies of a mostly white news force, many of whom embrace the same stereotypes of black Americans as the general population. Though drug addiction, unwed motherhood, bad parenting, undisciplined children, irresponsibility, illiteracy, and anti-intellectualism are national problems, they are often attrib-uted, by politicians and the media, to blacks exclusively. Whites complain about blacks depending on government handouts when the American white middle class may be the most heavily subsi-dized class in history. For example, while many blacks are denied home loans as a result of mortgage industry chicanery such as redlining, even when they have better credit ratings than whites, whites receive generous tax write-offs for payments they make on loan interest and property taxes. In one section, the narrator ob-serves "this [white] supremacy must be made permanent. Negroes must be taught that they need never look for any different state of things. New definitions were given to old words, new pictures set in old frames, new wine poured into old bottles."

How prophetic! Chesnutt foresaw a time when the enemies of blacks would spruce up their crude style by playing language games. For example, while in the old days the colonel might have been called a "nigger lover," today he would be called a "liberal."

An early assault on liberalism came from Tom Wolfe in *Mau Mauing the Flak Catchers*, in which he satirizes New York Jewish liberals for being too accommodating to blacks, in this case the Black Panthers. He followed this up with *The Bonfire Vanities*, in which he traces the downfall of Manhattan to a tendency among Jewish liberals to cater to black demands. His line has been followed in a number of neocon books, op-eds, and so on. It is obvious to me that "liberal" is a code word for those who are soft on blacks. Nigger lovers. Additionally, the convict labor industry, one of the main issues addressed by *The Colonel's Dream*, has become big business. In a story headlined "Incarceration Rates Fueling Economic Crisis" and subtitled "Suburban communities benefit from prison populations as money is drained from African American communities," published in the September 15–18 issue of *Black Enterprise*, Tamara E. Holmes quotes Justice Department figures for the year 2002.

"Midyear 2002, found that 12.9% of black males between the ages of 25 and 29 were incarcerated in 2002. While that number is staggering, it is even more disturbing when compared to other racial and ethnic groups. Among Hispanic males in the same age group, 4.3% were incarcerated in 2002. For white males in that age group, 1.6% served time in 2002."

Like the convict labor system of Chesnutt's novel, what Angela Davis refers to as the prison-industrial complex is one that depends on a high incarceration rate. California, for example, has the highest rate of incarceration in the United States. It is where the prison guard and corrections lobbies have great power due to their contributions to members of the state legislature and to Governor Gray Davis, who was recalled. Arnold Schwarzenegger, his successor, is supposed to be a tough guy, but even he found himself bowing to the contract demands of these unions. This came after local newspapers exposed the corruption in the corrections industry and the brutality dealt to inmates, who are mostly black and Latino.

Recent scandals in California prisons were cited in a report from an independent commission set up by the California state senate. Part of the report involved an investigation of the California state prison at Corcoran, which uncovered "staff and guard misconduct, violent cell extractions, medical neglect, inadequate diet and food tampering, preventable deaths, violations of health and safety regulations, lack of mental healthcare, lack of yard access, poor treatment of disabled prisoners, denial of due process, loss and destruction of personal and legal property, denial of access to legal property and resources, mail tampering."

In his article "The Prison Industry Goes Global," in *Yes* magazine, Stephen Nathan writes that "the privatization of the prison industry has created a situation where prison managers strive to earn profits for shareholders." This has led to abuses, including "riots, violence, the murder of prisoners and guards, sexual and physical abuse of prisoners by guards." Given these contemporary conditions, it becomes difficult to argue that the plight of black prisoners has improved since Chesnutt's time.

In *The Colonel's Dream*, the town's law enforcers, Fetter's henchmen, ensnare blacks into a cheap labor pool by using vagrancy laws. Historian Leon F. Litwack describes this system in *Trouble in Mind:* "Replacing the discipline of slavery, vagrancy laws, contract laws, and a variety of local ordinances reinforced the power of employers to procure, maintain, and exploit black workers." Only when prisoner abuse occurs abroad, as in the case of Abu Ghraib prison, where Iraqi prisoners were tortured and abused sexually, does the public seem to become repulsed by the actions of sadistic prison personnel. Similar abuse of black prisoners, even before Chesnutt's time, has been greeted with silence. Moreover, while the "down low" activities of black males are seen as contributing to the AIDS epidemic among blacks (a claim that writer Ta-Nehisi Coates attributes to shaky evidence yet is embraced by the media), the role of American prisons, where sadistic guards use rape to punish black prisoners who "get out of line," is rarely mentioned. In a CBS report, "[Mike] Wallace found that California prison guards were mistreating inmates in another way. They were allowing inmates to be raped by other inmates, as retaliation against those who had gotten out of line."

The details of this state-sanctioned rape became clearer during a special hearing on prison violence last summer in the California state senate. "The Department of Corrections was willing to allow at Corcoran State Prison those conditions to exist in which a prison inmate was encouraged knowingly to commit rape against another inmate. And get away with it," said state senator Quentin Kopp at the hearings.

One story involves Wayne Robertson, a convicted murderer and known sexual predator nicknamed "Booty Bandit." Investigators say he raped at least fifteen inmates, many of whom were thrown in his cell as a form of punishment.

Eddie Dillard was one of those inmates. He's out of prison now and has started a family, but back in 1993, Dillard was serving time for assault with a deadly weapon. When he got into a fight with a female officer, the guards at Corcoran State Prison locked Dillard up in a cell with Robertson.

Over a period of three days, Robertson raped Dillard twice and tried to force him into oral sex. "How can you expect for a person to be subjected to that type of cruelty and then expect them to come back out, back into society, and be productive after being scarred like that?" Dillard asks.

The reality of Dillard's nightmarish experience was corroborated by the testimony of former corrections officer Roscoe Poindexter, nicknamed the "Bonecrusher." Two years after he was forced to resign for excessive violence at Corcoran, a repentant Poindexter has gone public, admitting how cruel he had become. "I became insensitive, callous, uncaring, numb," says Poindexter. "Maybe I was in denial or maybe I didn't really care."

"After the incident happened, all of us sitting down and writing reports together, so we could be consistent. I was very much part of that," Poindexter remembers. "If I had to do it back over again, I would have separated the inmates."

Dillard is currently suing several of the correctional staff members, some of whom have been indicted by the California attorney general. But Dillard is not suing Roscoe Poindexter, whom he has forgiven for the things he did. Moreover, the privatization of the prison system has the same result as the old corrupt convict labor system, the major theme of Chesnutt's novel; it places private interests above those of the general public and leads to the exploitation of cheap labor.

Disenfranchisement remains a problem for African Americans almost one hundred years after the publication of *The Colonel's Dream*. The U.S. Civil Rights Commission reported that thousands of African Americans in Florida were denied the right to vote in the 2000 presidential election; Reverend Jesse Jackson and Senator John Kerry estimate that 1 million African Americans were denied the vote in 2000. Besides the traditional tactics of using vague balloting procedures, others were employed, including changing the place of balloting without notifying voters, setting up roadblocks in order to prevent black voters from gaining access to voting stations, requiring black voters to produce more identification than white voters, and, in Florida, denying the vote to blacks on the grounds that they were guilty of felonies, when they weren't. Molly Ivins wrote that "8,000 of the blacklisted voters had been convicted of misdemeanors, not felonies." Even more ominous is a report from *New York Times* columnist Bob Herbert that Florida's state police are seeking to intimidate black voters, even after the scandal of the 2002 election. He concludes that this effort has "the vile smell of voter suppression."

While white rural communities are making money by harvesting black prisoners the way fishermen harvest tuna, often on the basis of capricious arrests and prosecutorial and police misconduct, the economic health of African Americans has become dismal. Fifty percent of New York black men are unemployed. (Though think

tank operatives boast an expanding black middle class, their status
is always provisional. They're the first ones to suffer when recession
hits and their enemies sometimes use the rule of public domain in
order to pave over their progress in the name of regentrification by
paying less for their homes than the market price. The black middle
class success story in *The Colonel's Dream*, a barber, is reduced to
the status of a porter as a result of white mob violence.)

Employment discrimination is as prevalent today as it was in
Chesnutt's time. In the novel, black and white workers are pitted
against each other in a competition for jobs. Today, black men
must compete with immigrants, both illegal and otherwise, and
the millions of women who've entered the labor market. No matter how menial the job. I saw a pigtailed blonde shining shoes in
the Atlanta airport.

These are not the only issues addressed by this novel, published
in 1905, that remain contemporary. Chesnutt's prose soars when
he writes about the southern landscape. An early environmental-
ist, he deplored the ravaging of the land by developers in passages
that are unsparing: "When the colonel had traveled that road in
his boyhood, great forests of primeval pine had stretched for miles
on either hand, broken at intervals by thriving plantations. Now
all was changed. The tall and stately growth of the long-leaf pine
had well nigh disappeared; fifteen years before, the turpentine industry, moving southward from Virginia, along the upland counties of the Appalachian slope, had swept through Clarendon
County, leaving behind it a trail of blasted trunks and abandoned
stills. Ere these had yielded to decay, the sawmill has followed, and
after the sawmill the tar kiln, so that the dark green forest was now
only a waste of blackened stumps and undergrowth." Today, air
and water quality are among the chief issues of concern to the
public. As a result of the kind of reckless development depicted in
The Colonel's Dream, the ecology of the planet is in peril.

This and other issues did not receive wide circulation. "Chesnutt pressured the Doubleday, Page & Co. about the advertising

and promotion they were responsible for. The tone in many of his letters to the publishing company regarding his new book was written with disappointment and misunderstanding."

Charles Chesnutt's complaint to his publisher about the lack of advertising and promotion given to *The Colonel's Dream* is also a problem faced by contemporary African American writers, who belong to the tradition of Gwendolyn Brooks, Richard Wright, Margaret Walker, Chester Himes, and Charles Wright—the Tradition of Serious Concerns. This tradition is in serious jeopardy as publishers saturate the market with escapist chick lit, booty and bling bling books, which are little more than advertisements for brand names with some bad fiction added as filler. Chesnutt deplored the dime novels of his day in his first literary attempt, a short story he wrote at the age of fourteen. Such books competed with Chesnutt's books for white readers because publishers held blacks to be inarticulate.

But unlike Chesnutt, a black novelist in the Tradition of Serious Concerns is no longer totally dependent on large publishers. As a result of e-book and print-on-demand technology, writers like Michael Ross and Fred Beauford, who describe the plight of heterosexual black men, a subject publishers don't view as bankable, have been able to publish their books. Moreover, the rise of a multicultural readership, black book clubs, and black literary fairs, such as the Harlem Book Fair, free the writer from accommodating a limited readership—a readership that might find his vision uncomfortable.

The alleged angry rhetoric that offended white critics, who judged the novels and poetry written by black male writers in the 1960s, is absent in Chesnutt's work. The prose is polite and even deferential as Chesnutt attempted to woo the white book-buying public of his time. He even made his hero a white ex-Confederate colonel, an unlikely one for black writers, for whom the Confederate army ranks right up there with the SS and other nefarious and brutal institutions. His empathy extends to whites as well as blacks.

Of the cotton mill operated by Fetters, the book's villain, he writes, "He had seen the operation of Fetter's convict labour plantation, where white humanity, in its fairest and tenderest form, was stunted and blighted and destroyed."

So why did this novel, published in 1905, receive such a mixed, lukewarm, and even hostile reception? Chesnutt's experience as a novelist demonstrates that whether black novelists' prose is florid and Victorian, as in Chesnutt's style, or prone to stridency, their views are often at odds with those of "mainstream" opinion. This alienates the so-called white book-buying public, which today, as in Chesnutt's time, becomes uncomfortable when black writers expose the bigotry and the ugly side of the American experience. They prefer being soothed by a neoconservative black intellectual elite which proposes that racism is a thing of the past and that the problems of blacks are "structural" and "behavioral."

Just as Anne Frank's powerful diary challenged revisionist opinion that sought to minimize the suffering of the European Holocaust victims, Chesnutt provided a different witness to the South, both before and after the war, than the one that either sympathizes with the rebellion or justifies the way of life it sought to defend. This effort continues in films like *Gods and Generals*, where we view mass murderers like Robert E. Lee and Stonewall Jackson tearfully sing Christmas carols by the fireplace, and Ken Burns's *Civil War*, which earned Burns a membership in the Sons of the Confederacy.

Chesnutt rose to the challenge that black writers have always faced, and he did it magnificently. Regardless of the monopoly that those opposed to African American progress have over the dissemination of ideas and opinion, Chesnutt proves that a good writer can always present a version of history that challenges the official one. And if the writer is as extraordinary writer and as talented as Chesnutt, his appeal will transcend the times and address the needs of generations to come.

Miles Davis

A trip to Paris and a Miles Davis concert would determine the course of my life. It all started innocently enough. In 1954 I was chosen by the African American Michigan Avenue YMCA to be part of a delegation to a Bible study convention. The money had been raised by the older members of the Y, merchants, professionals, and clergymen who acted as the informal government of black Buffalo and negotiated with the white government that wielded power in the community. I was very active in high school clubs, and the Y was a second home, where I would go and swim and try to set down some chord changes on the piano. There were many eccentric characters who came to the Y. One was a guy who called himself Lord Johnny. He taught me some blues chord changes that I later learned were the ones Charlie Parker used. Parker changes.

I'll never forgot the day my young friend and future roommate Malcolm Ernie and I were standing in the lobby of the YMCA and he received a phone call from Emperor Haile Selassie. The YMCA was where I met my first wife, Pricilla Thompson. It was at the YMCA where our mentor was the late Fred Barkley and where, later, during my university years, poet Lucille Clifton and her husband Fred, and short story writer Ray Smith, performed in plays. We called ourselves the Buffalo Community Dramatic Workshop. Our director was Joe Byron, who was a doctor at Buffalo's Roswell

Hospital. Our performance of Lorraine Hansberry's *Raisin in the Sun* took place in the hospital's auditorium. It was only during last year, while accompanying my spouse Carla Blank to a meeting with Buffalo architects in connection with her book about women architects, that I learned the YMCA was designed by leading black architect John E. Brent. I knew his daughter, who was the mother of Janessa and Jennifer Rollins, friends of mine. Before the YMCA trip to Paris, I hadn't traveled to many places. Maybe to Chattanooga, where my mother and stepfather were born. Sometimes to Cleveland, where my stepfather's mother lived. Once to New York where the highlight of the trip was a glimpse of the boxer Sugar Ray Robinson standing in front of his bar. I was a shy person and was embarrassed by the attention paid to those of us who were going on the trip. We lived in the lower-middle-class neighborhood on Riley Street, having moved from East Utica where my parents had rented. We lived in the projects before that.

There was a woman who lived across the street. She looked like a young Etta James. It was difficult to avoid looking into her bedroom from where I slept on the sunporch. She wasn't modest. I had some serious fantasies about her. My interest in women was beginning, but the ones I found attractive were older than I. In Paris, I attended parties also attended by the students who lived at the Cité Universitaire. I was the youngest person there and would survey the French coeds as they danced with their partners. Walter Dukes, the basketball star at Seton Hall, was studying international law at the time. Just as I was about to hit on one of these French girls, he'd send me to my room. For some reason, he had appointed himself my chaperone.

But he couldn't always be on my case. I'd go to the jazz clubs, sometimes alone, sometimes with some white kids from Long Island with whom I'd begun hanging out. You'd be walking down a narrow street and you'd hear maybe Clifford Brown's "Parisian Thoroughfare" coming from one of the clubs. We once went to a club in Pigalle and watched nude dancers until we fell asleep over champagne. When we awoke, the club had emptied out and it was dawn. I remember riding on the metro and seeing one of the chorus girls who'd performed the night before. She pointed at us. When I got back to my room, my roommate, an older white man from Texas, said, "Some people are out all night." It was the first time I ever stayed out all night.

I have a memory from the proceedings that showed how things were before the drive for civil rights. Kids from all over the world elected me to head one of the conference committees. Some of the white kids on the southern delegation got angry.

When I returned to Buffalo, I was a different person. High school bored me, and so, out of the blue, I told a teacher who wanted me to be part of a delegation to go to Hyde Park to meet Eleanor Roosevelt, "I won't be here." I dropped out of high school and went to work at a library.

I bought a trombone and began to play with a group of young musicians. I had studied the trombone in high school and had played the violin in elementary school. I took up the violin again in high school and formed a string quartet. Members of the band played arrangements made popular by Stan Kenton, like "Intermission Riff." One of those on saxophone was Don Menza, who went on to play with Maynard Ferguson.

The star among the young black musicians was an alto player named Claude Walker. He was a prodigy. Sometimes he would disappear and we'd discover that he'd been in Rochester performing with the Eastman Symphony. But he liked jazz and was playing hard bop before there was a name for it. Claude later died in a fire. Before that he had a shootout with the police. His was a talent snuffed out as a result of being unable to graduate to a larger stage.

One of his friends was jazz pianist Wade Legge, who used to fascinate us with his stories about jazz musicians in New York. He was discovered by Milt Jackson while playing in a jam session at the musician's local. Wade died in his twenties. He said that he got fired from the Mingus band because he'd show up late for rehearsals. I still listen to Wade on the only solo album he made from Blue Note. He deserves more recognition.

If our group had a god it was Miles Davis. People can tell you what they were doing when Kennedy was shot or when the Twin Towers fell. I remember being in the house alone listening to a Buffalo jazz show moderated by Joe Rico, for whom Illinois Jacquet wrote "Port of Rico." I was in grammar school. He played a Miles Davis tune. I'd never heard a sound like that. The sound epitomized where I was and what I wanted to be. I played *Birth of the Cool* until it was worn out. And so when we heard that Miles was going to perform in Buffalo, we were excited. The night came: September 21, 1955.

We were all standing on the corner when this cab drove up and Miles got out. The black men we were used to were square working-class types and professionals who were a part of an emerging middle class. Buffalo was at that time a backward, dull town where there was little to do. When Jazz at the Philharmonic came to town, there was a scandal at Kleinhans Music Hall because the boppers began to dance in the aisles. Ben Webster was busted for possession of a few joints. It was a conservative town, where people went around assassinating abortion doctors, the Catholic Church being very powerful there. This was before Leslie Fiedler, John Barth, and others came to town. Fiedler also got busted for pot.

Miles was performing with Eddie "Lockjaw" Davis. Miles played these up-tempo numbers and Lockjaw seemed to fumble around his keys in an attempt to keep up with him. I don't think he did it out of any kind of malice toward Lockjaw. He wasn't mean like Diz when Miles did a duet with Satch and tried to show the old man up. I think that he did "Blue and Boogie." He also did some ballads like "Yesterday." We'd heard that Miles was mean and would KO people. My friends were scared to approach him. But I had been to Paris. I was fearless and worldly. And so I asked Miles for his autograph as my friends looked on in terror. He obliged. I told him that he was well-known in Paris. I wanted him to know that I had been to Paris.

Another incident tested Miles's affability. A man knocked over his trumpet, which was perched atop a piano. This guy is going to get it, we thought. But Miles was cool. He inspected the trumpet for damage and, seeing none, continued the break. Archie Moore and Rocky Marciano—who made his reputation fighting old black men who were in their forties yet gave Marciano all he could handle—were fighting that night. Miles paused during his concert to listen to the fight.

When I ordered a drink à la grenadine, which I had begun drinking in Paris, the waitress who served me was the woman from across the street for whom I had eyes. I was flabbergasted. It was like when I was dining at the Hayes Street Bar in San Francisco and an associate of the San Francisco Opera told me she wanted to introduce me to Kathy. I didn't know who she was talking about. Suddenly standing before me was Kathleen Battle, the diva.

Miles was at this club on William Street in Buffalo, I think the Casablanca. (About a mile away was the Zanzibar, where, as a teenager, I caught Kai Winding and Della Reese.) This was the most memorable concert for me even though I don't remember all of the numbers played. But Miles in his sharp suit and dark glasses and cool sounds convinced me that I wanted to be where all of that was taking place. That my hometown could not hold me. That I wanted the world.

Sonny Rollins

Three Takes

M y first interview with Sonny Rollins was published by *Vibe* in October 1996. I interviewed him again in 2000 for *Modern Maturity*, a magazine published by the AARP. The black editor who requested the interview left the magazine, and so the interview wasn't published. The most recent interview took place on February 12, 2007. It was meant to be an update for a book, *The Best of Vibe*.

THE COLOSSUS, TAKE 1

Bebop was my generation's hip-hop. It was more than a pastime; it was an obsession. I used to play trombone with bebop groups. When I turned sixty, I enrolled in Berkeley's Jazz School, where I studied with jazz pianist Susan Muscarella for nearly five years. I've continued with jazz pianist Mary Watkins. When I met Max Roach, I thanked him for keeping me out of reform school; we were too busy listening to bop to get into trouble. We'd spend hours at each others homes listening to the latest recordings. We dressed like the beboppers. We were clean. We went around looking like Gregory Peck in *The Man in the Gray Flannel Suit.* Our idea of a party was where they'd play "Moody's Mood for Love." We knew all the words.

Bebop musicians didn't walk. They came at you, dancing. When Sonny Rollins descended from his studio after our interview, he was wearing this great greenish raincoat that hit him near the ankles. Rollins, who had turned sixty-six in the September when the first *Vibe* interview took place, said that when he was a teenager, he was impressed with the way an older trumpet player shined his shoes. Beboppers were sharp, and we were their acolytes.

Theodore Walter "Sonny" Rollins first picked up the sax in 1944 as a sophomore in high school. By the 1950s he had come into his own, playing tenor with a variety of all-time jazz greats, including Art Blakey, Bud Powell, Thelonious Monk, and Miles Davis. When he left the Max Roach Quintet in 1957, he created his own unique trio (sax, bass, and drums) that spotlighted the versatility of his solos and hard bop style. Several years later, in an attempt to regain inspiration in his playing, he stopped recording and began practicing regularly while walking along New York's Williamsburg Bridge; his triumphant return took place in 1962 with an album titled simply *The Bridge*.

Rollins's early recordings show him developing what would become the Rollins style: a broad repertoire including blues, standards, and even spirituals and an intense devotion to melody. No matter how abstract his solos become, one is always mindful of the tune with which he started out—a trait he shares with Thelonious Monk. Though jazz solos may sound spontaneous, many are rehearsed and memorized. Some musicians are still recycling solos originated by Charlie "Bird" Parker. Rollins, on the other hand, is known for pure improvisation. He has a dedicated following but fame in the United States has been slow to come. For some of the white critics, who form the largest segment of the fraternity of jazz critics, Rollins has an attitude. He is recognized as one of the first artists to make reference to the growing militancy of the 1960s with his *The Freedom Suite*.

Both the Yoruba and biblical traditions hold that sometimes your worst adversary is inside your family—in this case, American fans and critics. The prophet is not honored in his own country. Abroad, though, it's different. Rollins's *Saxophone Colossus* is a best seller in Japan, which he has visited nineteen times and where he has appeared in computer commercials. Since 1996, when I first interviewed Rollins for *Vibe*, he has been the subject of interviews in the *New York Times* and a profile in the *New Yorker*, written by novelist and critic Stanley Crouch. At seventy-six, he still continues his vigorous touring.

But Rollins doesn't have to go anywhere if he doesn't want to. He's come a long way since his mother bought him that first Zephyr tenor. He can kick around his Germantown, New York, farm and continue to develop his music.

Rollins has accumulated a catalog of close to fifty albums. More importantly, he's one of the only surviving icons left from an era in jazz when genius was the norm and musicians like Miles Davis, John Coltrane, and Thelonious Monk were not only changing music but also affecting black culture and American society. When members of my generation tried to break away from the linear forms of novel writing, we did so because we were trying to keep up with the musicians and painters. How would it look if I did some refried Faulkner and Hemingway, when I lived in a community on the Lower East Side that included Joe Overstreet, Sun Ra, and Cecil Taylor? Kenny Dorham and I used to drink together at a dive named the Port of Call, and Albert Ayler and his brother were guests in my home. It's appropriate that the central image associated with Rollins is a bridge, because the beboppers, like the hip-hoppers, those who are not pushed in to a music that degrades by avaricious record producers, have established a bridge that reaches back thousands of years to the sound of the mother drum, the root of all black music. But sometimes it seems that in a white supremacist society, constantly on guard against minorities gaining the upper hand, even the creators of one form of homegrown music are denied credit for their invention. *American Experience* is currently running a program about the history of New Orleans. Based on the visuals, one would gain the impression that whites invented jazz. Photos of great black musicians like Jelly Roll Morton, Louis and Lil Armstrong, King Oliver, and others roll by without the musicians being identified. All one has to do is notice the names associated with the production to realize the problem.

REED: *There aren't many survivors from the great bebop revolution. Who is still left?*

ROLLINS: Well, J. J. Johnson [who, since this interview, has died] and Max Roach [died], Milt Jackson [died], Percy Heath, and his little brother Jimmy. There's not many of us left. Art Farmer, who I guess would be around my age. Johnny Griffin. [Since the first interview was conducted, bop pioneer Jackie McLean has died.]

REED: *Do you guys have a survivors guild? (laughter)*

ROLLINS: No, we don't have one. We should have something like that, 'cause in the old days in Harlem, they used to have all these clubs and everyone would be together, to help guys. There should really be some kind of federation. But people just see each other now and then, you know.

REED: *You've said your mind is like a computer—you have different programs and you snatch from everyplace. Tin Pan Alley, country and western—very eclectic. Do you consider your music to be at all political or satirical, like poking fun at institutions that take themselves too seriously?*

ROLLINS: Yeah, oh sure. Of course. I got a lot of criticism for *The Freedom Suite*, especially when I went down South on tour and we were playing mainly white colleges. A lot of people had me against the wall, asking, "What did you mean by that?"

REED: *We still get that with gangsta rap, and I remember the horrible things they used to say about bebop. When middle-class black people listened to bebop, they said the music was strange. They didn't like the culture, they didn't like the style; just a lot of hate.*

ROLLINS: In a way, because of the guys in that day using drugs and stuff, they might have associated the music with that culture. So maybe I can cut them a little bit of slack.

REED: *Let's talk about music here. One critic, Gunther Schuller, said that your method of playing, through melody rather than running harmonic changes, was a radical concept. What did he mean by that?*

ROLLINS: I guess what he's talking about is thematic improvisation. In other words, if I played "Mary Had a Little Lamb" [sings the melody], I might play for two hours from that same song, variations on that theme. What he meant was that I didn't just play the melody of a "Mary Had a Little Lamb" and go into the chord changes. I kept it as a theme. I think that's what he meant. But at the time he wrote that, I didn't know what he meant. I might have understood it, but it was so strange to have someone tell me what I was doing that it sort of tricked me for a minute.

REED: *Describe your apprenticeship with Coleman Hawkins. I know he influenced you a great deal.*

ROLLINS: I would say Monk was more like that. Coleman, he was sort of—I didn't really work with him. He was just my adult. But I actually used to go to Monk's house after school and rehearse with his band and stuff, so with him I would say it was more like a real apprenticeship. He was like my guru. Monk would say, "Yeah, man, Sonny is bad. Cats have to work out what they play; Sonny just plays that shit out the top of his head."

REED: *In the old days, the players and the gangsters were the real patrons of the art. And if you had talent, they would get you gigs in their clubs. Then a new kind of drug came on the scene. What was the impact of heroin on the jazz scene?*

ROLLINS: Devastating. Devastating.

REED: *When you got in trouble, was that peer group stuff?*

ROLLINS: To an extent, but you know, Bird [Charlie Parker] was doing it, Billie Holiday was doing it, but especially Bird. That's why Bird was such a distraught figure. Because cats were copying him, and he knew it was wrong but he couldn't stop. So we figured, yeah, man, Bird is doing it, let's go and get high. And I got strung out. I got fucked up. I mean, that's normal when you don't know better.

REED: *But you overcame it.*

ROLLINS: That was a rough one. The person that gave me pride to overcome it—besides Bird—was my mother, who stood by me after I had nobody. After I had ripped everybody off. People would see me coming down the street, they'd run. But my mother stayed with me all the way. And Charlie Parker.

REED: *You had a great reputation, but you went to Chicago and worked as a laborer. How did you feel about that?*

ROLLINS: Well, I had messed myself up so bad and burned all these bridges, so when I went to Chicago, I went there to kick my habit.

REED: *And then you went to the government rehab center in Lexington, Kentucky. And afterward made your comeback.*

ROLLINS: I came out and I was thinking about Bird, and what happened when I was in there. I thought, boy, wait till I come out. I'ma show Bird that I'm cool. And then he died while I was still in there. But anyway, I came out and still had to struggle with cats saying, "Hey, man, come on, let's step out," but I won that struggle. I wanted to work, and I had to come all the way back out myself. I knew how far down I'd been; I did janitor work and all of this—well, what else was there to really do?

REED: *What about your relationship with club owners?*

ROLLINS: I was blackballed by a lot of these people.

REED: *Why?*

ROLLINS: Because I was what you would call an uppity nigger or whatever, so a lot of these cats were keeping me from playing festivals and shit. This was for acting up and asking for money. Some cats be so glad to play that they don't say nothing.

REED: *People are so happy to play that they lower the standards?*

ROLLINS: It's not just in the past, either; I'm going through this shit all the time. They just called me to do a commercial for this car, Infiniti. They wanted us to go to Czechoslovakia to shoot it. There were no speaking parts; it would be this actor and myself sitting down in a jazz club at a table, and there'll be some Czech jazz musicians up there playing and then a voice-over about Infiniti; something like that. So naturally I didn't do it. I mean, for me to just be validating white jazz music. I'm not going to put myself in that position. I'm *glad* they still think I'm viable, but I'm not gonna do that shit, man.

I did one commercial some time ago, where I was playing on the bridge for Pioneer. They said, "Sonny Rollins really went to practice on the bridge and became excellent, like our product." Something like that is cool, where I'm identified and the people know it's me playing. But to sit down and validate somebody else's shit, it's just not *right*. It would get me a lot of exposure, it would be cash, of course, but I reached the conclusion a long time ago that I'm not rich, I'm not going to get rich, I just want to make enough to make it. Fuck trying to get into that race. I don't want it; I don't even want to speak to those people about it 'cause I don't like them.

REED: *Was that like a revelation—some sort of spiritual thing that led you to do that?*

ROLLINS: It happened because I was getting a lot of publicity at the time. I had a band with Elvin [Jones] and I was playing these places, and I remember the place I played in Baltimore and people didn't really get it, so I said, "Man, I'm not really doing it. I got to get myself together. First of all, I'ma go back and woodshed." That's why I went on the bridge. Some cat, a writer, was up across the bridge one day and saw me playing, but nobody wouldn't have even known it if it hadn't been for him. That's how it happened. It didn't have anything to do with trying to make it public.

REED: *Why are you so hard on yourself?*

ROLLINS: I'm hard on myself because maybe I been around a lot of great musicians, and I don't think I'll ever be at the level of some of the people I been around. So I'm trying to reach that level, I'm trying to reach a level of performance, and that's what it's about.

REED: *They used to have something called the "Pat Juba" in slavery days: the white slave owners made two black guys beat each other up and one survives, and the masters stand around and watch. I think that still goes on. When it comes to blacks it always seems to be a competition, fighting to see who's going to be the diva, like they're having a diva war to see who's going to be accepted. There can only be one dancer, one writer, one musician. They tried to do that with you and Coltrane, to play you against each other.*

ROLLINS: We didn't react to it. Coltrane was beautiful, a very spiritual person. He was like a minister. We were thinking about music. It was the writers who influenced the friends who . . .

REED: *Was it just a few writers who did this?*

ROLLINS: Probably. Remember when Coltrane and I came out, I was popular before Coltrane. We used to be referred to as the angry young tenors—we were against, like, the Stan Getzes, the *Birth of the Cool*; we were sort of a reaction against that. That was still going on at that time, so we were the angry tenors and nobody was thinking about that shit. But I noticed that without even realizing that's what they were doing in slavery days. I noticed that you could never have more than one person up there at a time.

REED: *Let me ask you about gangsta rap.*

ROLLINS: I like the content of rap because it's the black experience; what they're saying is the truth. Not everything—I'm talking about the political stuff, of course. We have to accept that 'cause that's what's happening.

REED: *What about the style, all this mixing and sampling and stuff they do?*

ROLLINS: Well, they sampled some of my stuff. This group Digable Planets did some of my stuff. I heard it in a store; I heard somebody playing some of my stuff.

Reed: *How do you feel about that?*

Rollins: It's okay, it's all right; I just don't want to be ripped off. I need my money. So I like the political thing and I like some of the rhythms them cats are playing. I can use it. I'm not an old fogy. I think jazz has done so much to bring people together, but jazz is only an art form. You can't change a society with jazz. The society is still backward on racial matters. I like to be democratic; I have a white boy playing in my band right at the moment. But it's not a personal thing. I find people personally who are great, but the oppressive society just makes it impossible to be real with people. It always fucks everything up.

(*After the* Vibe *interview, I kept in touch with Sonny. We've been corresponding over the years. He sends me these elegantly written letters in longhand on yellow legal paper. In 2000, he was seventy years old, which, given the depressing statistics about black male mortality, is like being Methuselah. The following is the interview conducted for* Modern Maturity.)

THE COLOSSUS, TAKE 2

Considered by some to be the greatest living saxophonist, Sonny Rollins, at seventy, continues to maintain a demanding schedule. He has been called the Colossus, not only because of his album by that name but because for five decades, he has towered over the modern jazz scene. He has witnessed some of the changes in modern music from the origins of bebop through its musical offspring, funk and hip-hop. Olly Wilson, Berkeley's music department chair, defines bebop as "the term used to describe the period that began in the early 1940s in which a new paradigm was established for the development of jazz. Fundamental to that development was a focus on virtuosity in performance, a return to small music ensembles as opposed to big bands, a conscious focus on innovation and the insistence by performers that this music be listened to carefully and taken seriously." After an early period of self-destructive behavior, Rollins has gone through a series of physical and mental renewals. He is always evolving, an attitude of self-discipline and intellectual curiosity that has found him constantly on the cutting edge of jazz.

Since its origins over one hundred years ago, jazz, a music based on African rhythms, has not captured the huge following that's been attracted to less cerebral art forms such as popular music and rock and roll, but its fans are as devoted to this music as acolytes to religion. For example, in 1993, I was traveling with the Conjure band, musicians and composers who set my songs and poetry to music. We were making appearances in Europe as preparation for the second of three Conjure recordings. We were in the bar of an Amsterdam hotel where some of the most famous jazz musicians in the world were gathered. Suddenly Max Roach appeared. Reverence and awe swept the room. I thought, this must have been what it was like when the Apostle Paul suddenly appeared before the early Christians. In fact, jazz fans use the language of the church to describe their love for jazz. Ted Joans, the (late) great jazz poet and the last roommate of alto saxophonist and bop innovator Charlie Parker, wrote his famous line "jazz is my religion." If jazz is a religion, then Sonny Rollins is a high priest, one of the surviving greats of this music that has inspired millions across the planet, as well as controversy and imitation.

Sonny Rollins was born September 7, 1930. His clan originated in Haiti and Rollins can identify a Haitian ancestor named Solomon, who practiced medicine. After a sojourn in St. Thomas, the family moved to the United States. His mother, Velma, was a domestic who worked on Park Avenue. Sonny used to accompany her when she went on these jobs. Though she supported his musical aspirations, his father, a career navy man, was opposed to them.

There is another family member who may have provided Rollins with his tone, which has been criticized as militant, harsh, strident, and even "grouchy." Others, however, have pointed to his sense of satire and humor. Rather than being those things, his is the tone of Marcus Garvey and Malcolm X: aggressive, insistent, and ironic. His rhythm struts. His music reveals a frustration that chords and scales won't yield more. A restlessness and anxiety that is like the spirit of our age. In early jazz all things were resolved. Duke was chastised for his weird harmonies. Rocking the boat. Rollins is in that tradition. He is the perfect musician for a world whose future is uncertain. A world that doesn't have all the answers. A world that is out of control. Nothing like Handel's *Water Music*. A music that says God is in his heaven and all is fine.

Rollins's grandmother, Mariam Solomon, was a follower of Marcus Garvey, a political leader of the 1920s who believed that integration was impossible and that the only hope for African Americans was to repatriate to Africa. During the height of the Garvey movement, the controversial black leader attracted thousands of African Americans to his banner. With this background it was perhaps inevitable that Rollins would follow the Booker T. Washington, Garvey tenet of self-proprietorship.

In 2006, Rollins established his own label, Doxy. Rollins also accompanied his grandmother to Harlem street corners where he was exposed to the oratory of political firebrands like Adam Clayton Powell Jr., the former U.S. congressman whose expulsion from Congress was overruled by the Supreme Court.

The young Rollins and his family also lived among the elite in the famed Sugar Hill section of Harlem. His neighbors included W.E.B. Du Bois, the educator and leader of the NAACP, and actor and singer Paul Robeson. The amazing Fats Waller played in a theater across the street from the Rollins home. Another neighbor was pianist and orchestra leader Duke Ellington. (Some of the leaps in music made by the beboppers, including expanded chord possibilities, were anticipated by earlier Ellington bands. As Rollins said during my 2007 interview, Ellington's voicings were advanced. He'd just seen the movie *Anatomy of a Murder*, for which Ellington wrote the music. (We both are puzzled as to why Ellington, who mastered every trend in twentieth-century music, from New Orleans jazz to postmodernism, is embraced by conservative critics devoted to the status quo in the arts.)

It was in this Harlem environment that Sonny Rollins's early musical education was formed. Then, as now, the American educational establishment was reluctant to recognize jazz as a legitimate art form, and so Rollins matriculated in the extracurricular academy. He was well schooled. He and his high school friends, the late alto saxophonist Jackie McLean and pianist Kenny Drew, names that are now part of the bop legend, served their apprenticeships under Thelonious Monk, a musician who placed melody first, a key element in the Rollins's style, and Charlie Parker, who was to modern jazz what Michelangelo was to Renaissance painting. Coleman Hawkins, whose 1948 work on Johnny Green's "Body and Soul" is regarded as one of the key moments in the history of jazz, was also available. Band leader Buddy Johnson heard Rollins, then a teenager, rehearsing on 133rd Street and liked what he heard.

Rollins was seventeen when he appeared on a record with scat artist Babs Gonzales. "Professor Bop" was its title and it was issued by Capitol Records. A few months later, he recorded with the great trombonist J. J. Johnson. The uncompromising new music of Rollins, Charlie Parker, Dizzy Gillespie, Miles Davis, Thelonious Monk, Jackie McLean, Milt Jackson, Kenny Clarke, Max Roach, and others alienated the older black and white musicians and critics at first. The young rebels were ridiculed mercilessly and chastised for what was considered their eccentric behavior. They were defiant artists who rejected the minstrelsy associated with their forebears, a minstrelsy that's making a comeback among some of the young commercial-minded musicians. The music was also difficult to perform. The beboppers used to put those attempting to join their circle through a demanding initiation in which they were required to play tunes and improvise at breakneck tempos.

Musical history is littered with the failed careers of those who were unable to pass the test.

Though Rollins has been cast by some as a bebopper exclusively, his restlessness and desire to avoid predictability have led him to include other styles of music in his repertoire, from the blues he heard performed in Chicago by Howlin' Wolf and Otis Spahn, to the music he heard in India while studying Indian meditation and philosophy. The Calypso grew out of the family's Caribbean experience. (The latest album, *Sonny, Please*, includes the make-you-want-to-get-up-and-dance Calypso "Park Palace Parade.") This intellectual curiosity has enabled him to perform with a variety of groups under a variety of circumstances from recording with saxophonist John Coltrane to the Rolling Stones. One reason Rollins has survived is that he is always contemporary. He told me that he enjoyed the music of George Clinton and Bootsy Collins, musicians associated with a style known as funk, a major influence on hip-hop culture; he also enjoys Prince, an avant-garde performer and producer of innovative music videos.

Rollins has come a long way since his mother bought him his King Zephyr tenor. His income enables him to turn down hundreds of thousands of dollars in projects whose "spin," he says, he might not approve. He once rejected an offer from the Rolling Stones to appear with them on a Home Box Office special.

He commutes between his Germantown, New York, farm and his studio in Tribeca, where I interviewed him on October 30, 2000, for *Modern Maturity*. This studio consists of a large room and a kitchen. The kitchen shelves are filled with different brands of mineral water. The studio has a commanding view of the Hudson River. On the wall is a poster that Rollins brought back from India. I was eager to find out how Rollins, who turned seventy on September 7, was able to maintain such a demanding schedule: forty concerts per year, during which he walks about on stage carrying a ten-pound instrument, an exhausting travel schedule, including sixteen-hour trips to Japan where he is very popular.

Some of the burden was carried by his late wife, Lucille, who served as his business manager. But still, Rollins isn't getting any younger. "How do you feel at seventy which, given the life expectancy of black men, is like 130?" I asked. (He gives the stress-relieving discipline of Buddhism credit for his longevity.)

"I feel pretty good. I have to work on things to keep myself in good form. I have to do all the right things, I have to be careful of my diet, but as long as I keep that together I feel okay." He says he stays away from red meat and rarely eats chicken; his diet consists mainly of fish, vegetables, and fruit. He also drinks a lot of water and fruit juice. He makes his own orange and grapefruit juice, freshly squeezed to preserve its enzymes, during this time of year when grapefruit and oranges are in season. During the rest of the year he buys juice. In addition, he supplements his diet with vitamin A, B-complex, E, C, flaxseed oil, and calcium/magnesium. Rollins condemns genetically engineered foods and pays tribute to Europeans who oppose these Franken foods. He believes that people in the states are apathetic on this issue.

I asked whether he still performed his legendary solos, some lasting two hours. He says he doesn't do that kind of thing as he did in the 1960s; instead, he does concerts that last three hours, which is like forty-five rounds in the boxing ring, an example of his physical endurance. He says he becomes so invigorated with his performance that he ignores the physical toll. His creativity gives him strength. The hardest part for him now is the traveling. Walking through airports with corridors that are becoming longer. Overcoming jet lag, trekking into hotels. Most of the time he has decent accommodations, but at other times "you have to deal with what's available." He's willing to endure all of this for the sake of his fans. The act of giving is where he gets his pleasure.

After that Conjure tour in 1993, I abandoned my fantasy about becoming a touring jazz musician. As soon as a concert is over, the musicians have to be prepared to move to the next town. They have to eat food backstage that may have been set out hours before.

Sometimes a hotel room is made available to them for a few hours, when they change and prepare for a concert. Then they have to show up sometimes hours before the concert to do sound checks. While singer "Little" Jimmy Scott and I would retire early, some of the younger musicians partied all night. Such a routine can wear a person down. Given their grueling schedule, demanding music, the indifference and sometimes downright disrespectful treatment, indeed, humiliation they receive, it's not surprising that some jazz musicians have resorted to self-medication.

Rollins's dedication to his fans makes the travail of traveling easier to take. He'd performed the previous week in Boston at the Berkeley School of Music performance center. Rollins is able to work in a variety of environments, clubs as well as museums. He talked about a funky place in Atlanta with beer bottles on the floor and untidy dressing rooms but it was the only venue in town. He did it because he wanted to make his music available to a grass-roots audience. "It doesn't matter where you play as long as you are inside of yourself," he says. I asked him about his use of hatha yoga, a discipline he learned in India, which "utilizes various body postures and purification exercises. Its chief goal as pursued by modern-day adherents is physical health." He says that hatha yoga taught him how to breathe properly. He doesn't sleep as soundly as he used to because of a physical condition that afflicts older men. He gets checkups twice a year. I asked Rollins why he thought so many African Americans avoid regular checkups. It's his opinion that because of the Tuskegee and other experiments in which blacks were used as unwitting guinea pigs, blacks don't trust the health care system. (A book, *Medical Apartheid* by Harriet A. Washington, which covers the "long, unhappy history of medical research with black Americans," and a report, *Unequal Treatment: Confronting Racial and Ethnic Disparities in Health Care*, indicate that such fears may have some basis in reality.)

Rollins blames some of the ailments that blacks suffer on their lifestyle choices. "You have to take care of yourself and don't fall in the trick bag of smoking and drinking a lot." Besides his vitamin supplements, Rollins drinks herbal tea, especially when on the road and in hotels.

A poem I wrote in the 1960s called "A Cowboy in the Boat of Ra," included the line, "The hawk behind Sonny Rollins' head." This was written during my Egyptian period, and the line was inspired by the face of an Egyptian pharaoh who could have been Rollins's twin. Rollins at seventy is still an imposing figure with a mixture of African and Native American features. His Van Dyke beard has almost become a trademark. I asked him about the handsome photo that appeared in *Vanity Fair.* It didn't seem to excite him; he's used to such attention. In the same issue appeared the standard piece about his mentor, Charlie Parker. From this piece you would conclude that Charlie Parker's chief role in the bop period was to inspire younger musicians to get hooked on heroin. It included one often repeated anecdote about how Charlie Parker shot up some drugs and went out and blew everybody away. Some critics, many of them white, seem to insist that the music innovators of the 1940s and 1950s reached their groundbreaking advances, not through study, discipline, practice, and exchange of ideas, but by getting high and playing anything that came to mind; that all of their work was the result of chance. Jazz criticism is the weakest form of art criticism, and because jazz is held in low regard in the country of its origin, anybody can play. Stanley Crouch was right when he said that most jazz commentators are not critics but fans, and some of them seem to have a depraved fascination with the moral failings of some of the great jazz musicians rather than trying to gain an understanding of their music. I sometimes feel that jazz criticism is a new form of white-collar crime. The *New York Times* inaugurated and then apparently dropped a "listening with" series in which Sonny Rollins was one of the respondents. This gave jazz fans an opportunity to hear from the musicians instead of from a critic who might or might not have played an instrument. Bobby Brookmeyer was also interviewed. He mentioned his apprenticeships in black jazz clubs when he was a teenager.

I doubt whether many white critics would have acknowledged that. When Chet Baker died, his obituary in the *Times* credited him with inventing the cool trumpet style that Miles Davis pioneered. In fact Baker copied Davis. The idea of African American intellectual deficiency is difficult to dislodge in a rampantly racist society; any sign of genius among a group viewed as backward (in order to enhance the self-esteem of others) is seen as a threat.

It's because of these slights and racism that some musicians in the early days turned to drugs. (Rollins complains about the "small indignities" he has to face while traveling. He's aware of the effects that such personal violations have on one's health.) Rollins had his bout with the demon, but ironically, as a result of Charlie Parker's disappointment with the young musician's drug addiction, he overcame this problem. While others of his generation were beaten down and destroyed, he has survived and flourished. There are a few others. Rollins says that stress killed the ones who didn't survive. They turned to alcohol. They had to play in funky, smoke-filled clubs and they didn't have a family life. Because of these hostile conditions, they perished.

Sonny Rollins, this prolific and versatile artist, has survived to tell their story and his. He has promised to write his autobiography. This book will not only provide a look at one of the most fascinating careers of modern music but give an insider's look at the great revolutions in modern music. His latest album, from Milestone/Fantasy Records, is entitled *This Is What I Do*.

THE COLOSSUS, TAKE 3

More accolades have come Rollins's way since these interviews were conducted. There was a *New Yorker* profile written by Stanley

Crouch. Rollins along with composer Steve Reich will receive the 2007 Polar Music Prize. The international award was founded in 1989 by ABBA's publisher-lyricist-manager Stig Anderson and is currently regulated by the Royal Swedish Academy of Music. Rollins will receive the award from King Carl XVI Gustaf—1 million Swedish crowns (equal to roughly US$140,000)—at a gala ceremony scheduled to take place on May 21.

His latest album, *Sonny, Please*, was released in 2006 by his label, Doxy. It was nominated for a Grammy but didn't win. An independent label doesn't have the political clout to determine the outcome of such awards. It was also odd that Paul Desmond (of whom I have been a fan since a teenager) received a Downbeat award when Charlie Parker was alive. Biographies of Colin Powell and Ralph Ellison show that no matter what black men achieve, they will still be subjected to slights and indignities. Unlike white jazz musicians, blacks don't have white cultural nationalists like Francis Davis providing a cheering section for their accomplishments. When the *New York Times* did a gushing puff piece on Ella Fitzgerald wanna-be Diana Krall, the great jazz diva Abbey Lincoln was mentioned only in passing. When I debated Francis Davis on WBAI radio, he challenged many of my comments. He is the kind of white critic who becomes upset when a black intellectual has a better grasp of a subject than he. I mentioned that Rollins told me he sold more records in Japan than in the United States. Davis heatedly disputed this comment. The day after our debate, CNN announced that jazz sales were higher in Japan than in the United States, probably because jazz shows that blacks are capable of highly sophisticated abstract reasoning. Such an admission by millions of Americans would challenge a cherished belief among many that blacks are motivated not by reason but by instinct, the kind of racist charge made against the largely black jury that acquitted O. J. Simpson of murder. Whites living in trailer parks aren't the only ones hopped up on the idea that blacks are prone to congenital feeblemindedness; intellectuals who are on the payroll of think tanks think so, too. People who are two or three generations from the peasant farms of Europe.

Having studied jazz theory for nearly ten years, I would compare jazz improvisation to high-speed chess.

I had a chance to talk to Rollins on February 12, 2007, the day after the Grammy Awards were announced. At the ceremony, Smokey Robinson was limited to a half a song while inferior performers were given extended time to compete with each other over who could scream the loudest at the audience. Sonny was at his home in Germantown, which he shared with his late wife. They bought a house one hundred miles away from New York City "to get away from people." Sonny says that when he went out on the back porch at night to practice, she'd come out and turn on the lights for him. He misses her turning on the lights. From his comments in the interview, Lucille Rollins was his right hand. I asked him whether not winning the Grammy Award had anything to do with forming his own record company, Doxy (after one of three compositions he wrote in 1955, along with two other bop classics, *Airegin* and *Oleo*. Rollins continues to compose. Four original compositions appear on *Sonny, Please*.)

Rollins replied, "It might have. It's possible. That's a good point, because we did have a nomination. But you know that's okay. I don't expect anything from these people."

Sonny Rollins's first instrument was the piano. I asked whether he used the piano when composing. He said he sometimes uses the piano and sometimes the tenor. At other times he writes compositions on manuscripts when traveling. He uses all three methods.

I noted that one of the compositions, "Nishi," a blues piece on *Sonny, Please* was written in the key of F on the piano.

ROLLINS: That's G for me. Sometimes I play blues in F. Other times in B flat and E flat.

REED: *Charlie Parker and John Coltrane have their trademark chord changes. For Parker they can be found on "Blues for Alice," and for Coltrane they're in "Giant Steps." Where are the Rollins changes?*

ROLLINS: I haven't gotten to the Rollins changes. This is something that I have to establish before I get out of here. I would say that the Rollins changes are still evolving.

(I sang a motif that appears in his songs repeatedly.)

ROLLINS: That's something I do? (laughter)

REED: *Frequently. You said that on* Sonny, Please *you became involved for the first time in postproduction, mixing, and mastering.*

ROLLINS: First time in a long time. I used to do it. I hate listening to the stuff so after many years, I got my old lady to the point where she could, and I trusted her, and she liked to do it and so I said okay you take care of that.

REED: *That's a tedious process.*

ROLLINS: Very tedious. See, when you have to listen to your own work you become critical. You know.

REED: *Did you take some things out?*

ROLLINS: Yeah. We kept the stuff that was the best we could get or else we'd still be in the studio. (laughter)

REED: *How much time did you spend recording?*

ROLLINS: We spent nine hours recording. It took a couple of days to mix it.

REED: *I'll bet Lucille used to insist that everybody show up on time.*

ROLLINS: Oh yeah, you know Lucille grew up with that American work ethic.

REED: *She handled the caterers and all that stuff?*

ROLLINS: She made sure everything was done on a business level.

REED: *Who does the managing now?*

ROLLINS: I'm doing most of it and my nephew Clifton Anderson helps. He plays trombone with the group. He's the next generation and so he helps me with the computer stuff.

REED: *His style reminds me very much of J. J. Johnson's.*

ROLLINS: That's his man.

REED: *Why didn't you use the piano on* Sonny, Please?

ROLLINS: Sometimes I do sometimes I don't; have been identified with the piano-less trio, that was my claim to fame in jazz. I switch back and forth piano to guitar. I'm in a guitar mode right now.

REED: *That piano player on Without a Song: The 9/11 Concert . . .*

ROLLINS: Stephen Scott.

REED: *He's smoking!*

ROLLINS: Another brother, man, he's not doing anything. He's not out here. There's not enough work out here for people.

REED: *You mean with his talent!*

ROLLINS: I know. It's shameful, man. It's a shame. You have to be fortunate to have talent and be able to get your life together.

REED: *A new biography of Ralph Ellison shows his contempt for bebop.*

ROLLINS: He got conservative toward the end of his life.

REED: *He says you can't dance to bebop. I first heard of Bird when he came to Buffalo to play for a dance. He played at a place where people had an inclination to get into fights. Cut each other. Pimps and prostitutes.*

ROLLINS: He's wrong. Because when we first came out cats used to do a dance called the Apple Jack.

REED: *I remember the Apple Jack. Cats used to stand in one place and slide their feet around, sometimes lifting the cuffs of their pants. They did the Apple Jack in Buffalo when Jazz at the Philharmonic came to the Kleinhans Music Hall, this seddity white supremacist space. After that bebop was banned from Kleinhans Music Hall. (laughter)*

ROLLINS: So you can dance to bebop.

REED: *He also says that bebop leaned toward dissonance. Most of the stuff I've heard doesn't come from the outside; it's played within the key.*

ROLLINS: That's unfortunate because someone he would like, Duke Ellington, was very much into bebop. His main man was Bud Powell.

REED: *The problem with his stance is that with the enormous power Ellison was given, he was able to deny beboppers support they should have received.*

One of the greatest concerts I attended was Sonny Rollins's free concert at Central Park, August 27, 2007. Victor Hernandez Cruz and I arrived to find Sonny playing before a couple thousand people in the rain. He had been on the stage for about forty-five minutes when we arrived. The crowd didn't want to leave and so he did encores, which lasted about as long as the original concert. After the performance, Victor, one of the wisest men I know, said, "Now I'll have a good night's sleep." It might have been the last great concert another man heard. I saw the late Ed Bradley walking out of the park. He was alone.

REED: *You must have been up on the stage for over three hours at that Central Park concert. You're seventy-six years old! Where do you get the stamina?*

ROLLINS: (laughter) I'm not sure. I'm like Lionel Hampton. They had to get him to the stage in a wheelchair. Once he got up on the stage he was ten years old.

REED: *The encores were as long as the original concert.*

ROLLINS: (laughter) That shows I don't think about anything but the music.

REED: *I wrote you that during the Central Park concert I thought you were playing the theme from the* Amos and Andy Show, *but it turns out to be similar to the actual Noel Coward piece you played, "Someday I'll Find You." But the melody sounded similar to the theme of that show, "Angel's Serenade." I thought you were having an inside joke.*

ROLLINS: (Hums the theme from the *Amos and Andy Show*, demonstrating his encyclopedic knowledge of music, popular and underground. He's able to hip-o-cize music that most would consider corny.) We used to listen to *Amos and Andy*. (laughter)

REED: *I loved it. Unlike the material today, which is all gangbanging or presents black men as lethal sexual predators, it presented different classes and types of African Americans even though Kingfish ridiculed the middle and upper classes.*

Are you going to travel to Sweden to collect the award from the king of Sweden?

ROLLINS: We're accepting that. We're going over there in May.

REED: *That's great! That's really great!!*

ROLLINS: I like it because it has nothing to do with politics. It's all about merit. I like that kind of prize. This other stuff is a lot of bullshit politics. Sweden and those European countries appreciate the music and when they give you a prize you know that's what it's about.

REED: *You still touring?*

ROLLINS: I'm off right now, but I go back in April. I'm trying to take care of my house up here, take care of my taxes. Things I have to do by myself.

REED: *Jackie McLean died since we last talked. What are your memories of Jackie?*

ROLLINS: (The interview was lighthearted up to this point. However, Rollins's voice cracked a bit as his thoughts turned to the musicians of his generation who had died.) We go back so far, we sort of came up together. We enjoyed Miles together, we were all hooked on drugs together. I didn't really know he was that sick. I still can't believe that I can't call Jackie up and talk to him. I can't comprehend that. I know his voice and talking to him, it's something that I haven't come to terms with yet. It's like a lot of people you know well; one good thing is he's always there, all I have to do is think about him, you know, it's a big thing in life, that kind of eases the thing about losing people like Miles and Trane. I've had dreams about Monk and Trane. The dream I had recently was about Walter Bishop Jr., the pianist. I saw Walter in the dream, it's like you know it's him, but he looks different, but then I realized it was him. It was like he was in another sphere. Jackie and these other people—they're still close to me and they're still part of life to me.

REED: *Sonny, what do you want your legacy to be?*

ROLLINS: Well, my legacy is to be a guy who got himself together after being messed up. Stopped drugs. Someone who did what he wanted to do. I went on the bridge and quit the scene. I used my conscience to do what I needed to do. That's what I'm proud of. That's what I represented. The music part that's a talent; of course I worked on it. But the other part—trying to get through life—that's where you really have to bust your ass. That's my legacy to me.

REED: *Thanks, Sonny.*

Ishmael Reed debuts as a jazz pianist on the CD For All We Know, *with Carla Blank on violin, David Murray on tenor, Roger Glenn, flute, and Chris Planas, guitar. Konch Records*

A Playwright of the Blues

As a young man living in New York during the 1960s, I was always struck by how some critics approached the work of then Soviet poet Yevgeny Yevtushenko. Most emphasized content and not form. His poems were treated as intelligence about political trends within our then enemy, the Soviet Union.

I suspect that the same thing happens here. What's up with the sisters and brothers? seems to be the question some critics ask when inspecting an African American writer's work or, as Adolph Reed Jr., put it, "What do those drums mean?" And minority writers perennially ask, What is the motive of mainstream white critics for favoring one minority artist over the other?

I've seen plays by Adrienne Kennedy, Suzan-Lori Parks, Amiri Baraka, Thulani Davis, Aishah Rahman, and August Wilson. I worked with Ed Bullins during his 1980s California sojourn when he ran a truly grassroots theater. While New York critics seem to be able to choose the best of these playwrights or "Black America's Best Playwright" or "The Poet of Black America" or "The Country's Greatest African American Playwright," I would have difficulty doing so. Under a grant from the Lila Wallace Foundation, I accompanied Second Start adult literacy students to a play a month for three years. One of the most outstanding was Marvin X's *One Day in the Life*. I doubt whether New York critics who anoint this playwright or crown that one have ever heard of Marvin X, let alone seen his plays. That probably goes for Marie Evans and Aishah Rahman as well. I doubt whether Robert Brustein, August Wilson's debating partner, was familiar with many black playwrights when he implied that they are recipients of a theatrical affirmative action. (Brustein opposed affirmative action at Yale.) Not that Robert Brustein is a malevolent man. My partner Carla Blank and I had a good lunch with him when I taught at Harvard.

But Brustein is like other American critics who judge African American art on the basis of a tiny sampling and prejudice. I don't think it has much to do with race. Just as critics in Asia, Europe, and Africa have a better grasp of African American literature than white American critics do, French critic Genevieve Fabre knows more about black theater than any white American scholar or critic. She's white. Moreover, Brustein seemed to use a double standard when debating Wilson. While opposing Wilson's call for an ethnic theater, he admitted that the "roots" of his play *Nobody Dies on Friday* were in Yiddish theater (http://amrep.org/past/Friday/Friday4.html). Why is it all right for Brustein to write an ethnic play yet oppose Wilson's call for an ethnic theater? Is Brustein saying that Yiddish plays have more universal import than black ethnic theater has? During the Town Hall debate, Brustein said, in an attempt to distance himself from his ethnic roots, that though his people came from Poland, he didn't consider himself Polish. *Newsweek* critic Jack Kroll wrote, "Wilson might have answered that Brustein's heartbeats were not Polish, but Jewish."

Though their approaches to theater are radically different, Wilson says that he was influenced by Amiri Baraka, yet the critics who praise Wilson have ignored Baraka for years. When they finally decided to give a *Dutchman* revival some print, the *Times* hired a radical white feminist academic to trash it, which was like turning an Arab over to the guards at Gitmo. And from the writings of black critics (some of whom examine work by black authors as a sideline), one gains the impression that they haven't seen a play by Baraka since the 1960s.

Toward the end of his life, Wilson seems to have been contemplating writing a play with a more postmodernist bent. From his description, it sounded like something akin to Kennedy's *Funnyhouse of a Negro*.

Nicholas Lemann in his book *Redemption* says that white southerners have an innate fear of a "black uprising," even though organized slave revolts historically were few. The traditional way to handle such fears has been to appoint, in the words of Paul Laurence Dunbar, "the Big Negro." Maybe the same thing happens in the art world as well. I wouldn't be the first to point to the historic trend of "mainstream" critics choosing a token, like an ox with garlands around its neck, who will eventually be led to artistic slaughter. Usually, leading black academics and critics certify the choices that arrive from the literary Big House like members of a neo-colonial government rubber-stamping the choices of their imperialist masters. John A. Williams recognized this tendency some years ago. Williams is a much more polished novelist than Ralph Ellison, whom the New York intellectual machine has crowned the King of Black Novelists. But those who choose black tokens find Williams's content too strong. Or how do they say it, "controversial."

And so the question remains: Are some writers being praised because a conservative period calls for plays that don't upset what the late Lloyd Richards called the "plastic card crowd" (white middle-class theatergoers)—plays that preach individual responsibility and blame all the problems in the black community on the behavior of black men? One can read that in Wilson's plays *Fences* and *Jitney*, where members of an older generation preach responsibility to their children, whom they accuse of abandoning the values espoused by their elders. The younger generation conversely accuses the older generation of acting in a passive manner when confronted with white male aggression, which is the conflict between *Jitney*'s Booster and his dad, Becker.

One of the abiding myths among outsiders who write about black life is that the fatherless home is an exclusively black phenomenon, despite new census figures that show married families in the minority throughout the country. These tough-love exhortations also appear in a number of op-ed columns and books written by black and white academics and the pundit elite. White male critics welcome plays by black women in which the image of black men is similar to that found in post-Reconstruction popular culture, that of a reckless, thieving rascal, misogynist, and rapist. (Reviewing this essay, theater critic John Simon went apoplectic over this claim, forgetting that he had said something similar.)

But if Wilson was one of the writers who merely tell white people what they want to hear, why would he eventually break with some who had praised him? He wouldn't be the first. Langston Hughes, Claude McKay, Richard Wright, Chester Himes, and Amiri Baraka did the same. After James Baldwin rebuked those who helped him become a literary star, his sponsors (according to the late Truman Capote, in an exclusive interview printed in a magazine published by Al Young and me) treated him like "shit."

In 1997, I talked to August before he departed to New York to engage in that fateful debate with Robert Brustein, which followed some unfavorable remarks about Wilson's theatrical abilities made in the *New Republic*, a publication that thrashes blacks regularly. (Martin Peretz, the publisher, got into trouble for accusing black women of having "cultural deficiencies.") I warned Wilson that it was an ambush, that he would be subjected to a hometown decision. I suggested he insist that the debate be held in St. Louis. Sure enough, after the debate, the same cultural machine that set up James Baldwin set him up: Wilson was subjected to hit pieces by white supporters who deemed him ungrateful for advocating a black nationalist theater during his Town Hall debate with Brustein. What probably bothered them even more was his favorable reference to Elijah Muhammad, the Nation of Islam leader who had been stereotyped by the media as hating white people. (In connection with a book I'm writing about Muhammad Ali, I have discovered that Elijah Muhammad entertained whites and Jews at his dinner table.) And from the amen corner, he was hit equally as hard by black surrogates. Frank Rich, the critic who was responsible for Wilson's fame, wrote:

> On the surface, Mr. Brustein, the artistic director of Harvard's American Repertory Theatre, won on most points. He argued for an integrated American culture that prizes multiculturalism but does not tolerate racial hatred or separatism or a waiving of artistic standards. Mr. Wilson, the Pulitzer Prize–winning author of such plays as *Fences*, *The Piano Lesson* and *Two Trains Running*, argued for a self-segregated black theater in which black actors would play only black roles and only black writers would write about black characters. Even as he presented his case, it was contradicted by both his own career (in which he had chosen to present his plays to integrated, mainstream theaters) and by the debate's moderator, Anna Deavere Smith, the black artist known for her brilliant portrayals of people of all races and genders.

During the week of March 12, when Don Imus was fired from MSNBC and CBS for calling the Rutgers women's basketball team nappy headed hos, I wrote Frank Rich, who is a regular guest on the Imus show. I wanted to know why he criticized August Wilson for supporting black nationalism but enabled Imus's yahoo bubba white nationalism. He didn't answer.

Margo Jefferson, Mr. Rich's colleague at the *Times* wrote:

> Mr. Wilson cast himself as the warrior-king of all people of African descent living in the United States. He spoke as though he embodied every experience every one of them had ever had (no one contains that many multitudes), and as though all authentic (and by implication great) black art were being forged in the smithy—or the slave ship—of his soul.

A Princeton site accused Wilson of anti-Semitism:

> One reason some were disturbed was the subtle but insistent join-
> ing of Wilson's vivid evocations of genetic memories of the slave
> trade with such anti-Semitic code words as "financiers," and a de-
> scription of black artists as "victims of the counting houses."

(This is the information I received from a Princeton site. The
comments about counting houses were attributed to the following: These stories by Simon Saltzman and Nicole Plett were published in U.S. newspapers on January 22 and April 16, 1997. All
rights reserved.)

Perhaps the most scathing, even cruel response to Wilson's position was written by Henry Louis Gates Jr. for the *New Yorker*.
Gates flogged black nationalism and the black arts movement,
one more time, accusing Wilson of aligning himself with those
groups, which Gates considered homophobic and misogynist
(though gays and women were active in both movements). After
the article appeared it was announced that Gates, Brustein, and
the debate moderator, Anna Deavere Smith, were going to share a
Ford theater grant amounting to more than $1 million. Ironically,
Wilson's insistence that he was a member of a culture that had
been segregated was corroborated by the *Times*, the publication
whose critics took exception to his speech. In their obituary, Wilson was not called a black playwright, not an American playwright. August Wilson was criticized as a nationalist by those who
can be the fiercest of nationalists, and criticized as a segregationist
by those who, at the time of the debate (and still) run a segregated
arts scene.

I think the 1997 debate was his way of distancing himself from
the neocons and neoliberals who had claimed him as a member of
their ranks. For some African Americans, including myself, white
conservatism is a euphemism for racism. Unlike traditional conservatism, American conservatives seem to have one issue: out-of-

wedlock births in the black underclass, about which they still write op-eds and long, ignorant books, even though the black teenage pregnancy rate has declined while that of white and Hispanic women is soaring.

And so, if August Wilson's plays have a conservative line, it was not an appeal to critics who misread him but a reflection of the attitudes of a large segment of the African American community. Wilson's conservatism was *his*, that of Booker T. Washington, Elijah Muhammad, Malcolm X, and Marcus Garvey, all of whom preached self-help and individual responsibility, and all of whom did business with white people; not *theirs*, which often took the form of vicious and nasty comments about the underclass. As Wilson said, "The ground that I stand on has been pioneered by my grandfather, by Nat Turner, by Denmark Vesey, by Martin Delaney, Marcus Garvey, and the Honorable Elijah Muhammad."

It is easy to see why some neocons and white conservatives regard Wilson as one of their own. Surely George Will, Hendrik Hertzberg, David Brooks, and other conservatives would applaud the juicy lines Wilson gives Doub:

> The white man ain't paying you no mind. You ought to stop thinking like that. They been planning to tear these shacks down before you was born. You keep thinking everybody's against you and you ain't never gonna get nothing. I seen a hundred niggers too lazy to get out the bed in the morning, talking about the white man is against them. That's just an excuse. You want to make something of your life, then the opportunity is there. You just have to shake off that "white folks is against me" attitude. Hell, they don't even know you alive.

Since this kind of speech recurs in Wilson's plays, one might assume that this is his position—that anybody can make it by working hard and taking advantages of opportunities.

Of course, it's not as simple as that. Even the Bush II administration admits to the existence of racial profiling; the *New England*

Journal of Medicine has documented racial disparities in health care; the Center for Responsible Lending has issued a report about the unequal treatment of blacks by the mortgage-lending institutions, even to those who work hard and play by the rules, and so on. When the Youngblood character bought that house in Penn Hills he probably had to pay a higher interest rate than Pittsburgh whites who had the same credit rating as his. Black and white conservatives accuse blacks of wallowing in a cult of victimization. Hell, judging from the facts that I have studied, they are victims!

While many whites are not against black people (or are indifferent to them), there are those in key positions who appear to be. Doub suggests that Youngblood use a GI bill to attend school. Ira Katznelson writes in *When affirmative Action Was White* (still is):

> the G.I. Bill did create a more middle-class society, but almost exclusively for whites. Written under Southern auspices, the law was deliberately designed to accommodate Jim Crow. Its administration widened the country's racial gap.

Seems as though some of the whites who designed the GI Bill were "against" blacks.

Though Wilson says his plays are not about politics, the politics are implied. For instance, blacks don't have the power to make decisions that would determine whether a neighborhood is subjected to public domain or urban renewal, a major issue in *Jitney*. Some argue that urban renewal, by dispersing the black community, is responsible for the problems experienced in the cities. Wilson would agree that integration, which led to the separation of middle-class blacks from the so-called underclass blacks, had bad effects.

Some of the themes in *Jitney* are as contemporary as gentrification. Others are as ancient as rape, as in the Scottsboro case of the 1930s, in which black men were falsely accused of rape. In *Jitney* also, which takes place in 1977, a white woman screams rape when her liaison with a black man, Booster, is exposed (but I doubt whether the 1960s warriors would consider Booster's murder of a rich white woman heroic, the generation that their elders believe has gone astray). According to *The Trouble Between Us* by Winifred Breines, a rare look into the conflict between black and white feminists, a dirty little secret is exposed (one that I challenge Henry Louis Gates Jr. to explore): the main complaint that black men and women had against the white women who joined Freedom Summer, set up in 1964 to register African Americans to vote, was that they got in the way and tried to run things. Booster's murdering of a white woman who accused him of rape feels more 1930s, like Richard Wright's Bigger Thomas, the murderer of two women in *Native Son*.

Another recurrent theme is the fratricidal arguments between the men. These disputes erupt over trivial incidents but signify deeper subterranean issues, though sometimes these issues are not dredged. In *Jitney*, people fight over a thirty-cent cup of coffee or a fifty-cent unpaid fare. (Fox Butterfield of the *New York Times* says that fighting over small things is a style that blacks inherited from southern Celts.)

But Wilson's greatest triumph is the creation of characters that are complex and human. A great ear helped. He must have spent thousands of hours tape-recording in that brilliant mind of his the back-and-forth among black male characters. The tall tales: Fielding says that he was such a good tailor that Count Basie canceled engagements to wait for a suit that he was making for him. The dreams: Booster says that he could have become a heavyweight champion or Albert Einstein. The arguments: Lena Horne's beauty versus Sarah Vaughan's. Wilson captures the small talk as well as the philosophical musings and poetry that go on whenever black men gather.

I don't know where August got his blues from. He says he listened to records. You can listen to all the records you wish, but that doesn't guarantee you'll be successful in getting the blues down on paper. Wilson has to rank with Langston Hughes and Ernest Gaines as a writer—his ear was so good that his characters' words could be set to music. Shealy's monologue in the first scene of *Jitney* is an example. Not only did August excel stylistically in bringing the blues to paper, but all the *issues* of the blues are presented in this play as well.

Since I signed up with XM Satellite radio, I've been able to listen to the blues whenever I wish. Sexual jealously, especially songs that address a lover's absence (usually about women staying out all night and, the worst, coming home the next morning with bloodshot eyes), money, betrayal, death, getting drunk, boasting about material possessions (especially automobiles, specifically Cadillacs) seem to be the main themes. Sometimes they are soul-wrenching cries like Ray Charles's "A Sinner's Prayer." Sometimes serious events like death are treated humorously: "Don't Send Me No Flowers When I'm in the Graveyard." But there are also good-time songs: "I Ain't Drunk, I'm Just Drinking," "Give Me a Pig Foot and a Bottle of Beer." In *Jitney*, one character says that the two issues that can get you killed are money and women. Wilson has the blues covered.

Wilson could have coasted along, continuing to receive the accolades and prizes and keeping his views to himself. But to his credit, at a crucial point, he turned to those who had misread him, and during the Town Hall debate he made it clear that his conservatism had different roots from theirs.

I Was a Victim of
Unfair Lending Practices

Victim \vik·təm\ n. 2: a person who is deceived or cheated

—*Random House Webster's College Dictionary*

Since the publication of this essay, discrimination against blacks and Latinos by the banks has led to a recession in the American economy. Unable to obtain loans from conventional banks, even though they may have had the same credit ratings as whites, led these customers into the high-risk loan market. Though the talk shows blame the debacle on customers receiving loans they couldn't afford, the *Wall Street Journal* reports that 65 percent of the victims of predatory lending had good credit. These and other issues affecting blacks and Latinos are ignored by a handful of black academics, who claim that we have entered a postrace period. Theirs are the views that are favored by the neo-liberal pages of the *New York Times* and the *Washington Post*, which recently established a far-right black site, including a scholar who believes that the problems of the black "underclass" are behavioral and refers to himself as an intellectual entrepreneur; a black writer who fronts for a think tank that supports race science quackery; and a best-selling writer who claims that the beating of Rodney King and the shooting of Amadou Diallo had nothing to do with racism. Apparently, as Jack Nicholson said in the movie, these media can't handle the truth when it comes to commenting about African American culture.

One of the buzzwords used by think tank moles who have nothing to do besides hang around dimly lit bars on Capitol Hill is "victimization." Every time blacks complain about a particular injustice, somebody like Shelby Steele or John McWhorter pops up like a duck in a carnival booth, shouting "victimization." What would they call the Department of Agriculture being more inclined to extend loans to white farmers than black farmers? What about this *New York Times* article: "The New York attorney general, Eliot Spitzer, said yesterday that the Countrywide Financial Corporation, a large mortgage lender, would adopt measures to prevent discriminatory pricing for minority borrowers. Mr. Spitzer began investigating Countrywide after federal mortgage data from 2004 showed that black and Hispanic customers in New York were more likely than white customers to receive higher-priced sub prime loans." What would Steele and McWhorter call those black and Hispanic customers, using not the Orwellian word games of their financers, but the plain old dictionary definition? Or are they saying that blacks should ignore deception and injustice and move on? McWhorter attacked me on a radio network and in a magazine in which the injustices committed against some of his sponsors are mentioned regularly. Are they engaging in victimization? And why can't Steele and McWhorter persuade some of those who sponsor them to move on? Why is it always blacks and Hispanics who are encouraged to move on?

In 1979 I bought a dilapidated five-bedroom Queen Anne Victorian house in Oakland's inner city. The house was in such bad shape that it rained in the living room. It would have remained that way had I not obtained a low-interest rehab loan from the City of Oakland. I got some free paint along with the deal. With the loan and other improvements, I have come close to restoring the house to its 1906 state. It's a sturdy old thing, having survived two major earthquakes and hundreds of small ones. The 1989 earthquake left a few cracks in the plaster.

Last August 26, I decided to take advantage of low interest rates and approached a lending agency. The loan officer said I could lock in a fifteen-year fixed rate loan at 5.8 percent. Fine. I did the paperwork and waited for the loan to close. On September 19, I received a contract in the mail from the bank for a 6.875 percent variable interest rate. I was instructed to sign the papers and return them to the bank. I called the loan officer and asked for an explanation. Obviously embarrassed, she said the computer had made a mistake and the initial rate was still good.

Mystified, I decided to approach the bank where I'd obtained the rehab loan in the mid-1980s. Perhaps they would have better computers. I didn't think that I'd have trouble there. After all, I'd paid off the loan long before it was due.

The loan officer there and I agreed on "a good faith estimate" of a fixed 5.4 percent interest rate for fifteen years. He requested that I pay some upfront fees so that he could close that day. In the weeks following, some glitches occurred. Although my credit and work history are excellent—I've been a senior lecturer at the University of California for thirty-four years—the bank required additional paperwork which, curiously, duplicated what I'd already submitted. Papers sent from the bank took forever to arrive. The calls I made to the loan officer weren't returned. I had to track him down at the bank to get a hold of him. Finally I received a contract, but instead of the 5.4 percent interest rate that he was eager to close on the day of our first meeting, a 5.8 percent interest rate was listed.

I called and asked why. He said he'd have to ask the underwriter. After consulting the underwriter, he said that the forty-five-day limit for the loan commitment had passed. I informed him that the delays were caused at his end and that I had been prompt at every step. He then explained that the rate was higher because the house was considered a duplex instead of a single-family residence. I told him that none of the loans I'd gotten in the past had cited that difference, that I didn't rent space and that the home was my primary residence. He then said that he'd appeal the decision from the underwriter. I never heard back.

At this point, I vented my frustrations to the realtor who helped me acquire the home in the first place. He recommended a broker whose office is located in one of the more upscale districts of the East Bay. The broker had read my books and was excited to do business with me. I told him the problems I had with the other lenders and he sympathized. I got a great rate and the loan closed within ten days.

So what was going on? Had I been redlined by the lending companies because I live in the Oakland Flats, an African American neighborhood, instead of the Oakland Hills, a predominately white section of the city? It was impossible to know for sure. Banks have never been models of efficiency and many people have trouble with their mortgages. Still, it's hard not to rule out something more insidious. After all, there's plenty of evidence that redlining is alive and well.

In just one of many studies, a housing advocacy group in Washington, the Center for Community Change, last year examined federal data on mortgages and found that regardless of income, black people were statistically more likely than whites to obtain high-interest loans when they refinanced their mortgages. A 2001 study by another advocacy group, the Association of Community Organizations for Reform Now, found that lenders rejected prospective black home buyers more than twice as often as white applicants nationwide.

According to these studies, if I were redlined, there are millions of African Americans like me. We have great credit ratings and work histories. As an owner of a small business, I even pay taxes to the City of Oakland.

But there are those who try to convince us that because Halle Berry receives leading roles in Hollywood movies, "we're getting there" in terms of race relations and equality? As I reach for the popcorn, I'm rejoicing. But when it comes to important issues like the lending practices of the mortgage industry, blacks are still in the back of the bus.

Showing White Students
Some Love

In March, CNN ran a story about prostitution in Chicago. While the face of the black prostitute was shown, those of her customers, white Johns, were hidden behind dancing checkers.* This is the way white and black dysfunction have been treated since the 1880s. Black social problems and criminality are played up while white problems are minimized, if reported at all. Even the *New York Times,* whose typical representation of a black man is a mug shot, sounded an alarm about the thousands of white babies abandoned by parents addicted to methamphetamine. *Times* columnist Joyce Purnick reported that 77 percent of those addicted to the drug are white. Yet there followed an op-ed by *Times* columnist John Tierney dismissing meth addiction as "a fad in some places." A letter writer, Bill Hansell, challenged Tierney. "I urge him to venture out to America's heartland, where meth abuse is anything but a fad. Meth is destroying families in counties all across America. Statistics show that meth use is increasing, yet the dangers associated with this drug are given short shrift by Mr. Tierney." It was Mr. Tierney who blamed the plight of the black Katrina victims on

*The CNN story appeared on March 1, 2006.

the Great Society programs of the 1960s, when 80 percent of those who've benefited from Medicare, Medicaid, and Social Security have been white! But for *Times* columnists David Brooks and John Tierney to admit that meth use among whites in the heartland is a serious problem would dispute the neocon formula that the red states are all God-fearing and virtuous and the blue states secular and decadent, or that whites dwell in a sort of Lake Woebegone utopia, while the problems of blacks are traceable to their culture.

David Brooks attributed the 2004 Bush victory to states with "high white fertility rates . . . people who wanted to escape vulgarity." He blamed the riots in France on gangsta rap.* I invited six French intellectuals to give their take on the riots and published their essay in my magazine *Konch*. They traced the current problems confronting immigrants to France to the occupation of Algeria. None mentioned gangsta rap.

Recently Orlando Patterson, one of those blacks whose op-eds reflect the *Times* editorial policy regarding the problems of blacks, attributed what he called the "self-destructive" behavior of some black males to hip-hop culture. The sharp rise in killings among black men, the result of competition over crack markets, began in 1984. Hip-hop artists and gangsta rappers were in elementary school at that time.

William Bennett is an old hand at blaming the country's social problems on black behavior. When he was education secretary he blamed whatever problems were occurring in education at the time on blacks, and when he was drug czar, drug addiction and sales were painted black. So it came as no surprise when he said that aborting black babies would reduce the crime rate (and was rewarded with a regular commentary spot on CNN). Even those white progressives who responded to Bennett failed to point out that 70 percent of those who commit crimes in the United States

---

New York Times, November 10, 2005.

are white.* If white babies were aborted, wouldn't there be an even more significant plunge in the crime rate?

Neocons like Brooks Tierney Bennett, and a tiny class of black intellectuals, their proxies, have succeeded in persuading the public that the only problem confronting American education is the gap in scholastic achievement between white and black students—a gap that is narrowing. The majority of the columns written by Samuel G. Freedman, the *Times* education columnist, trace the main problem confronting American education to that of young blacks' unwillingness to assimilate. Those who have been swayed by the numerous articles and books making this claim must have been astonished to read a recent study that shows 50 percent of the nation's white students (in Cleveland it's 74 percent) reading below proficiency level.** In another study, only one-third of college graduates were found to understand what they're reading or, in the words of this study, "read a complex book and extrapolate from it."***

Perhaps these white students view being able to read as "acting white." California State University reports that "less than half of their freshman are ready for college-level work in both math and English," which calls into question the effectiveness of the SAT in predicting success in college (*Oakland Tribune*, March 15, 2006).

No one who follows the annual reports in *Education Week* is surprised by these results. Since 2000, below-average reading proficiency levels have been reported in states with little black

---

*According to the latest statistics from the U.S. Department of Justice, of the men and women behind bars approximately 44 percent are black, 35 percent white, and 18 percent Hispanic. Whites, however, make up nearly 70 percent of all persons arrested and 60 percent of those arrested for violent crime (Diane Watson, *Huffington Post*, October 7, 2005).

**"New York Schools Narrow the Racial Gap in Test Scores," *New York Times*, December 2, 2005.

***Lois Romano, *Washington Post*, December 25, 2005, A12.

population. This emphasis on what editorial writers call black culture as being the culprit behind the country's educational failures has diverted attention from the deepening crisis in American education. According to Cathy McMorris, coauthor of the American Competitiveness Amendment, one-half of Chinese graduates obtain their degrees in math, science, and engineering, while only 16 percent of American undergraduates pursue these fields.* If these trends continue, she says, by 2010, 90 percent of scientists and engineers will be Asians. Black culture cannot be faulted for this dismal situation. Moreover, black culture includes scientists, businessmen, astronauts, writers, artists, philanthropists, and teachers, as well as those who regularly appear on the crime pages of newspapers, which, when it comes to diversity in their newsrooms, are fifty years behind the South.

What puzzles me is why no tough love op-eds and oversize books have been published lecturing white students for their lack of literacy skills, their lack of "personal responsibility," and their being prone to "self-inflicted problems." Where are Abigail and Steven Thernstrom and their adopted black intellectual son, John McWhorter, when we need them? What is the position of the right-wing Manhattan Institute, which sponsors all three?

Some of the scolding of black Americans was printed under the guise of "tough love." Some years ago, the symbol of tough love toward black students was a school principal who went around threatening them with a baseball bat. Right-wing and conservative writers applauded him. Don't these writers love white students? If whites continue to dominate the major economic social and cultural institutions, what is the future of these institutions if they are under the leadership of people who can't read or can't understand what they are reading? What will happen to the quality of our national life if the numbers of white males attending college continue to decline?

---

*C-Span, March 29.

The situation has become so dire, NPR reports, that some colleges have begun outreach programs with the aim of recruiting white males.*

The late principal of a black school in Chattanooga, Tennessee, told me that he had to end corporal punishment when integration occurred because the bruises on the white children were visible. This is how the media treat their problems. They are reluctant to address the social problems of the white community because they see it as their main consumer base and feel that unpleasant "tough love" might alienate them.

Andrew Hacker has written a dozen or so articles for the *New York Review of Books* repeating the same charge: the main problem confronting higher education at the University of California–Berkeley, where I taught for thirty-five years, is affirmative action, which he sees erroneously as a black program. However, white women faculty members attribute the declining numbers of males on California campuses to Proposition 209, which outlawed gender and racial preferences in California higher education. But the white family has become so dysfunctional that even Andrew Hacker, writing about rising illegitimate births among white women, says that "if Senator Moynihan were around, he could write about *The White Family: A Tangle of Pathology.***

While black students have athletes, entertainers, neocons, and just plain charismatics competing with each other to flagellate them with tough love, white students are failing without any affection being lavished on them.

---

*"Women Continue to Outpace Men in Graduating College," *Weekend Edition Sunday*, January 23, 2005. The gender gap at universities and colleges around the nation is now favoring girls. Increasingly, women graduates outnumber men, and that gap is widening, as reported by Beth Ford, KPBS, San Diego.
**Andrew Hacker, *Mismatch: The Growing Gulf Between Men and Women* (New York: Scribner's, 2003), 149.

Assisted Homicide in Oakland

Some gallows humor making the rounds in Oakland contends that one way to reduce Oakland's murder rate would be to offer free shooting instructions to the shooters. Maybe the teacher would be a suburban high school shooter. One of those white kids who can hit a target at a thousand feet. That way, innocent bystanders, some of whom have been the brightest among Oakland's young people, would be spared.

Certainly the dealers who shot up my block on the afternoon of December 12 could have used some firearms guidance. They shot into my neighbors' homes and cars but wounded only one of those they targeted. The police have suggested that this shooting was the result of a feud between gangs in the district. On April 1 another youth was murdered around the corner from my house. I wasn't surprised to read a report issued by the Oakland police that some neighborhoods receive more police service than others.

The police claim they don't have the resources or the budget to attend to our needs. Yet when a member of the African American elite, Chauncey Wendell Bailey Jr., a black journalist employed by the *Oakland Post*, was murdered, the police raided a black Muslim bakery and rounded up suspects the day after the murder. Governor Schwarzenegger acceded to Mayor Dellums's request for California Highway Patrol officers to buttress the Oakland police, which had been criticized by the local press and citizens for its lackluster performance in solving murders and its slow response in responding to other problems. A few days after the murder, the police got a confession from the alleged killer (which he later retracted, claiming he was tortured by the police), a nineteen-year-old who described himself as a soldier. He told police that he murdered the journalist because Bailey was about to expose criminal activities associated with the bakery, including kidnapping and murder. Some of those associated with the Nation of Islam (NOI) have been accused of roughing up writers and journalists since the 1960s, but this was the first time such intimidation ended in death. The Mass of Christian Burial was held at St. Benedict Catholic Church, which had such an overflow crowd that at one point I had to step outside to avoid being crushed. A defiant minister, Father Jay V. Matthews, compared Bailey to the early Christian martyrs and suggested that there would be more martyrs. Bailey's uncompromising stance was saluted by the minister, who quoted Irish American playwright Eugene O'Neill as well as the Scriptures. The audience agreed when he said that the community would not be silenced. Paul Cobb, the publisher of the *Post*, compared Bailey with Helen Thomas, the aggressive journalist whose questions have rattled a series of presidents, and said that the *Post* would continue to expose "the wicked," no matter how many death threats Cobb was receiving. This remark was greeted with thunderous applause by the fashionably dressed audience of Oakland's black movers and shakers. With performances by Oakland's Interfaith Gospel Ensemble, an interracial group, accompanied by drums, saxophone, and keyboard, the church rocked. It was like one of the old civil rights rallies. It took the murder of one of their own for Oakland's African American establishment to awaken to a murder epidemic that has plagued Oakland's impoverished neighborhoods for over a decade.

If Chauncey Bailey could have his life snuffed out, one of them might be next. Still the Oakland police came under criticism by some of the mourners and even Bailey's widow. If the Black Muslim bakery, from which other Oakland members of the NOI have disassociated themselves, had been under surveillance by the Oakland police for months, why weren't they aware of the conspiracy to murder the journalist? Also, why was the fact that Bailey was investigating police corruption at the time of his death ignored by the press? These and other questions were being raised by some members of the crowd who milled about the entrance of the church.

There have also been tensions between the politicians downtown and the police union, which local columnist Chip Johnson accused of being more concerned with its members' needs than the safety of Oakland's citizens. So powerful is the union that some say that it intimidated the former law and order mayor, Jerry Brown, who tried to portray himself as Giuliani west. In July 2007, the union balked at a plan devised by the new mayor, former black Congressman Ron Dellums, and the chief of police, Wayne Tucker, that would deploy officers on the streets in a way that combated crime more effectively. Commenting on the union's stubbornness, the chief said that "the union's position was self-serving and not in the best interest of the city." The union appeared indifferent to a crime rate that the *Oakland Tribune* described as "skyrocketing." There were 148 homicides in 2006, a 57 percent increase over 2005. Overall crime rose 9 percent. With downtown indifferent to our needs, neighborhoods like mine are on their own, "marooned," the word given to communities set up by runaway slaves who selected their own kings and queens (lowercase). As part of my duties as neighborhood block captain, I attended a neighborhood meeting with the police in the aftermath of the December shooting. Though the two officers seemed hardworking and sincere, they told us in so many words that their hands were tied. That as soon as they arrive on the scene the drug dealers scatter, or that they have to be mindful of the suspects' civil rights.

The Oakland Police Department is still under scrutiny as a result of the Riders case. Outlaw officers called the Riders were accused of

beating and kidnapping drug dealers, and the city had to settle with
their victims for $10 million.

Some Oakland residents cannot abide the violence that erupts in
Oakland neighborhoods. Impatient with police inaction, forty-
nine-year-old North Oakland black homeowner Patrick McCullough, an attorney who had been trying to rid his neighborhood of
drug dealers, shot a sixteen-year-old after a physical altercation with
him in front of McCullough's home. When I met McCullough, he
proudly introduced himself as "the vigilante." He has become a local folk hero. A shooting incident on my block that occurred on
February 18 indicates that others have the equipment to make the
same response. Two men armed with a shotgun held up a Korean
American neighbor. He handed over his wallet but resisted their demand for his car keys. He ran toward the middle of my block
wounded from a gunshot that had grazed his finger and abdomen.
His screams attracted the attention of an African American family
headed by Chauncey Crosby, a twenty-year Marine veteran who
saw combat during Desert Storm. He and his wife, Dawn, are the
parents of four children. Chauncey talked about the incident when
I interviewed him on March 31, 2007. He said that he heard the
gunshot while he and his son were changing tires. Then he saw the
neighbor, whom he had befriended, running in a hunched over
posture. He asked the man if he was okay. "No man, I've been shot."
His hand was bleeding. Crosby sent the wounded neighbor into his
home and prepared to meet his attackers with lethal resistance. This
is the kind of heroic story that happens every day among the marooned. Crosby, who is employed by a diesel company, attributes
the upsurge in Oakland crime to the lack of jobs and services like
sports and recreational programs for Oakland's youth. In one meeting I attended, a county supervisor, Keith Carson, said that as a result of cuts in social programs, there would come a time when
someone would assault you over the contents of your refrigerator.

The situation in the country's inner cities is more complicated
than reports issued by think tanks or upscale black and white op-ed

writers would have their subscribers believe. Recently, when the *New York Times* addressed the crime rate in Oakland, it consulted three armchair academics, one of whom lives in Cambridge, instead of those of us who live "in the finite thick of things." They hadn't a clue as to why violence exists in the inner-city neighborhoods like mine when it's obvious that it is the result of competition over drug markets, which in Oakland were deregulated when the local drug kingpin, Felix Mitchell, was busted. He kept a lid on things while he was alive, but after he was murdered, wildcat operations erupted.

They say that people in neighborhoods like mine lack the work ethic. If American business operated as effectively as crack operations I've witnessed, there would be no trade deficit. These members of the chattering classes are people who believe that the farther you are from a issue, the more profound your observations. For example, our problems would be less chronic were suburban gun dealers to quit flooding our neighborhoods with illegal weapons. A local newspaper, the *East Bay Express*, traced a number of illegal weapons used in the commission of Oakland crimes to a gun dealer in San Leandro, a neighboring town. "According to the federal Bureau of Alcohol, Tobacco, and Firearms, the San Leandro sporting goods store is the nation's second-biggest source of crime guns—that is, weapons either acquired or used illegally. Last year, law enforcement agencies traced 447 crime guns to Trader Sports. There were 481 traces in 2004 and 496 in 2003. That's more than one a day," reported the *Express*. The guns end up in Richmond, Oakland, and San Francisco.

Nothing has been done to stop this dealer. Trader Sports is still open. The voters of San Francisco, across the bay, approved a ban on handguns but a judge overruled them. Trader Sports is one of an extremely small number of gun shops that account for the large number of weapons used in crimes, according to a government report. Though black and Hispanic children have been mowed down in the streets since the introduction of crack, which occurred in the mid-1980s, it took the martyrdom of white children at Virginia

Tech to impel the House of Representatives in June to pass a modest bill that "would improve state reporting to the National Instant Criminal Background Check System to stop gun purchases by people, including criminals and those adjudicated as mentally defective, who are prohibited from possessing firearms." But in July, the *Times* reported that "a key Congressional committee dealt a major blow to Mayor Michael R. Bloomberg's campaign against illegal firearms . . . refusing to allow police departments broader access to data that tracks guns sales." Why? Is Mayor Bloomberg the only American politician who is not controlled by the gun lobby?

Another outside group that contributes to the murder rate is absentee landlords, many of whom are suburbanites who rent their homes to criminals, who not only practice their trade before neighborhood children, who pass these houses on the way to school, but dwell in houses that blight our neighborhood. We've complained to the police about a row house that not only degrades our neighborhood but is a scene of drug dealing. It's still in operation. Another problem is elderly homeowners who are too frail to prevent their younger relatives from turning their homes into drug marts.

This is not to excuse the youngsters whose illegal actions led to a shootout on my block. But to blame the drug trade solely on this group is like blaming drugstore clerks for Fen-phen. The high murder rate in Oakland involves black men killing black men, but they are receiving supplies and assistance from the outside. (Though the federal government didn't participate in drug sales, officials looked the other way while their allies did.)

After the murder of Chauncey Wendell Bailey Jr., one that unsettled Oakland's black power elite, the kind of people who brought down the Jim Crow South—people who are not to be fucked with—the change in the city's attitude toward crime was breathtaking. If the role of a martyr is to lay down their lives to effect change, then Reverend Matthews was right. Chauncey Wendell Bailey Jr. was a martyr.

Black Philanthropy

Old Money, New Money

Since the beginning of the European occupation of North America, whites have received enormous subsidies. While blacks were enslaved and Indians were being driven off their lands, whites were benefiting from a number of free land acts and were permitted to seize property from which blacks and Japanese Americans and other unpopular groups had been forcibly removed. In the twentieth century, whites benefited from the New Deal reforms inaugurated during Franklin Roosevelt's administration, the Great Society programs, and the Federal Housing Administration, which until recently discriminated against blacks while allowing whites to accumulate assets through equity and mortgage interest deductions. And although affirmative action has been propagandized as a black quota program, white women are the ones who have received the fruits of this program. And with the declining numbers of white males enrolling in colleges, outreach programs have been extended to them. Yet it's blacks who are marked as the dependent class lacking self-reliance and personal responsibility.

Such stereotyping by conservatives, neocons, and their African American proxies ignores black philanthropic efforts dating from the colonial period to the generosity exhibited by the new millionaires, some of whom have made their money via the hip-hop industry.

Jonathan S. Coit, writing in *Encyclopedia of African American Business History,* says, "Black organizations and institutions, churches, benevolent societies, and fraternal orders have been the focus of much of the study of black philanthropy. Historians have documented their efforts to establish schools and hospitals and provide relief for the poor and indigent." Among mutual aid societies, Coit cites Charleston's Brown Fellowship Society, founded in 1790, and the Woolman Benevolent Society, founded in 1818. Among the more prominent black philanthropists of the eighteenth century were Paul Cuffee, who made a fortune in shipping. "In 1815, he transported 38 African Americans to settle in Sierra Leone, becoming the first American of any color to sponsor a settlement in Africa."

Many leading black philanthropists have been women. Mary Ellen Pleasant came into a "sizable estate" when her husband, James Smith, died. In San Francisco, she ran a boardinghouse and laundries. With her income, some from investments earning 10 percent interest, Pleasant financed black businesses, including the black newspaper *Pacific Appeal.* Almost one hundred years before Rosa Parks challenged racism in public transportation, Pleasant sued the North Beach & Mission Railways, after a streetcar failed to stop for her. An early freedom fighter, Pleasant helped finance John Brown's ill-fated raid on Harper's Ferry.

Perhaps the most famous and fabulous patron of the arts was not a member of the black elite or the talented tenth, but a woman whose mother, Sarah Breedlove Walker (Madame C. J.), built a fortune selling hair products. Walker donated thousands of dollars to civic groups, colleges, church organizations, and the NAACP. She also contributed to Tuskegee Institute, Mary McLeod Bethune's Daytona Normal and Industrial Institute, the Haines Institute, and the Palmer Memorial Institute.

Her daughter, A'lelia, threw parties at which poets of the Harlem Renaissance networked with patrons and sponsors. Langston Hughes was one of those who attended and described a typical gathering: "A'lelia Walker, however, big hearted, night-dark, hair-straightening heiress, made no pretense at being intellectual or exclusive. At her 'at homes' Negro poets and Negro number bankers mingled with downtown poets and seat-at-the-stock-exchange racketeers. Countee Cullen would be there and Witter Bynner, Muriel Draper and Nora Holt, Andy Razaf and Taylor Gordon." When A'lelia died, the Harlem Renaissance ended, according to Hughes.

While the typical black philanthropist accumulated money through legitimate sources like Cuffee and Walker, those who tapped into illicit economies have also made sizable contributions, according to the oral tradition. Faced with hostility from the legitimate routes to capital, black entrepreneurs sought loans from operators of the underground economy, the original venture capitalists. But when white ethnics discovered that money was to be made at the lottery, they used violent methods to take it over. The film *Cotton Club* is about the fight between gangsters Dutch Shultz and Lucky Luciano. Their attempt to seize the numbers racket was opposed by the "Queen of Harlem," Stephanie St. Clair. These underground capitalists not only financed black businessmen but also were community philanthropists. My mother, in her book, *Black Girl from Tannery Flats*, describes how Buffalo numbers bankers supported church and charity events. Unlike the new crack capitalists, whose cars and jewelry and other bling bling end up being seized by the authorities (a policy that began when young blacks entered this illicit business, according to attorney Kip Lenoir) and sold off at suburban auctions, none of these men displayed conspicuous wealth. They blended in within the community and could be found serving as officers in the Elks or the Masons.

Philanthropic numbers bankers were present in every big city of the North. According to Michael Flug, senior archivist for the

Harsh Collection at Woodson Regional Library, "The economy of the black community of Chicago in the earlier part of the twentieth century was so circumscribed by segregation and economic discrimination that the policy industry really generated a lot of the ready cash that flowed around Bronzeville." Curtis Lawrence, who wrote the story about Chicago policy kings as venture capitalists for the *Chicago Sun Times,* added, "The policy kings put a lot of their earnings into legitimate enterprises, such as funding writers, car dealerships and churches." It was these gangsters who sponsored the African American musical that took the name *Jazz* during its Chicago sojourn. Jazz and blues were art forms that were disdained by the elite black classes and so it was left to these "bad people" to support them.

Louis Armstrong in his autobiography talks about how the New Orleans underground economy supported jazz during the early years. But Louis Armstrong noted the hazards arising from such sponsorship. He claims that he was forced to go play at Harlem's Connie's Inn at gunpoint.

There are many stories about the friendship between Louis Armstrong and gangster Al Capone who booked Louis in his clubs, but less known are the black underworld figures who patronized jazz. Alan Lomax gives credit to the Elite Club, a black Chicago club, for sponsoring the newly arrived talent from New Orleans.

Even as members of underground economy supported the arts, leaders of the black upper classes, who have been satirized and ridiculed mercilessly, have done their part especially in the support of literacy.

At the beginning of the 1900s, literary societies were "likely to bear the names of such famous blacks as Frederick Douglass, John Mercer Langston and Blanche K. Bruce, or Paul Laurence Dunbar. In 1907, a black journalist calculated that there were at least 800 literary societies named for Dunbar."

In Washington there was the Bethel Literary and Historical Association, the Monumental Literary Association in Baltimore, and the

Women's Club in Baton Rouge. According to Prof. Reginald Martin, these clubs did much to improve the literary skills of black women in a period when the education of women was discouraged.

These clubs did not confine their efforts to literature. In 1901 Mrs. Andrew F. Hilyer, after meeting with the black composer Samuel Coldrige-Taylor in London, joined her husband and their friends in forming the Samuel Coldrige-Taylor Choral Society. The society persuaded the composer to come to the United States in 1904 and 1906, when his Hiawatha became "one of the most popular works with choral groups of both races."

Some leading black capitalists of the twentieth century continue this patronage. Perhaps the most prominent have been the late Reginald Lewis, Oprah Winfrey, Bill and Camille Cosby, Tiger Woods, Michael Jordan, and the late Richard Pryor, who contributed to the animal rights movement and to violence prevention in Los Angeles schools. The late Reginald Lewis, president of Beatrice international and one of my benefactors, supported public and private institutions; $3 million went to Harvard Law School, which, at the time, was the largest gift to Harvard from an individual. Other grants went to Virginia State College, the NAACP, and WNET-TV.

The August 2005 issue of *Black Enterprise* article entitled "America's Leading Black Philanthropists" provided a list of philanthropists and their contributions for the year 2003. Oprah Winfrey contributed over $10 million to education, the arts, public health, and women. William and Camille Cosby, $215,000 to education and dyslexia awareness. Philanthropists connected to the hip-hop industry have also made contributions to various causes. Sean "P. Diddy" Combs contributed $1,333,333 to youth and education. Russell Simmons supported art, education, and youth with $388,798. Chris "Ludacris" Bridges gave $121,830 to abused and homeless children.

Many of the top millionaire rappers and hip-hop artists are missing from this list. So are some of the white producers who receive the lion's share of the profits made from their art, people who remain unscathed when syndicated black columnists fall over themselves chastising the music. The record of these new million-aires remains to be seen.

Lisa Y. Sullivan, writing in the fall issue of *Responsive Philan-thropy,* makes this point: "As this generation of black millionaires turns to philanthropy, however, their legacy remains to be seen. In many ways these hip-hop entrepreneurs are no different from their white Generation X dot-com counterparts. They look at business and government differently than their parents, preferring a new ethic of self-reliance. Lacking confidence in government's ability to solve problems or guarantee a secure economic future, white Internet entrepreneurs and black hip-hop entrepreneurs believe in ownership, money and clout. The members of this gen-eration will undoubtedly have the means to finance a new move-ment for justice and equality; whether or not they do so depends on their ability to build networks and institutions that combine hip-hop sensibilities with a broader understanding of how wealth and power operate in society at large."

Reporter Darryl Fears of the *Washington Post* cites another cause for concern, referring to a 2004 study by the Coalition for New Philanthropy which documented minority giving in the New York area. "Black Americans of all age groups contributed slightly more than the nation's other two major groups, Latino and Asian. But art museums and cultural centers were low on the priority list of all minority groups, who give instead to churches, schools, and scholarships." While contributions to churches, schools, and schol-arships are commendable, it's regrettable that contributions to culture fall short. Ethnic museums provide black and Hispanic students with information about African and African American cultures that aren't covered in public schools.

Black theater is approaching extinction, and African American actors and playwrights cannot find venues where they can hone their talents. Athletes and entertainers who make hundreds of millions of dollars seem lackadaisical about rescuing institutions like the Harlem Boys Choir and the black dance troupes that are struggling for survival. Dick Gregory has spoken out about a leading black golfer who sometimes drops $10 million at Las Vegas gaming tables in one night. I'm not one to scold people about how they spend their money, but I can dream, can't I? With $10 million you could establish a permanent arts colony in a place like New Hampshire, where, the last time I checked real estate prices, you could buy a place like Mount Vernon for $300,000.

The new black millionaires don't seem to realize that a group's worth is defined by culture, not money. We don't celebrate the method of exchange in ancient Egypt, but the sculpture, painting, and writing. Zora Neale Hurston, Langston Hughes, Duke Ellington, and Aaron Douglas represented the African American spirit of the 1920s. Those old numbers bankers knew that the arts reflect the soul of a people.

The Last Days of Black Harlem

When blacks began moving into Harlem in the 1900s, American whites responded in their usual way when those of a different race moved into their neighborhoods. They fled. Now that real estate interests have sent housing prices soaring and the far-right antipoor and antiblack policies of the Manhattan Institute have taken effect, blacks have found it difficult to remain, not only in Harlem but in the rest of Manhattan. The Manhattan Institute also influenced the policies of former mayor Rudolph Giuliani, a candidate for president in 2008.

Under Giuliani's fascist regime, thirty-five thousand black and Hispanic men were stopped and frisked without cause and Giuliani, who threatened to close museums that sponsored exhibits not to his liking, sided with the police when they killed black and brown men. Yet Giuliani's reign has been praised by writers for the *New York Times,* including cultural critic, A. O. Scott. This wasn't the first time blacks have met a hostile reception in a city that was once a slave port.

In 1863 Irish American mobs that blamed blacks for the Civil War ran amuck in New York, killing every black person they could find and burning down a colored orphan home. Again in 1900, blacks were subjected to an orgy of carnage by roaming white mobs.

Writer Wallace Thurman, a figure in what has become known as the Harlem Renaissance, wrote an article entitled "Negro Life in Harlem," for the October-November-December 1927 issue of *Haldeman-Julius Quarterly*, which gave an account of how the black population started out in Greenwich Village and reached Harlem. (In 1927, the black population of Harlem was two hundred thousand.)

After Greenwich Village, they moved to the Twenties and lower Thirties west of Sixth Avenue and to West Fifty-third Street. They settled in Harlem in 1900. Blacks moving to Harlem caused panic among whites. Writes Ann Douglass in *Terrible Honesty*, "Opposition from Harlem's white tenants and other white New Yorkers to the black influx was fierce. The *Harlem Home News* exhorted its readers in July 1911, 'The Negro invasion . . . must be valiantly fought . . . before it is to late to repel the black hordes.'"

The white press, the traditional lynch mob leader, habitually referred to the newcomers as niggers and coons: the enemy. Though many American whites are drunk on the lost cause of Anglo supremacy (though many of them were only recently admitted to the club; their ancestors were considered "white trash" in Europe), they have traditionally been enthralled by black culture, from the early plantation days, when southern planter families "cavorted among the darkies," to today's hip-hop craze. Therefore when *Shuffle Along,* a musical written and performed by blacks, opened in 1921, it was widely appreciated and imitated. George Gershwin and Irving Berlin were influenced by this groundbreaking low-budget musical, which, like many black creative inventions, earned millions for its white imitators. Choreographer and producer George White and Florenz Ziegfeld made fortunes bringing black dance to the stage in musicals that were imitations of *Shuffle Along,* which was written by Flournoy Miller and Aubrey Lyles, with music and lyrics composed by Noble Sissle and Eubie Blake. Featured in the musical was Florence Mills and among those in the chorus line was Josephine Baker. Ivy Anderson, a singer with Duke Ellington, was the show's soubrette. A young Paul Robeson also appeared. Writer and activist James Weldon Johnson hailed the musical as a breakthrough. Playwright Loften Mitchell credited *Shuffle Along* with launching the Harlem Renaissance.

So did Langston Hughes. He said that *Shuffle Along* excited interest in black books, African sculpture, music, and dancing. Among the writers were Hughes, Jessie Fauset, Helen Johnson, Rudolph Fisher, Countee Cullen, W.E.B. Du Bois, Zora Neale Hurston, Claude McKay, Hale Woodruff, Aaron Douglas, W. H. Johnson, and Augusta Savage, who did busts of sociologist, historian, poet, and novelist W.E.B. Du Bois and black nationalist Marcus Garvey. Du Bois was a critic of some of the younger Renaissance writers. Another Renaissance figure, Charles S. Johnson, edited the important magazine *Opportunity*. In 1921 Garvey, using some of the capitalist ideas of Booker T. Washington, began the Negro Factories Corporation that provided loans to develop a chain of cooperative grocery stores, a restaurant, a laundry, a tailor and dressmaking shop, a millinery store, and a publishing house.

Harlem's official photographer was James VanDerZee and its filmmaker was Oscar Micheaux. Charles Gilpin, Paul Robeson, and Ethel Waters were its actors and among the dancers were George Snowden, Herbert White, and Earl Tucker. The most famous dancer was Bill Robinson. Perhaps the greatest artist to emerge from the Harlem Renaissance was Duke Ellington. He performed at the Cotton Club, which opened in 1924. The exuberance of the period is captured in his piece "Rockin' in Rhythm," which included "Jungle Music." The Cotton Club was off-limits to black patrons and Ellington had to play to audiences in a stereotypical manner. For example, dancers were required to dress in grass and banana skirts; Cotton Club entertainers reproduced a blackness as the racist Hollywood industry defined it. One of those who defined the Harlem Renaissance was critic, philosopher, and educator, Alain Locke (1885–1954). He supported Countee Cullen, published Zora Neale Hurston's first story in his magazine, *The Stylus*, and introduced Langston Hughes to his patron Charlotte Mason. In the March 1925 issue of the *Survey*

Graphic he wrote, "Here in Manhattan is not merely the largest Negro community in the world, but the first concentration in history of so many diverse elements of Negro life. It has attracted the African, the West Indian, the Negro American; has brought together the Negro of the North and the Negro of the South; the man from the city and the man from the town and village; the peasant, the student, the business man, the professional man, artist, poet, musician, adventurer and worker, preacher and criminal, exploiter and social outcast. Each group has come with its own separate motives and for its own special ends, but their greatest experience has been the finding of one another. Proscription and prejudice have thrown these dissimilar elements into a common area of contact and interaction. Within this area, race sympathy and unity have determined a further fusing of sentiment and experience. So what began in terms of segregation becomes more anymore, as its elements mix and react, the laboratory of a great race-welding."

I had heard of this "laboratory of a great race-welding" when growing up in Buffalo, New York, about five hundred miles north of New York. But as a result of a Eurocentric education, I had never heard of the writers of the Harlem Renaissance. From reading magazines I learned that my hero Sugar Ray Robinson, considered by many to be the greatest fighter, pound for pound, of all time, lived there. In 1959 my mother and stepfather took me to New York. We visited their friends in Harlem and then while driving down Seventh Avenue, I spotted Ray Robinson standing in front of his bar. He'd returned from Europe where, in London, he had been defeated by Randy Turpin.

In 1962 I met an ambassador from Harlem, minister of Muhammad's Mosque 7, Malcolm X. We had never seen a personality like that in Buffalo, New York, but when I arrived in Harlem, I found many who were endowed with intelligence and wit.

My second trip to Harlem occurred when I rode uptown from the East Village, where I was living. I was so overwhelmed that I immediately returned home, but after my initial shock, I returned often, sometimes to hear Malcolm and others speak on street corners. There was much cultural and intellectual ferment and some were calling it a Second Renaissance. Former roommates of mine, Ray and Charles Patterson and Askia Toure, were on the staff of the Black Arts Repertory theater and belonged to the Umbra workshop, where I came in contact with one of the surviving members of the Renaissance, Langston Hughes. He was responsible for my first novel being published. Later, I met two other surviving members, Bruce Nugent and George Schuyler, and ran into Duke Ellington when leaving my dentist's office.

Harlem didn't exactly go dark when the vibrant days of the Renaissance ended. Hughes says this occurred in 1931 with the death of hair products millionaire Madame Walker's daughter, A'leila Walker, one of the Renaissance's patrons. Indeed some of the most important developments in art culture and politics occurred after the Harlem Renaissance. While the patrons of the Harlem Renaissance were wealthy white and black New Yorkers and included at least one numbers baron, Casper Holstein, in the 1930s the federal government in the form of the Work Projects Administration subsidized black artists living in Harlem. A black artist collective called the 306 Group, under the leadership of Charles Alston, was organized to paint murals. Among Alston's students were Romare Bearden, Jacob Lawrence, and Charles White. In 1935 the Harlem Suitcase Theatre presented the plays of Langston Hughes. In 1939 the Salon of Contemporary Negro Art was founded by Augusta Savage. The 1940s and 1950s saw the rise of Richard Wright, Ruth Brown, Dean Dixon, Joe Louis, Sugar Ray Robinson, Adam Clayton Powell Jr., Sarah Vaughan, Pearl Primus, James Baldwin, Canada Lee, Alice Childress, Pearl Bailey, Lena Horne, Gordon Parks, Gwendolyn Brooks, Willie Mays, Roy Campanella, John Oliver Killens, Eartha Kitt, Marian Anderson, Malcolm X, Ivan Dixon, Alvin Ailey, and others. For Harlem, the Renaissance never ended. Until now.

From their first entrance to Harlem in 1900 until today, blacks have made Harlem an artistic and political Mecca that has influenced the world. Now that they are being forced out, they will take the Renaissance elsewhere, leaving a New York that will become little more than a tepid theme park and tourist trap.

The Colored Mind Doubles

How the Media Use Blacks to Chastise Blacks

I TiVo Don Imus as much as I can because his putrid racist offer-ings are said to represent the secret thinking of the Cog-noscenti. Maybe that's why journalists like Jeff Greenfield and others admire him so much. He says what they think in private.

On any day, you might find Bernard McGuirk, the man who, ac-cording to *60 Minutes,* Imus hired to do "nigger jokes," doing a lame imitation of New Orleans Mayor Ray Nagin, using a plantation-type dialect. The blacks who are satirized by McGuirk and others are usually displayed as committing malapropisms. Although white writers appear daily on the show, I've rarely seen a black author.

In the past twenty years, black authors have received every prize available to authors. McGuirk's idea of a black author must be the same as the producers of the movie *The Tenants:* Snoop Dogg.

Recently McGuirk referred to Reverend Joseph Lowery as a "shameless skunk," and a joke was made about the manner in which Betty Shabazz, Malcolm X's widow, was murdered. Black athletes are referred to as "knuckle draggers," which, the Irish and Scots members of Imus's crew (they discussed their ethnic her-itage on C-Span) might be surprised to learn, was the way the British referred to their groups. When an exhibition of great apes was presented in London, the British commentators said that the

Irish formed the link between ape and man. But their being Irish and Scots-Irish makes sense because it was members of these groups who used to entertain the Anglos by blackening up. Maybe that's why Imus has listeners in Kennebunkport. Bush I is a fan.

Another fan is former congressman Harold Ford, whom Imus endorsed so as to deflect attention from the show's lowbrow racism. I'm sure Ford understands what Imus is all about, but he needed the country and western vote in rural Tennessee when he ran for the U.S. Senate. Imus has a big following among this constituency. So did James Earl Ray.

Why pick on Imus? His approach to black issues and personalities has become mainstream. But instead of using the Irish and Scots-Irish, the traditional white trash mercenaries who stand between the Other and the Anglos (when given their social and economic position, they should strike common cause with blacks), the network and newspaper executives use people who resemble blacks to chastise blacks. This colored auxiliary functions as their mind doubles and iPod people.

I'll bet the executives got the idea from President Bush's cynical political handlers. Those who advocate torture on behalf of the administration, for example, are Vietnamese, Chinese, and Mexican Americans. The former domestic policy adviser who was recently arrested for scamming a department store is black, and the secretary of state is black. When they come before congressional committees, the idea is that congressmen would be reluctant to submit them to harsh questioning for fear of being called racist. That way, they can promote the administration's megalomaniac foreign policy with little criticism. I'm sure that's Karl Rove's thinking.

Unlike Condoleezza Rice, whom I dubbed "the Manchurian candidate," in an exchange with her at a Stanford luncheon sponsored by the National Association of Black Journalists, about a year before she joined the Bush campaign, journalist Barbara Reynolds is a progressive. She said that she was fired from *USA*

Today because she didn't appeal to the demographic group from which the paper gets its sales: angry white men. The black syndicated columnists who remain have become the gofers for backlash journalism, all of them competing with each other to blame the country's social problems on black behavior.

Clarence Page and others regularly blame the victim. Harvard's Orlando Patterson is also brought in by the neocon op-ed editors at the *Times* to characterize the problems of African Americans as self-inflicted, using the kind of argument that would be ripped to shreds in a freshman classroom.

Even Bob Herbert, a liberal and the token black on the *New York Times* neocon editorial page, has to take the brothers and sisters to the woodshed from time to time in order to maintain credibility with his employer. He, too, says that gangsta rap is the cause of society's woes. (David Brooks, who promotes some of the same ideas as David Duke but has a more opaque writing style, even blamed riots in France on gangsta rap.)

For these writers, black people's style is the irritant. If we could only get Cynthia McKinney to find a new hair stylist.

Michel Martin, who was assigned to beat up on McKinney by the producers of *Nightline,* spent half the interview on McKinney's hair even though McKinney has spoken out on a number of serious issues. Can you imagine Martin interviewing Trent Lott, the last person on the planet to use Wildroot Cream Oil, or Joe Biden, and spending half the time on his hair?

If Martin had subjected a white male congressman to this kind of sarcastic interview, complete with hostile body language, Martin would have gotten the same treatment from her bosses that Connie Chung received when she interviewed Newt Gingrich's mom, who denounced Hillary Clinton as "a bitch." (Martin appeared on a program with "white militant" Joe Klein, who lied about his authorship of *Primary Colors.* When Klein talked about "the poverty of values within the inner city," she just sat there and took it.)

Before Chung interviewed Newt's mom, the network executives, according to a media publication issued by the Freedom Forum, wanted someone like Connie Chung for their shows. She still hasn't recovered and has been assigned to a Saturday morning show on MSNBC. Oblivion.

Cynthia Tucker of the *Atlanta Constitution* was also solicited by *Nightline* to join the McKinney ambush. Tucker, who blames the Hudlin brothers, producers at Black Entertainment Network, for the problems confronting some black kids, is the syndicated columnist who relied on the usual inflammatory and racist reporting to describe those who sought refuge in the New Orleans Superdome as "bestial." The *New York Times,* the New Orleans *Times-Picayune*, and the LA *Times* all discounted these rumors and the LA *Times* even apologized, saying that such reporting would never have occurred had the Superdome hosted members of the white middle class.

Tucker never retracted her false accusation, nor did Jeff Koinage, the reporter CNN has assigned to cover all of Africa. He replaced the African American reporter who was covering the Superdome because this reporter presumably wasn't sensational enough.

While one can see African leaders, intellectuals, scientists, parliamentary sessions, and cultural events on the BBC, CNN's view of Africa is on par with that found in the Tarzan movies. When CNN bade Koinage farewell on the occasion of his new assignment, they presented the highlights of his Africa coverage. One picture showed him staring at a crocodile. Another showed him grinning at a monkey. No wonder the American public's knowledge of the world is on par with their president's.

You'll also notice that the moderator of the *Nightline* show where McKinney was grilled is of South Asian origin. According to a memo I have from a Cuban reporter who was fired from CNN, the executives there, led by Jonathan Klein (the new head of CNN who is trying to boost his ratings by running mug shots of black males all day, while dropping the story about the middle-class white kids caught on video beating up homeless people, killing one of them; they were sent to psychiatric counseling), prefer South Asians as anchors, especially women, and particularly on CNN International.

CNN Atlanta features a South Asian anchorwoman who giggles while the male correspondents exchange remarks with her that are loaded with sexual innuendo, certainly an issue that feminists should take up.

Even C-Span, the only network where you can obtain a variety of viewpoints from African Americans (though tank blacks like Shelby Steele receive disproportionate exposure) has gone Imus. Last week, Jadish Bhagwati, a South Asian professor at Columbia who supports Bush's plan to bring Mexican slave labor into the United States to serve his big agribusinesses contributors, shared laughs with host Pedro Echevarria and a caller, a white employer, who was voicing the kind of jokes about black work habits featured on the Klan's Nigger Watch website. Both Bhagwati and host Echevarria are black, but that didn't prevent them from enjoying the kind of barbs against African Americans heard on the Imus show.

Of course one should avoid generalizing about South Asians. But obviously the British, who referred to them as "niggers," trained some of them very well and they're not the only "people of color" who serve as stooges for the corporate media. Michel Malkin, instead of a hard-hitting antiestablishment writer like Emil Gulliermo of *Asian Week,* represents Filipino Americans. For Muslim Americans they give us Irshad Manji, who refuses to debate the young playwright Wajahat Ali. For Mexican Americans we are awarded the syndicated Ruben Navarrette Jr., who believes that black people are too dumb to compete with the cheap Mexican labor that has been brought in to New Orleans. He is a fan of Rudolph Giuliani, even though under Giuliani's regime the civil liberties of thousands of Hispanic men were violated. People who work off the books for less than minimum wages and are subject to blackmail by their employers. People who threaten to wipe out all of the gains that American workers have fought for over the past one hundred years. Apparently there is no room for the views of Patricia Gonzales and Roberto Rodriquez, who are to the left of Navarrette.

African Americans have a number of individuals who are willing to serve as mind doubles. Some are supported by right-wing think tanks like the Manhattan Institute's John McWhorter, black front man for the eugenics movement. The Manhattan Institute boasts that it can provide enormous publicity for its fellows—the kind of clout that enables them to impose their viewpoints on discussions about black issues—by using proxies who are unknown to black Americans. When McWhorter attacks me in *Commentary*, a magazine that praised Charles Murray's *The Bell Curve*, where do I go to get equal time? He once challenged me to a debate, threatening "to wipe up the floor" with me. But when I accepted, he backed out.

Another proxy person of color intellectual for right-wing interests is Shelby Steele of the Hoover Institute. He just got three hours on C-Span to explain his one-note theory that blacks complain too much about their "victimization." He accused blacks of expressing victimization when they complained about being robbed of their votes in Florida during the 2000 presidential election, even though there is abundant evidence that they were victimized.

But even Shelby Steele isn't as popular with the right as Ward Connerly, who is so firmly associated with Proposition 209, the measure that ended affirmative action in California, that lazy journalists claim he started the drive that led to its being passed. He didn't. He was brought on when the real sponsors suffered a lapse in their notion of a color-blind society long enough to realize that a black face on their proposition would aid in its adoption. Before Connerly came on, the proposition was failing. One of the two white founders of the proposition said that he did so because a woman got the job he was qualified for. (Lydia Chavez, the author of *The Color Bind: The Campaign to End Affirmative Action*, an excellent book about the sinister maneuvering that led to Proposition 209, says the woman has never been found.)

Connerly, viewed by the media as the martyr who braved the scorn of black accusers to follow his conscience, only agreed to support the proposition if its supporters raised $500,000. Newt Gingrich helped to raise the money. He was also supported financially by President Clinton's nemesis Richard Mellon Scaife. Rupert Murdoch contributed $200,000 and the Pioneer Fund $35,000 to the campaign to end affirmative action in California, so that now Duke University and "Old Miss" have a higher black enrollment than the University of California.

In his book *The Nazi Connection,* Stefan Kuhl says that "today, the Pioneer Fund is the most important financial supporter of research concerning the connection between race and heredity in the United States." Until the 1960s its largest contributor was textile magnate Wickliffe Draper, who worked with the House Un-American Activities Committee to demonstrate that blacks are genetically inferior and ought to be "repatriated" to Africa.

The Pioneer Fund also supported Charles Murray's *The Bell Curve,* the book beloved by publications that hate Louis Farrakhan so much. In his book, Charles Murray floats some of the same stereotypes about blacks that were once aimed at his Scots-Irish ancestors.

Another supporter was Andrew Sullivan, who came to the attention of the mainstream electronic media after he did such a good job bashing blacks in the the *New York Times Magazine,* which portrays blacks as cannibals and crack addicts.

Obviously Ward Connerly, who has become wealthy from being associated with Proposition 209, is supported by such ultra-right individuals and groups that he has been reluctant to list his contributors.

Such is the power of their right-wing backers that Steele, Connerly, and McWhorter get more media attention than black elected officials. When Congressman Jesse Jackson Jr. and Connerly appeared on C-Span on the same day, it was Connerly who was featured.

I remember the press conference David Duke held when he announced that he was abandoning his quest for the presidency. Only a few news people attended. Duke complained that he had to quit because the mainstream candidates had coopted his program about a growing black underclass threatening civilization. (Nazi colleague Tom Metzger disagreed with him. He said on Larry King's show that the average woman on welfare is a white woman whose husband has abandoned her.)

The same might happen to Don Imus, whose nigger jokes are sponsored by American Express and other famous brand names. Who needs a white man when there are plenty of people of color willing to take up the slack?

THE FUROR OVER THE "COLORED MIND DOUBLES"

The backlash on multiculturalism has even affected the arts. Except for a few tokens, most of those listed as writers invited to conduct workshops and do readings at conferences are white. One exception is the Naropa Institute's summer workshops held in Boulder, Colorado.

Poet Anne Waldman is probably responsible for this being the most diverse of summer workshops. Another is the literary festival held in Flagstaff, Arizona, where I appeared from April 21 to 23. Flagstaff is located eight thousand feet above sea level near Hopi and Navajo country. An elderly white woman, a passenger on the shuttle that takes three hours to transport passengers from the Phoenix airport, complained about Native Americans operating casinos, an opportunity denied to whites, according to her. This is Goldwater country. But unlike many of today's conservatives, who use the label as a cover for racism, Goldwater was unpredictable.

Flagstaff is a place where you can catch a glimpse of ancient America. Twenty minutes from town, one can find pictographs carved on rock faces, left by the Anasazi who dwelled in this area for six thousand years before leaving in the 1300s.

The town's revenues are mostly derived from tourists who arrive from around the world to visit the Grand Canyon. I didn't notice any blacks when I arrived and so I remarked to our host that I felt like James Baldwin must have felt in Switzerland.

I've had this experience on other occasions in the West. In Laramie, Wyoming, when I was invited to speak there; in Grand Forks, North Dakota, Missoula, Montana, and Pullman, Washington. When I was about nineteen, traveling from San Francisco to Buffalo, New York, our car was stranded in North Platte, Nebraska. Being a black person gave me celebrity status.

Though eastern op-eders and intellectuals criticize black separatism, one can find hundreds of white separatist towns throughout the United States, though they are not considered as such. James Loewen, in his *Sundown Towns,* documents a number of communities from which blacks, Chinese, and other groups were driven out by force, or made known that they weren't welcome.

These towns still exist. It shouldn't come as a surprise that some of those who've migrated to places like Flagstaff did so to escape blacks, who have been the targets of an unprecedented media and think tank battering. (The old lynch mobs didn't have access to cable.) They escaped urban America, only to face what some Flagstaff residents view as a Mexican invasion. A younger passenger, a white woman who was also on the shuttle ride to Flagstaff, said that she and her husband were heading back to St. Louis.

This is happening all over the West, so that within twenty years nearly everything west of the Rockies will be northern Mexico. The Spanish were here before the Anglos arrived, bringing with them the virus of white supremacy (though many of them weren't considered white in the east, just as some South Asian natives get a Brahmin upgrade when they arrive in the United States; so it was with ersatz whites in the nineteenth century when they moved to the West).

Visitors to San Francisco will notice a number of places named Berryessa. The Berryessas are among the families that arrived with the De Anza expedition in the 1770s. They were given large tracts of land by a Spanish king, but this land was stolen by the American invaders. I interviewed Rose Berryessa, a descendant of this family who is now a schoolteacher in San Francisco, for my book *Blues City: A Walk in Oakland*. The interview wasn't used. She talks about how her great-grandfather was murdered by Kit Carson during a trip to a prison where his son was being held by the Americans without being charged. Given the status of land disputes in the West, one can argue that the real illegal aliens are the Americans who, I suspect, will begin leaving the West for a prosperous Europe before the century is out.

For three days I forgot about politics and basked in the brilliance and fellowship of readings by fellow writers, among them Naomi Shihab, whose poem about sending Johnny Carson to Iraq got a rousing reception from those attending the readings and panels. Heidi E. Erdrich gave a brilliant statement about the concept of beauty. Ted Koosier, the U.S. poet laureate, was supposed to appear but had to cancel because of illness in the family. He was replaced by a wonderful poet, Li Young Lee. The board of the Northern Arizona Book Festival did everything possible to make ours a comfortable visit. The events were held at the Orpheum Theater, part of a funky revitalized downtown of restaurants, shops, and bars. The Orpheum has the distinction of housing the original popcorn machine. As I was being dined and feted, Little did I know that the article I wrote for *CounterPunch* had ignited a blog firestorm eight thousand feet below, but awaiting the plane for my return to Oakland reminded me of why my observations about the media had to be made.

Maybe if those who manage airport services and the presidents of the airline companies knew how it feels to sit in a place like the Phoenix airport as the sole black person while watching CNN's airport service parade stereotypes of black men, for ratings, surrounded by people who look like Bush supporters, they would end this service. At home you can always change the channel. Here you're stuck.

Within an hour CNN broadcast stories about the alleged rape of a black college student by white members of the Duke University lacrosse team. The report was biased in favor of the white players. When a black man is suspected of a crime, the cable networks are pro-prosecution. When whites are involved, like the kids who killed a homeless man in Florida, the kind who are attacking the homeless all over the country, the suspects are given the benefit of the doubt by the media. The story disappears after a day or so.

CNN continued to run footage of the arrests of two black security guards who were the initial suspects in the Valerie Holloway kidnapping, *even after they had been released*!

Evan Thomas, who, judging from comments he made to Don Imus, believes, like the *New York Times,* that the typical perpetrator of domestic violence is a black male, when statistically black men have a better record than men of a number of ethnic groups. According to a study issued by a scholar from SUNY, they have a better record than white men. But nobody has told the *New York Times* where the typical face of domestic violence is black (and the new U.S. postage stamp with the domestic violence theme also shows a black figure). I tried to set the record straight with an op-ed I sent to the *Times,* using their statistics! It was rejected.

When it came to the white lacrosse players, Thomas just about wrote their defense in *Newsweek.* He cited Thomas Wolfe's ugly, mean-spirited, and bigoted *Bonfire of the Vanities* to suggest that racism doesn't happen to black people the way the college student claimed the Lacrosse players raped her. She made it up! (But even if this turns out to be true, Susan Smith, who claimed black men kidnapped her children, isn't used to challenge the credibility of all white women.) Thomas's view is reminiscent of Heather MacDonald's claim that racial profiling doesn't exist, even when the Bush administration says it does! MacDonald is John McWhorter's colleague at the Manhattan Institute. As for Wolfe, he writes in the tradition of Reverend Thomas Dixon, author of *The Klansman*. His novel *A Man in Full* is a perfect match with Dixon's book. Black rapist, incompetent black government, the works.

During this CNN airport broadcast, even Condi Rice, their favorite black person, was accused of leaking classified documents to members of the Israeli lobby. Mexican "migrants" were shown handcuffed and there was a story about how a new program allows women in prison to maintain contact with their children. Black and Hispanic mothers.

There was a story about the runoff race between Mayor Nagin and Lieutenant Governor Landrieu that was pro-Landrieu. The reporter, Susan Roesgen, in a previous broadcast abandoned any pretense of objectivity by criticizing Nagin for his "chocolate city" remark, yet neither she nor others who grilled Nagin for this remark, including Chris Matthews, have paid much attention to the citizens of Gretna, Louisiana, who prevented black New Orleans citizens from seeking safety there. By gunpoint. And the city council of Gretna supported this action that was meant to maintain Gretna as a vanilla city.

There was also a story ridiculing Cynthia McKinney for her run-in with a Capitol policeman, which, if she had been a white congresswoman, would have been dismissed with a joke. This is another example of the double standard by which blacks and whites are treated by the criminal justice system. A black drug addict gets jail, a white defendant like Rush Limbaugh gets rehabilitation, or a black congresswoman gets the grand jury, while the same gesture by a white congresswoman would have been considered a sign of endearing eccentricity. But for all of its presentation of blacks as buffoons and criminals, this particular program was an improvement over one I saw on CNN's airport service in Atlanta, Georgia.

I was returning from Spain in 1988 and had a stopover at the Atlanta airport. The CNN airport service was doing a feature called "Christmas on the Plantation," about how wonderful it was during Christmas in the antebellum South. It made sense. Ted Turner, who headed CNN at the time, is a big supporter of the Lost Cause myth. He pours millions of dollars into such projects as *Gods and Generals,* a film that glorifies the war criminal Robert E. Lee, who, in his own time, was considered an incompetent, responsible for the Confederate defeat at Gettysburg.

Maybe Turner doesn't realize that the black man who, according to *Jet* magazine, helped raise him wouldn't have had such a wonderful time at the old plantation Christmas. He would have been a slave!

When I returned home, I received an e-mail from Earl Caldwell, a former reporter for the *New York Times,* who now has a show on New York's WBAI, indicating that my *CounterPunch* article had ignited a controversy. (Nobody's going to give Earl Caldwell or George Curry a syndicated column). I did a Google search and found some of my comments and the excerpted reply from Michel Martin, whose interview with Cynthia McKinney was criticized in my piece, at a website operated by the Maynard Institute. The title was "Black Journalists Push Back at Ishmael Reed."

Martin's interview with Cynthia McKinney came to my attention originally after I received an e-mail from the brilliant young social and media critic Joseph Anderson, who was offended by it. After viewing the interview at the ABC website, I agreed with Anderson that Martin was curt, rude, and sarcastic to McKinney. I sent him an e-mail saying that if she had used this tone during an interview with a white male congressman she would have received the Connie Chung treatment. Readers may consult the show online and decide whether they agree. Ignored during this interview was the fact that McKinney's political views, not her hair or her minor altercation with a Capitol policeman, have earned her persecution from one of Washington's most powerful lobbies and ridicule from places like CNN, whose president views dissing blacks as a way of raising the fledgling ratings of the network. Had it not been for the O. J. trial, CNN would have tanked long ago, and they've spent much time since then, searching for an O. J. or a Michael Jackson, or Clarence Thomas, Kobe Bryant, or another black male who would attract a viewer lynch mob to their product.

They celebrated their twenty-fifth anniversary with a visual montage that was supposed to include photos of the most important events of the last twenty-five years. A photo of Anita Hill was larger than the rest.

Does CNN believe that the Anita Hill controversy, however significant, was the most important event in twenty-five years—overshadowing natural disasters, wars, an attack on the American homeland, and the impeachment of a president? Does this mean that the morbid fascination with blacks involved in scandals borders on a sickness, something that needs to be studied in a clinic examining room? Is it those who furnish the public with this junk who are sick, or it is the market that craves it?

Why, asked the late Rick James, during an interview with a CNN bimbo, was the Michael Jackson trial more interesting to the public than the war in Iraq? Good question.

Martin is right when she says that she wasn't obligated to answer Joe Klein when he made one of his frequent generalizations about black morality, the kind of remarks that earned him the title of "white militant," from For Accuracy In Reporting. Klein recently said that the black inner city should be turned over to the churches. This from one of the biggest liars of the 1990s. I don't know whether Klein or his neighbors attend church or temple, but around here my neighborhood is deserted at 11:00 A.M. on Sundays.

Martin is also correct to rebuke me for misspelling her name. I blew that one and I apologize (though the word "chastise" was spelled correctly in the copy I sent; I didn't write the headlines). As an author of millions of words, I have made mistakes, but may I suggest that my record of accuracy is superior to that of some of her employers?

I remember criticizing ABC for locating all of American drug use in the black community and I presented statistics to show that most drug users in this country are white. My comments were broadcast on Pacifica network that had an ABC ombudsman to follow me. He repeated this suburban legend about blacks and was corrected by some policy wonks who followed him.

I also appeared on *Nightline* on December 10, 1993, with the kind of pretty boys they hire to do the news. In England these people would be called newsreaders. They offered no resistance when I confronted them in regard to the folklore they spread about black life in this country. Since that show, I've noticed that these men haven't the slightest interest in acquainting themselves with the facts.

Howard Kurtz was a member of that *Nightline* panel. Kurtz is the "media critic" who ridiculed black journalists at NPR when NPR aired one of the nastiest, most irresponsible hits on black people ever broadcast. It was something called "Ghetto 101" produced by David Isay, who armed two black kids with microphones and encouraged them to record all the sleazy aspects of Chicago project life they could find—or create some. Insensitive to the black employers' complaints, NPR did a sequel that was even worse. When I sent an e-mail complaining about the sequel to "Ghetto 101," NPR got mind double Hispanic Ray Suarez to reply to me. He defended the show and in the course of his reply disparaged Bryant Gumbel and Ed Bradley. Called them "showcase blacks." Another participant on that broadcast was Jeff Greenfield. He became agitated over an issue I raised and described himself as a "white man" who had the guts to bring up black crime. By contrast, in a *New York Times* op-ed, he was soft on insider trading, the kind of crime that nearly destroyed the American economy.

Black people are not good at crime. Been here since 1619 and haven't produced a single Martha Stewart or Ken Lay.

So I think I have a good record for accuracy. Why else would NBC call me after I appeared on a network show and request that I share my data with them? They never reimbursed me for my faxing expenses. I'm just an ordinary black person living in the ghetto while they have hundreds of millions of dollars at their disposal, and media stars who might not be informed but are good actors. These pretty boys stick together. Notice how they fell over each other to congratulate Tony Snow on his new job as Bush press secretary. They don't mention that he was part of the right-wing conspiracy against President Clinton. He's the fellow who, according to Sidney Blumenthal in *The Clinton Wars*, introduced Linda Tripp to Lucianne Goldberg.

But what do we expect from the outfits that employ Martin? Tim Russert, for example, accosts every black guest about out-of-wedlock children in the ghetto without mentioning that the rate among black women has plummeted more than that of any other group. You can't get him to mention that the out-of-wedlock birthrate among white women is soaring. He must have gotten his dated information from his late mentor, Daniel Moynihan. Moynihan was the senator who accused black women of "speciation." Of producing mutants. Little Russ's idea of a panel on black America included the Manhattan Institute's surrogate John McWhorter, intellectual godson of far right-wingers Abigail and Stephan Thernstrom, and Taylor Branch, one of the media-appointed experts on black America. Only one guest, Marian Wright Edelman of the Children's Defense League, knew what she was talking about.

When Russert did an Easter special with a panel composed of Christian ministers and Rabbi Michael Lerner, not one black minister appeared, not even their favorite, Bishop Jakes. It was the black church that defined twentieth-century American Christianity.

We expect NPR to offer more superior programming than the networks that make money by offering hi-tech lynching of black people, twenty-four hours per day.

I'm glad that Michel Martin is with NPR. Maybe she can convince Ira Glass that there is more to black life than gangs. He said recently that he was "mesmerized" by ethnic gangs, which shows how blacks and Latinos get defined by people who only see them as perpetrators of crime, athletes, and entertainers; this image of blacks hasn't changed since the 1880s. Booker T. Washington, W.E.B. Du Bois, and Marcus Garvey might have had disagreements, but they all criticized the media presentation of blacks. The villains of two of Charles Chesnutt's novels, *The Colonel's Dream* (1905) and *The Marrow of Tradition* (1901), are newspaper editors. The inflammatory editorials in one lead to the lynching of a black man and the yellow journalism in the other causes a riot. Chesnutt had in mind an actual massacre of blacks that took place in Wilmington, North Carolina. Instead of pushing back on me, maybe the black journalists who belong to the NABJ can get the Newspaper Society of America to issue an apology for all of the civil discord, riots, and lynching in the past century that were perpetrated by an inflammatory press.

Martin might ask Nina Totenberg, who praised *The Bell Curve*, whether she believes that Anita Hill, whom she outed as the anonymous author of a statement about Clarence Thomas's character, has a low IQ.

Martin also feels that I was hard on Bob Herbert. He, too, is bound in journalistic shackles, in my opinion. He did a smear job on former congressman Kweisi Mfume about his children born out of wedlock, which is fair game, but he listed the children's names. Does Herbert believe that Mfume is the only Washington politician to father children by unmarried women? Would the *Times* permit him to write about the moral transgressions of white Washington politicians? Could he, for example, comment on the irony of Bush I spending millions of dollars to force some black women to help sting ex-mayor Marion Barry while, according to Kitty Kelly, author of *The Family*, Bush II was snorting coke at Camp David?

So when Martin says that I am imprisoning black journalists, I would suggest that it's her employers who are confining African Americans to a few areas of media coverage and that she and some of her fellow black journalists are the ones who are in jail.

They can only express tough love toward blacks when the "tangle of pathologies" that exist in some black communities exist in many American ethnic communities. When Greg Lewis of the *San Francisco Chronicle* pointed out that most perpetrators and victims of drive-by shootings are Hispanic, he caught hell. They'd probably be surprised to learn that Filipino American enrollment and women faculty numbers were also affected negatively by Proposition 209, because the propaganda line has it that affirmative action is a black program and that Asian Americans are a "model minority." Among Asian American groups in California, Filipino Americans constitute the largest.

Finally, Martin says that I treated Cynthia Tucker harshly and says that Tucker was a Pulitzer Prize finalist. That doesn't amount to beans, lady. They gave a Pulitzer to Janet Cooke for her story about black people being so low down that they injected a child with heroin. Robert Maynard objected but he was overruled by the white men who also gave an award to a novel that depicted black men as incest perpetrators and rapists, though it was not the author's fault that her individual characters were taken to represent all black men by Gloria Steinem and Steinem's feminist followers (for the goods on Steinem and her power to create black divas, see Cecil Brown's interview with Toni Morrison, *Massachusetts Review*). Maybe Tucker was nominated because she called the black victims of the Katrina flood "bestial," or maybe for one of her recent columns, "Idle Black Men, Tragically, Aren't Just a Stereotype," an insult to the millions of black men who, like my stepfather, worked thirty years at a crummy job so that he could feed his family. The column was about black men in New Orleans who were too lazy to compete with Hispanics for jobs.

Martin also objects to my treatment of Jeff Koinage. Jeff Koinage reported widespread looting and mayhem in New Orleans taking place in an area where even white reporters said they found no evidence. Maybe the Pulitzer Committee will create a Jayson Blair award for people like him.

Martin also says that I dislike her. That's news to me. I find Martin to be a highly professional journalist. I admire her. But her talent is being imprisoned by the men who run the outfits where she is employed. Men whose opinions are more aligned with those of white power columnists Joe Klein and David Brooks than with hers. Joe Klein, who feels that his morality is on a higher plane than that of blacks, said that Kerry lost the election because of Whoopie Goldberg's double entendre on Bush's name and Janet Jackson's exposing her breast at the Super Bowl.

Don Imus and his friend Little Russ, David Brooks, Joe Klein, and others are bullies because they know that the victims of their attacks don't have the media power to respond. They're like their role model Ronald Reagan who began his political career as an informer and rose to power by picking on welfare mothers. My *CounterPunch* article was criticized by a Republican party blog. Their remarks amounted to the usual towel-snapping fratboy-type put-downs and wisecracks that you hear from Tucker Carlson.

They disputed my claim that Charles Murray's *The Bell Curve* was supported by the Pioneer Fund, a foundation with Nazi links. I sent them the evidence, but they didn't print it. I don't understand why the Democrats have trouble with these people. They have to be fought the way Holyfield fought the bully Tyson. Bullies can't fight, backing up.

How can Martin's considerable talents be put to good use? I have a suggestion. Since she is friends with Bill Kristol, maybe she could ask him about his father's ties to the far-right Bradley Foundation, which he encouraged to finance a propaganda attack on black Americans. For more on the Bradley Foundation, *CounterPunch* readers should go to the Media Transparency website. Here's an excerpt about the foundation and its support of Murray's book:

> The book argued that poverty is the result, not of social conditions or policies, but of the inferior genetic traits of a sub-class of human beings. The book was widely seen as a piece of profoundly racist and classist pseudo-science, and was denounced by the American Psychological Association. It had relied heavily on studies financed by the Pioneer Fund, a neo-Nazi organization that promoted eugenicist research. Immediately after its publication, Bradley raised Murray's annual grant to $163,000.

Irving Kristol is a former Trotskyite who became a neocon. He's the one who said that a neocon is a liberal who has been mugged by reality. His buddy John Q. Wilson, who believes that black people have damaged genes, thought it funny to add there are no more liberals because they have been mugged. This is the man who was the philosopher behind Mayor Giuliani's fascist roundup of New York's black and Hispanic men. This would be a truly challenging assignment for Martin, something worthy of her talents. She could even ask Shelby Steele about his ties to the Bradley Foundation.

And how can Martin defend *USA Today,* after the treatment they accorded Barbara Reynolds, treatment she writes about in her book, *Out of Hell Living Well*? Of her firing by *USA Today* she writes: "On cue, a blond guy in a crisp blue blazer appeared at the meeting to escort me out of the building. I was not allowed to go back to my office. I was escorted out of the door, into the parking lot. No more was I a founding editor, who had worked day and night, traveling thousands of miles to help start the paper. I was now being treated like a criminal, busted, kicked to the curb all for having an opinion unlike those of my white comrades. Diversity was not only over; it had become virtually a treasonous offense.

By that evening I was in the emergency room with tubes hanging off of me."

I would also recommend that Martin read a book I published last year. It was written by eighty-year-old Jerri Lange, the dean of West Coast black journalists. It's called *Jerri: A Black Woman's Life in the Media*. It's about how Lange rose to the pinnacle of media success in San Francisco until she made a speech before broadcast executives about the limited portrayal of blacks in the media. After that speech the same thing that happened to Barbara Reynolds and the late Carl Rowan—who said that he was fired because he was "too old and too bold"—happened to her.

Maybe Martin will have Lange as a guest on her show. Maybe the National Association of Black Journalists will find a way to honor Reynolds, Rowan, and Lange just as they just honored Cynthia Tucker. As Carl Rowan once said of the media, "Blacks have been out propagandized."

Color-Blind Coverage?

Because many whites believe a fact only when someone who resembles them informs them of it, black opinion makers are wasting their time when they talk about the racist features of the New Orleans calamity. It's better to leave that job to Maureen Dowd, writing in the *New York Times*, Francis Fox Piven, appearing on KPFA radio, and, remarkably, Don Imus on MSNBC.

As a result of an industry of heavily financed think tanks and a media intimidated by conservatives—institutions that have conspired to destroy the credibility of black leaders—many Americans are convinced that American society is color-blind. Many progressives agree, maintaining that issues involving gays, lesbians, transgender persons, and white middle-class women are more pressing than those affecting blacks. I'm against discrimination against anyone, but I've noticed that most of those being evacuated from New Orleans—people who couldn't get out— were black, both gay and straight. Yet, when Jesse Jackson raised the issue of the racist treatment of black residents, he got swift boat–type retaliation from Bill O'Reilly and Newt Gingrich, who appeared on O'Reilly's show. (Of course we learned from the documentary *Outfoxed* that sliming Jackson and Al Sharpton are part of the Fox playbook.)

As someone who is acquainted with the inflammatory media coverage of civil disturbances involving blacks since Reconstruction,

I was prepared for the inflammatory, sensational, and racist coverage accorded the Hurricane Katrina tragedy, much of it lining up with that of the online comments about the flood and its aftermath by ex-convict David Duke, a leader of the Eurocentric movement in the United States. White residents of Louisiana were so fond of this man that they almost elected him governor.

Also, I'm not surprised that there was very little difference between the former Ku Klux Klan leader's comments and commentary earlier this week by elite *New York Times* columnists Nicholas D. Kristof and John Tierney. Conservatives might view the *Times* as liberal, but, in my opinion, the *Times* leads the nation's media when it comes to scapegoating blacks for the country's social problems.

Kristof endorsed a deal suggested by the clueless Rich Lowry of the *National Review* in which the left would devote "greater attention to out-of-wedlock births . . . in exchange for the right's support for more urban spending." Missing from this proposal is the fact that out-of-wedlock births among black teenagers have plummeted more than that of any ethnic group, while those among white women are on the rise, according to the latest figures from the National Center for Health Statistics.

Kristof also praised *Times* writer Jason DeParle, who has made a good living identifying welfare as an exclusively black problem. Meanwhile, some members of the Vietnamese community are in a crisis because their five years of receiving checks are about to expire. (When he appeared on C-Span, I asked DeParle why the *Times* always accompanies welfare stories with a black face. He squirmed as callers from around the country referred to other ethnic groups with large numbers on the welfare rolls, including immigrants from Russia.)

Tierney praised Rudy Giuliani, a man whose poll numbers were about 40 percent before the 9/11 attacks, for reducing New York City crime, when the reduction began under the David Dinkins administration. Without facts, Tierney lamented the failure of the

Great Society programs. Not only did those programs enlarge a black middle class, but Medicaid and Medicare benefited whites the most, just as whites are the principal beneficiaries of the social programs begun during the Roosevelt administration. Because American whites may be one of the most subsidized groups in world history, one wonders why they're not the object of cornball lectures about self-reliance from right-wing and neocon commentators and their persons of color auxiliary.

Neocon *New York Times* columnist David Brooks repeats some of the stereotypes listed by his colleagues and adds some of his own. For instance, he believes that among the American population, only white middle-class men are monogamous.

About the members of the Kennedy administration who were considered "the best and the brightest," Sam Rayburn, longtime speaker of the House, said "they may be just as intelligent as you say. But I'd feel a helluva lot better if just one of them had ever run for sheriff."

I feel the same way about those who write tough-love op-eds about the black inner city from Cambridge, Greenwich Village, the Upper West Side, Georgetown, and beach houses in Santa Monica and Monterey. I suspect that some of them are composing columns and articles maintaining that Katrina was not an act of God, but the result of blacks' personal behavior.

I wish that some of these smug individuals would serve as block captain in an inner-city neighborhood for a year, as I have since 1989. They would discover that the official indifference and apathy and neglect expressed toward the black residents in New Orleans happen on a smaller scale to black neighborhoods throughout the nation. That nation is not color-blind. It's colored blind.

Imus

How Imus's Media Collaborators Almost Rescued Their Chief and How Media and Academic Blacks Fell for Imus's Talking Point That It Was All About Hip-Hop

Some of us relish the naughtiness.
—HOWARD KURTZ ON DON IMUS

I n his 1995 book *Hot Air*, Howard Kurtz wrote that "Imus' sexist, homophobic, and politically incorrect routines echo what many journalists joke about in private." Later, host Don Imus brought up McGuirk's prior impersonations of African American poet Maya Angelou by asking, "Who was that woman you used to do, the poet? . . . We used to get in all that trouble every time you'd do her." As McGuirk launched into the impersonation, Imus said, "I don't need any more columns. Come on." But Imus did not stop McGuirk, who delivered his impression in verse:

Whitey plucked you from the jungle for too many years. They took away your pride, your dignity, and your spears. With freedom came new woes. Into whitey's world you was rudely cast. So wake up now and go to work? You can kiss my big black ass.

What began as a firestorm against Don Imus's remarks against the members of Rutgers women's basketball team ended, thanks to Imus's friends, who controlled a bogus "national dialogue about race," and media and academic blacks, who hadn't been paying attention to his vile racism over the years, with a referendum on gangsta rap and the morals of Al Sharpton and Jesse Jackson. By Monday, April 16, 2007, an all-Imus buddy panel appearing on CNN—including John Roberts, Paul Begala, and James Carville—engaged in a tribute to Imus. All that was needed were champagne glasses. On the same day, John Roberts and his colleague Wolf Blitzer described the murder of thirty-one students at Virginia Tech as "the worst massacre in American history," ignoring mass killings of blacks and Native Americans that had been far worse. Moreover, the fact that the shooter Cho Seung-Hui was a fan of Guns N' Roses (he named a play, "Mr. Brownstone," after one of the band's songs) didn't inspire the 24/7 castigation of white heavy metal music that was dealt to hip-hop music in the wake of Don Imus's firing. Ignoring the misogyny of heavy metal music is in keeping with the media's two-hundred-year policy of playing up black pathology and playing down pathology when it occurs among whites; when white journalists aren't doing the job, their African American farm team is summoned.

The president of NBC News, Steve Capus, was disingenuous when he claimed that Don Imus, the shock jock, was fired solely because employees at NBC were outraged at Imus's description of the members of the Rutgers women's basketball team as "nappy headed hos." That might have been part of it. But it was the multibillion-dollar purchasing power of African Americans and organizations like the National Association of Black Journalists, a more difficult target for Imus's fans than Sharpton and Jackson, that gave the African American community its greatest victory against a racist media that has been its bane since the first slave ships arrived.

Before television and radio, it was the newspapers that raised lynch mobs on African Americans. In Charles Chesnutt's novels, *The Marrow of Tradition* (1901) and *The Colonel's Dream* (1905), the villains are newspapermen. The inflammatory coverage of one led to a lynching; the editor in the other caused a race riot. *The Betrayal of the Negro*, a book by Rayford Whittingham Logan, indicts some of the nation's most prestigious newspapers for inciting civil strife during the twentieth century based on malicious and false reporting.

The "national dialogue" that MSNBC held after the Imus outburst about the Rutgers team was a telling example of this historic trend. The so-called dialogue was dominated mostly by white talking heads, including white women who seem to be prospering at MSNBC, receiving as much airtime as the men. (Even so, Gloria Steinem maintained in a recent *New York Times* op-ed that white, middle-class women and blacks share the same social predicament. Really? The college enrollment of white women is higher than that of both white men and blacks.) Instead of the opinions of black academic feminists like bell hooks, Michele Wallace, Sandra O'Neale, Paula Giddings, Joyce Joyce, or Sonia Sanchez being solicited to comment about Imus's remarks, Naomi Wolf, a white feminist bell hooks has criticized in *Ms.* magazine, spoke on behalf of black women.

It's fortunate that the money people at General Motors and Bigelow Tea, DirecTV, Ameritrade, Staples, Sprint, American Express, and Proctor & Gamble stepped in. Had they not, Imus groupies like Mike Barnicle, David Gregory, Bo Dietl (the author of a vicious anti-Muslim tirade during Imus's last weeks), and Joe Scarborough would have rescued their buddy by following their leader's talking points. (Keith Olbermann reported that Dietl was even reprimanded by right-wing fixer Dick Morris for using Barack Obama's middle name, "Hussein," to make even more anti-Muslim comments.)

Imus griped that he was a victim of African American male culture, where—according to a man who has a lengthy record of making misogynist remarks—men mistreat women. Yet a recent State
University of New York study reveals a different reality: white men
commit most of the assaults on women in this country.* According
to the study conducted by Lois Weis, professor of education at the
University of Buffalo–New York, and Michelle Fine, professor
of social psychology in the Graduate Center at the City University
of New York, white women are afraid to talk about the abuse. Weis
and Fine found that 92 percent of the white women interviewed
said that "serious domestic violence" had been directed against
them, their mothers, and/or sisters, either in their birth households
or in later relationships. By comparison, 62 percent of black female
subjects reported similar levels of violence in their lives. The authors of the study said they were surprised because these were
white women largely from middle-class homes. I sent this study to
feminists at National Public Radio, Pacifica Radio, and other places
where they give the brothers a hard time and only one writer, the
late Susan Lydon of the *Oakland Tribune*, replied.

By now it must be obvious that the feminist movement, which
has singled out black men for their misogyny, has a Stockholm
syndrome relationship with white men. Maybe that's why little
has been made about the falling murder rate of black women by
their husbands and boyfriends, while the murder rate of women
by white men has remained about the same. One reason for the
falling rate of domestic abuse among blacks is that black women
are more likely to retaliate.** This drop in black domestic violence

---

*Patricia Donovan, "Domestic Violence Found in Stable White Fami-
lies," *Reporter*, January 16, 1997.
**That black men are a class unto themselves when it comes to homicide
will not come as a surprise to most Americans. Black men are America's
primary crime victims. Black men over eighteen are only 4 percent of
this country's population. Yet more are hospitalized for assault injuries

has been reported in the *New York Times*, yet the face of domestic violence in the pages of the *Times* continues to be painted black.

Do you suppose that MSNBC will ever conduct a "national dialogue" about white domestic violence? Maybe *Newsweek*? One of its writers, Evan Thomas, recently told Imus's audience that black men in the inner city enjoy beating up their women. It's obvious that as long as wealthy white men control the media, it will be used as a weapon against black men, while the crimes against women committed by them will be hidden. Why should anybody be surprised that black actors perform in HBO projects like *The Wire*? Black actors performed in D. W. Griffith's *Birth of a Nation*. In *The Wire*, written by three white men, black men engage in cruel treatment of black women, yet the head of HBO had to resign recently because he beat up a woman in the parking lot outside of a Las Vegas casino. Maybe HBO should do a series about that incident?

Given the remarks about women made by Imus's stable of Celtic American commentators, I wouldn't be surprised to learn that women in Celtic American households have a harder time than women in black households. And what about Imus's constant on-air berating of his wife Deirdre as a "whore" and a "moron"? Why isn't this kind of verbal battery reported domestic abuse?

Imus also set himself up as the arbiter of dating among black men. Of course, the majority of blacks have some European heritage: my mother has Irish American ancestors on both her mother's and father's sides. But black people didn't become a Creole nation as

---

each year than women and girls of all races combined. More black men died from homicide in 2004 alone than all the children age ten and under in the previous five years. Even domestic violence, which accounts for a fraction of homicides nationally, appears to have resulted in higher death rates for black men than for white women in recent years. Jill Levy, "Don't Believe the Hype About Murder," Salon.com, December 14, 2006, www.salon.com/opinion/feature/2006/12/14/homicide/index.html.

a result of black men and white women having sex. Indeed, the first deadbeat dad of an African American household was almost certainly English, Irish, or Scots-Irish. Both Frederick Douglass and Booker T. Washington's white, slave-owning fathers had nothing to do with them. And though some black men are abusive to their families, I don't know of any who have sold their own children for profit.

White men and women who believe that domestic violence is a peculiarly black phenomenon must get their information about black life from Stephen Spielberg's film *The Color Purple* or like-minded novels. These are works of fiction. Spielberg's portrait of the book's villain, Mister, even offended the book's author, Alice Walker. When is Spielberg going to make a movie about the abuse of Jewish women in Jewish households, in both the United States and Israel?

When I first visited Israel in 2000, the murder of Israeli wives by Israeli husbands had become such an issue that the then prime minister, Ehud Barak, was compelled to comment about it. Moreover, Jewish feminists assert that the abuse of women in Jewish households is a "dark secret." Shouldn't Spielberg expose this "dark secret" on the screen?

After a version of this chapter appeared in *CounterPunch*, I received no mail from black men or Celtic American men that disputed my comments. I did receive some angry mail regarding my comments about domestic violence in Jewish American and Israeli households. One writer said that the abuse of Jewish women happens when they marry outside of their religion. Another writer said that Jewish women are abused because they marry black men. I sent the letter writers an extensive bibliography about domestic abuse occurring in Jewish American families compiled by Marcia Cohn Spiegel of the Minnesota Center Against Violence and Abuse, which refutes their claims.* Moreover, some of the harshest criti-

---

*Marcia Cohn Spiegel, *Bibliography of Sexual and Domestic Violence in the Jewish Community* (2000; Minnesota Center Against Violence and Abuse, 2004).

cism of black male misogyny has been made by Jewish American feminists: Gloria Steinem, Tammy Bruce, Susan Brownmiller, Amy Goodman, and others, yet they seem to look away from domestic abuse that occurs in their ethnic group. These feminists have a lot of educating to do.

While Spielberg used Alice Walker's book as an excuse to create one of the most sinister black male characters since the black actors who appeared in *Birth of a Nation*, black veterans complain that the director ignores their fighting role in his war movies. One black veteran expressed his frustration at the HBO blog:

There is one big huge problem about *Band of Brothers* and *Saving Private Ryan* that bothers me. Where are the black GIs? In *Band of Brothers*, the story line was from 1943–1945 and no black troops. *Saving Private Ryan*—no black troops during D-Day? It's hard to take *Saving Private Ryan* & *Band of Brothers* seriously. WWII films such as *Pearl Harbor, U–571, Hart's War* and including *The Dirty Dozen* showed black WWII soldiers. I rewinded the beach scene in Saving Private Ryan to find dead black soldiers and I did not find one. That is sad if I had to rewind the scene to find dead black soldiers because there weren't any black soldiers seen period. Tom Hanks and Steven Spielberg should try looking at WWII through a different lens because I don't think they've got it right. It's sad to see African American WWII vets ignored in the public eye. Not only the African American vets, all minority vets of WWII ignored. The minority vets of WWII are the real Band of Brothers. They fought two wars—The American military Jim Crow Law attempts in England (racism, segregation and bigotry in our arm forces during WWII) and the Germans. What does Easy Company vets got to say about that? My family lost six, one family member lost his legs and four made it back safe. Today, out of eleven vets in my family, only one is alive (My oldest cousin who is a WWII vet and was over in Europe in 1943–1946). He remembers Easy Company during Bastogne. My cousins regiment was the unit that bailed easy company out of heavy fire and other white units. If it wasn't for my cousins unit, easy company would of been nil. I was surprised Spielberg & Hanks did not add that big piece of history in the *Band of Brothers* series. Back to my point, my cousin saw *Saving Private Ryan* and he was disappointed. My cousin didn't want to see *Band of Brothers*. He called the show "Disney Liked," unreal. Eleven family members gave there life to this country during WWII and Tom Hanks & Spielberg couldn't add black soldiers as extras in there WWII films. Before making these films, they should have made sure the events are correct. Film directors should not try rewriting history to suit there own egos.*

The other talking point set forth by Imus was that his smearing of the Rutgers team was his first offense and an apology should have been enough. On March 14 Tom Foreman parroted this line after yet another ignorant CNN rant about hip-hop. Foreman complained that Imus was being punished for "a few ill chosen words," thus obscuring the fact that his firing was a culmination of years of KKK-type comments about Jews, blacks, Muslims, and gays. The Rutgers slur was merely the straw that broke the camel's back. Though Imus's defenders claim he is an "equal opportunity abuser," his ridicule of gays, lesbians, and blacks, and especially black men, was a daily feature of his program. Yet gays and lesbians, whose organizations have been complaining about Imus for years, weren't invited to participate in the "national dialogue" because the networks and cable channels have found that they can make more money by promoting the racial divide.

Don Imus's acolytes, like the former NYPD cop Bo Dietl, were all over television insisting that the Rutgers team should be the final judge of whether Imus remained on the job: young women who were not fully acquainted with Imus's résumé of past offenses

---

*HBO Bulletin Board, March 23, 2005.

against black women and more were likely to cut him some slack. These young women might not have known that Imus called Gwen Ifill "a cleaning lady," a term that certainly wasn't inspired by rappers. The Rutgers team probably wasn't tuned in to Imus when he and his crew joked about the murder of Betty Shabazz, Malcolm X's widow, jokes that don't appear in any hip-hop song yet.

Attorney Constance L. Rice, in an opinion piece defense of Imus published in the *Los Angeles Times*, described Imus's racism as "good-natured." I doubt whether Betty Shabazz's children or many of her admirers would find anything good-natured about Imus and his friends joking about her murder. Rice must not have been listening when he and his buddy, the contemptible Bernard McGuirk, laughed over an obscene parody of Maya Angelou's poetry or when Sid Rosenberg thought it clever to suggest on the Imus show that the Williams sisters pose in *National Geographic*. Those Green Zone blacks—coddled academics, journalists, opinionators, and intellectuals—who are out of touch with everyday life in African American communities and who trace all of society's misogyny to hip-hop would be hard-pressed to find a hip-hop song suggesting that the Williams sisters pose in *National Geographic*, nude.

Though the American cognoscenti wallowed before Imus, even calling him "bookish," Imus was apparently ignorant of Maya Angelou's highly acclaimed body of work, although she was President Clinton's inaugural poet.

The other Imus talking point was that it was all about Al Sharpton and Jesse Jackson. Kill the messengers, even though the National Association of Black Journalists made the initial call for Imus's firing. Researchers at MediaMatters.org, according to the *Wall Street Journal*, posted the transcript and clips of Imus's remarks on their website. This brought the matter to widespread attention, yet Media Matters didn't receive the scolding accorded Sharpton and Jackson.

Frank Rich, another Imus stalwart, took a shot at Sharpton and defended Imus in the Sunday *New York Times* of April 15, 2007.

Rich claimed the Rutgers basketball team and Don Imus were the only ones, during the entire episode, who weren't hypocrites! Why isn't the effort by Imus and his posse to deflect the attention from Imus to Sharpton and rap music deemed hypocritical? Why wasn't Imus's pretending to distance himself from the man *he hired* to do "nigger jokes" considered hypocritical? Why wasn't Imus condemned for attempting to blame black men for misogyny instead of apologizing for his own verbal abuse of women? Frank Rich, who provided intellectual heft to the Imus show, is former theater critic at the *New York Times*. Rich was the one who condemned the late August Wilson for proposing a black nationalist theater. I asked him in an e-mail how he could criticize August Wilson's black nationalism but cooperate with Imus's crude, yahoo-bubba white nationalism. Rich didn't respond.

After this cowardly display by Imus's defenders—Rich, Maher, Carville, and others—how can they claim moral superiority to their usual targets: George Bush and Dick Cheney (Vice President Cheney and his wife Lynne also appeared on the Imus show)? Neither Cheney nor Bush ever called a black athlete a "nappy headed ho" or referred to black men as "gorillas," at least not on national television.

NBC reporter David Gregory, like a prize poodle, used to appear on Imus's show and receive pats on the head for engaging in testy exchanges with White House press briefers. Gregory ran a television marathon defending Imus and castigating gangsta rap. Another claim was that his critics were depriving Imus of his right to free speech. White men control the means of expression in this country from *Newsweek* to *Rolling Stone,* for all three networks and cable channels from the mainstream newspapers to *The Nation,* where the majority of the writers are white men (two of whom joined in the attack on hip-hop during the entire "Imus week") even though it's edited by a feminist.

It's those who are abused by the media—blacks and Latinos, who have consistently complained about the one-sided presentation of their groups—whose free speech is denied. In the Imus case, they used one of the few avenues of expression open to them: a threatened boycott of the offender's advertisers. MSNBC allowed Imus's pals and regulars like Gregory and Joe Scarborough to moderate panels where they prosecuted Imus's critics, even though they were Imus's collaborators. One night a screaming Joe Scarborough totally lost it when he accused a puzzled Joan Walsh, editor of Salon.com, of enjoying hip-hop music. (Yes, this is the same Joan Walsh, a TV "progressive," who agreed with writer Stanley Crouch that an Albany jury was right to acquit the NYPD cops who shot the unarmed Amadou Diallo forty-four times.) Gregory (whose unconscionable role in this affair I believe violated basic journalistic ethics) and Scarborough were among this faux cowboy posse, and the cable networks allowed other Imus groupies to fan out across a number of shows to defend their boss. Instead of treating their audience to a nonstop interrogation of Imus critics, the networks should have convened panels to examine the role their own pundits played in the enabling of Imus.

The list of Imus enablers is a long and star-studded one, including *New York Times* writer Maureen Dowd; David Brooks, who has set himself up as the country's ombudsman for morality; Tom Friedman and Frank Rich; James Carville and his wife, Mary Matalin; Craig Crawford; Tom Browkaw; Brian Williams; Jeff Greenfield; Bo Dietl; Tom Oliphant; Imus sidekick Charles McCord; and others who tolerated his and McGuirk's crude skinhead tirades against blacks, Jews, gays, and lesbians for years. These journalists should be given the same scrutiny as Imus. Instead, Imus's groupies were allowed to dominate a bogus, one-sided "national dialogue about race." Didn't historian Douglas Brinkley know better than to enable Imus? The *New Yorker's* David Remnick? Presidential historian Michael Beschloss? Michel Martin, after mentioning the guests who went on the Imus show to plug their books and pretended to have no knowledge of what was what on the show, asked, "Who's the ho?"

Bill Maher, who appeared on one of Imus's last shows, even after the Rutgers put-down, pretended that Imus's remark was his only offense, a kind of misdemeanor for which a simple apology was enough. Maher and some admiral who appeared on the same show assured Imus that their Negroes supported the shock jock. Maher contends that blacks are more homophobic than members of other ethnic groups, which only means he hasn't examined the homophobic attitudes of other ethnic groups.

MSNBC then brought in members of its African American bench to endorse the talking points set down by Imus. John Ridley and Niger Innis certified the posse's line that black male culture is responsible for Imus's problems! Both men made ad hominem attacks on Jackson and Sharpton. Ridley was described as a screenwriter and commentator. His essay, "The Manifesto of Ascendancy for the Modern American Nigger," a piece clotted with the usual "tough love" generalizations and stereotypes, was considered so offensive that author Jill Nelson, whose book *Involuntary Slavery* is a scathing indictment of racism in the newsroom at the *Washington Post*, among others, called for a boycott of *Esquire*, which published the article.

Ariana Huffington, another former conservative turned television liberal, apparently hasn't noticed her black sisters' outrage; she has provided John Ridley with a platform at the *Huffington Post*. Joe Scarborough and the producers who brought Ridley on their show probably enjoyed the article. They probably thought it provocative.

Maybe the Pulitzer Committee will award Ridley a prize next year, as it did Cynthia Tucker, editorial page editor for the *Atlanta Journal-Constitution*, who got one this year for calling black men "bestial" and "idle" and for regularly criticizing black leaders and personalities. While the *Atlanta Journal-Constitution* is rough on the brothers and sisters, it treats whites like children. The *Atlanta Journal-Constitution* killed a story about how thousands of blacks were chased from American cities through mob action in the early part of the twentieth century. The judgment at the paper was that this unpleasant news might hurt the feelings of white readers.

The *Atlanta Journal-Constitution* has a history. This is, after all, the newspaper that endorsed President Rutherford B. Hayes's withdrawal of Union troops from the South, an action that left blacks to the tender mercies of white terrorism. The paper also praised Dinesh D'Souza's screed *The End of Racism*, a book so racist that its publication prompted two black conservatives to resign from the American Enterprise Institute, one of D'Souza's main patrons. D'Souza, who became a millionaire for writing hateful comments about blacks, thought he could attack whites. As a result, the same white critics who praised his *End of Racism* killed his new book *The Enemy at Home: The Cultural Left and Its Responsibility for 9/11*. For its part, one of the main sponsors of the American Enterprise Institute, beer manufacturer Peter Coors, was arrested recently for drunk driving. Maybe the institute, which preaches family values to blacks, should address his morality.

Cynthia Tucker wouldn't be the first black tough love merchant to receive a prize from the white men at the Pulitzers. They gave one to Janet Cooke, the former *Washington Post* fabulist who concocted a story about black parents supplying an eight-year-old with drugs. That year, the token black members of the Pulitzer Committee tried to warn the men who controlled the prizes that her story was a phony; they were overruled.

This year, the Pulitzer Committee cited Tucker's "courage," which implies that the black community is of such monolithic opinion that it takes guts to criticize its leaders and culture when that's all we get from the media and their journalistic mind doubles, those mercenaries and overseers who have an editorial whip ready to flog the underclass blacks in the field. Lewis Lapham, the former editor of *Harper's*, said of one Colored Mind Double: "He says what we say in private." Another black guest, Steve Perry, author of a book called *Man Up*, blamed Imus's problems on the content of the Rutgers basketball team's iPods! Rarely mentioned during this "national dialogue" about race, which Imus and his defenders successfully turned into a referendum on rap music, duping media blacks and academics into underwriting this effort, was Bernard McGuirk, who was hired by Imus to do "nigger jokes."

McGuirk's ugly tirades about gays, lesbians, blacks, and women far exceeded insensitive remarks that Jackson and Sharpton have made in the past. Jesse Jackson is still being hounded for his "Hymietown" remark, for which he has *repeatedly* apologized. Yet former secretary of state James Baker, who once snarled, "Fuck the Jews," according to former Mayor Ed Koch, is still considered a statesman.

TIME magazine editor Jon Meacham, an Imus all-star, swooned that being in the presence of Billy Graham must be like being in the presence of God when peddling his interview with Graham by saying such things as, "He is what God looks like—white hair, blue eyes." This is the same Reverend Graham who once confided to Richard Nixon in the Oval Office that the Jews are satanic and own the media. According to H. R. Haldeman's diaries, Graham agreed to Nixon's request that he, Graham, select a black leader. The media and the establishment select black leaders and when these leaders mess up blacks are called on to criticize selections they hadn't made in the first place.

I e-mailed "Noah" at Rabbi Michael Lerner's *Tikkun* magazine. Rabbi Lerner had picketed Cornel West for joining Minister Louis Farrakhan's Million Man March. I asked whether Lerner was going to protest Imus's anti-Semitism. No answer.

Bernard McGuirk prefaced Imus's comments about the Rutgers team with a description of them as "hard-core hos." He's the one who constantly smeared black athletes as monkeys, gorillas, and "knuckle draggers" and called Lindsay Davenport, the tennis champion, "a big dyke," with no prompting from Snoop Dogg. He's the one who led Imus's crew in ridiculing the features of a black woman who had launched a sexual harassment suit against Isiah Thomas, the coach of the New York Knicks. At TomPaine.com, writer Philip Nobile has chronicled outrages on the Imus show dating to 2000. TomPaine.com published an ad in the *New York Times* and even bought time on the Imus show to address the sewage spewing from Imus and his crew.

In an article on May 16, 2000, Nobile wrote, "Just about anything goes—from saying that [African American former basketball player] Larry Johnson ruined [white female TV news personality] Willow Bay for white men, to asking the borough president of the Bronx if he felt 'like the mayor of Mogadishu.' Epithets like 'brillohead,' 'dark meat,' 'dingos,' 'mandingos,' and 'Uncle Ben' are okay on Imus."

And though it was an insult about black women that got Imus fired, black men were ridiculed on the show daily. Often it was about their mythical sexual prowess, which extended to jokes about Deirdre Imus in bed with black sexual partners. When Deirdre said that Harold Ford would make a good president, McGuirk chimed in, "Yeah, and you can be his first lady." McGuirk seemed to have a pathological obsession with the alleged sexual gifts of black men, returning to the subject time and time again.

When New Orleans Mayor Ray Nagin confused the word "cavalry" with "calvary," a common error, McGuirk seized upon the verbal slip to cast the mayor as an illiterate. Using an old plantation dialect to imitate the mayor, McGuirk ridiculed Nagin mercilessly. In one scene, he had the mayor in bed with a white prostitute only to have Nagin's family show up. McGuirk had Nagin say, "It was all right, because we wasn't doing nothin'," a remark Imus and his crew found hilarious and perhaps another example of Imus's "good-natured" racism. In another scene, Imus and his crew were in stitches as McGuirk had Nagin searching for his dead mother after the floods of Katrina. When Imus complained about Marcia Clark and Chris Darden "blowing" the O. J. Simpson case, McGuirk interjected, "They blew each other, too," referring to Darden and Clark vacationing together in San Francisco.

McGuirk's sexual obsession harkens back to the old Confederate fear of miscegenation. McGuirk is the son of Irish immigrants. It was an Irish immigrant named David Goodman Croly who, according to Harvard professor Werner Sollors, coined the term "miscegenation" and perpetrated "the great miscegenation hoax of 1863." Croly was the author of a phony pamphlet that exposed a plan by Lincoln's party to invade northern bedrooms with black women. Lincoln was forced to defend the party against the charge. From *The Journal of Negro History*:

> The pamphlet claimed that the goal of Abraham Lincoln and the Republican Party was the 'interbreeding' of 'White' and African Americans in the United States. Many people thought the pamphlet, "Miscegenation: The Theory of the Blending of the Races, Applied to the American White Man and Negro," was written by abolitionists who supported the idea. On February 17, 1864, a Democratic congressman denounced the pamphlet in a speech delivered to the House of Representatives. He claimed it represented the social philosophy of the Republican Party. The actual authors of the pamphlet were an editor and reporter from the *New York World*, a pro-Democratic Party newspaper. They wrote it to stir up racist attitudes among White voters as part of the newspaper's opposition to Abraham Lincoln's reelection campaign.*

Contrast McGuirk's reactionary bile with the views of Gerry Adams, leader of the Sinn Féin Party. He told a U.C.–Berkeley audience about the renting of the alliance between the Irish and the blacks who worked on southern plantations by slave masters, who turned them against each other. When Gerry Adams visited the United States, he stopped off to see the late Rosa Parks to thank her for inspiring the Irish movement.

---

*Sidney Kaplan, "The Miscegenation Issue in the Election of 1864," *Journal of Negro History*, July 1949, 274–343.

McGuirk is not the only one out of touch with his heritage. Imus admirer Chris Matthews, another Irish American who gets to comment on race more than African Americans, confessed that he admires Rudy Giuliani because he brought "a little fascism" to New York. Of course it was black and Hispanic men who were the primary victims of this "little fascism." Maybe Matthews has forgotten that it was the Irish who, about a hundred years ago, were targets of fascism, attacked by mobs for practicing their faith and rounded up and thrown into "paddy" wagons. Yet Matthews gets to comment and make judgments about blacks when he is apparently ignorant of Irish history.

Somebody ought to remind McGuirk and Matthews that the nineteenth-century solution to the race problem was to have an Irishman kill a black man and get hanged for it. Another joke at the time was that an Irish American is a Negro turned inside out.

Instead of criticizing McGuirk, the pro-Imus claque at MSNBC reserved their harshest treatment for Sharpton and Jackson. MSNBC reporter Lisa Daniels, who was assigned to interview students at Rutgers, followed this line by attempting to goad the students into attacking Sharpton and Jackson.

Tucker Carlson, whose show is a "lite" version of the Imus show (he attracts attention to his opinion product by picking fights with blacks under the cover of opposing political correctness), brought on a black sportswriter named Jason Whitlock to call Jackson and Sharpton "terrorists." After this bizarre outburst, Tucker the Wiseass, in an arrogant colonial manner, nominated Whitlock to become a black leader. But Carlson was right about one thing. While the liberal Imus protectors stood by their man, the same crowd drove Senator George Allen, the Virginia Republican, from public life, even though his demeaning "macaca" crack was mild in comparison to Imus's daily portrayals of blacks.

Boston Globe columnist Tom Oliphant, who pledged "solidarity" with Imus on one of his last shows, thought it clever to cite neo-Confederate novelist Tom Wolfe's *Bonfire of the Vanities,* in which a character named Reverend Bacon is crudely based on Reverend Sharpton. Every time Oliphant popped up during the "national dialogue on race," which, given the segregated media, was dominated by talking heads belonging to one race, he said, "You know, this whole thing reminds me of *The Bonfire of the Vanities*." This book proposes that as a result of Jewish leniency, blacks get away with hustling white guilt. At one point, Oliphant seemed to be sending out marching orders to the Imus legions, inviting a white backlash against Imus's firing.

Craig Crawford of the *Congressional Quarterly*, another Imus regular, was given hours at a time to repeat his claim that he didn't know what was going on during the segments in which he was not a participant. Crawford said that Imus didn't make racist comments while he was on the show. He didn't have a clue. This was the line closely followed by other Imus collaborators. Mary Matalin, another frequent guest, said she had no idea what was going on. Perhaps Matalin was spending all of her time keeping up with Jesse Jackson, whom she attacks obsessively.

In a column appearing in the April 16 edition of the *San Francisco Chronicle*, Eugene Robinson wrote, "While we're in the business of blunt truth, do the big-time media luminaries who so often graced Imus' show have some explaining to do? You bet, and so do the parent news organizations, including my own, which allowed their journalists to go on a broadcast that routinely crossed the aforementioned line. All these trained observers couldn't have failed to notice Imus' well-practiced modus operandi. 'He never said anything bad while I was on,' doesn't cut it as a defense."

At one point during MSNBC's "national dialogue on race," which included no Hispanics and no gays or lesbians—groups routinely abused by the Imus show, when Jesse Jackson challenged MSNBC to hire more black anchors and talk show hosts, Imus buddy Mike Barnicle said that it was not necessary; this from a man who referred to the black wife of a former defense secretary as "a Mandingo." *The Village Voice* reported, "Talking about the marriage of former secretary of defense William Cohen (who is white) and his wife, Janet Langhart (who is black), Barnicle remarked, 'Yeah. I know them both. Bill Cohen. Janet Langhart. Kind of like Mandingo.'" Yet, incredibly, at one point CBS considered appointing Barnicle (who was fired from the *Boston Globe* for plagiarizing columns) as Imus's successor on the radio!

For his part, Jesse Jackson has been a longtime NBC watcher. Jackson recalls the time when *NBC Nightly News* executive producer Jeff Gralnick referred to Somali military leader Mohammad Farah Aideed as an "educated jungle bunny," saying, "the rest of the jungle bunnies are not like this at all. They're illiterates" (*Washington Post*, October 16, 1993). Jackson described Gralnick's racist outburst as part of a mind-set at NBC.

When Jesse Jackson asked Keith Olbermann, one of the few white talking heads who had urged the firing of Imus, the same question about the networks hiring more black anchors, Olbermann (another former sports reporter) said that he permits Alison Stewart, a black woman, to take his place when he's on vacation. Yet Stewart's approach was no different from those of Don Imus's groupies. This poor child has no power at MSNBC. Another Colored Mind Double, she moderated a discussion between Paul Waldman from *Media Matters,* who supported the firing of Imus, and Imus pal Craig Crawford. She reserved her toughest questions for Waldman and permitted Imus groupie Craig Crawford to interrogate Waldman.

By five o'clock on March 12, when David Gregory again substituted for Chris Matthews on *Hardball,* he'd learned that Imus had been fired from CBS. This gave Gregory an excuse to prolong his seventy-two hour marathon effort to garner sympathy for his leader. But by that time, like the man who was sent on a mission to sell Dracula some insurance, the teeth marks on Gregory's neck were apparent. The panel in this part of the "national dialogue on race" included only one black man, the soft-spoken Eugene Robinson from the *Washington Post*, and what seemed like an Imus alumni reunion: Pat Buchanan, Gregory, Oliphant, and Senator Chris Dodd, all Imus regulars. On March 13, Gregory continued to blame his buddy's ordeal on Sharpton, Jackson, and rap music— the line that had begun to gain traction as the Imus collaborators began to fill hours of talk show time by blaming Imus's victims for his ouster.

But as a result of the press conference held by the members of the Rutgers team, Imus was doomed like the pathetic cowboy in the film *Down in the Valley* to wandering around on horseback amid condominiums and urban sprawl, an anachronism in an age that has left him behind. Imus vowed to his followers that he'd be back. And he probably will be. Imus will survive as a result of the spite that many whites hold for African Americans.

The same kind of spite led some white citizens of Memphis to respond to the civil rights movement by erecting a statue of General Nathan Forrest, whose massacre of black men, women, and children at Fort Pillow, even after they'd surrendered, was called "the atrocity" of the Civil War.

The white men and women in charge of the "national dialogue," conditioned by degrading images of black kids in the news media and grungy products like HBO's *The Wire*, seemed shocked by the young women on the Rutgers team who were committed to scholastic excellence. African Americans aren't shocked. Most of my nieces and nephews either have degrees or are enrolled in college. Both my daughters have a college background.

In the end, Imus is a throwback with fans who cling to the lost cause of white supremacy. Like the old-timers who show off their medals at reunions of Stalin's veterans, like residents of Madrid who tell you that Franco kept the streets clean, or the sad people who write books that end with a Confederate victory, Imus's fans get off by listening to bullies like Imus ridicule and humiliate people who don't have the media power to fight back.

Don Imus's defenders point to his charitable works. They remind me of Stonewall Jackson's admirers, who point to the Con-

federate general's donations to a black Sunday school as proof
that the insurgent, who fought to defend the institution of slavery,
loved black folks. The National Basketball Association and its
players have contributed hundreds of millions of dollars to charity, but instead of receiving praise in the media, the NBA is de-
rided as a collection of knuckle draggers, chest-thumping pimps,
rapists. The media don't like their style of dress. They diss their
way of speaking. They envy their wealth. When Allen Iverson was
late for a game, McGuirk quipped, "His Bentley broke down?"
McGuirk called Iverson's mother "a crack ho."

Moreover, the *Wall Street Journal* raised troubling questions
about the charity-spending practices of the Imus ranch, suggesting that much of the money was going to support the lifestyle of
the Imus family. Imus responded to the article by calling the
writer a "punk." The *Journal* stood by the story: "The managing
editor of *The Wall Street Journal*, Paul Steiger, said that the article
was accurate and fair and that Mr. Frank [the reporter] had had
many detailed discussions with Mr. Imus' representatives during
the two months he worked on the article. In addition, Mr. Steiger
said, Mr. Frank spoke twice with Mr. Imus at length the day before
the article was published."

After Jeff Greenfield finally abandoned Imus, he reminded the
shock jock that the kind of black voice-overs that he and his colleagues engaged in harkened back to the minstrel shows, when
Irish immigrants entertained audiences by getting up in blackface.
McGuirk does his blackface with his tongue. Another ship jumper
was Harold Ford Jr., the former congressman from Tennessee. For
his disloyalty, Imus denounced him as a coward.

Michael Eric Dyson exposed the problem that occurs when the
media refuse to diversify. In terms of integration, the media are
fifty years behind the South and resemble a Mississippi bus station
of the 1940s with its "Whites Only" sign. Both David Gregory and
Ed Shultz, another putative "progressive," lashed out at Sharpton
and Jackson for not holding hip-hoppers to the same standard

they held Imus. In the sharpest exchange of what amounted to an Imus farewell victory lap, Dyson exposed their ignorance.

> You said earlier, Mr. Gregory, that you didn't—that you weren't aware that Al Sharpton and Jesse Jackson—and you're pretty much on the news beat—have been protesting this. That's part of the problem: a smart person like you, who is well informed, doesn't know that there has been a huge movement in African American culture against this kind of vitriol that has been expressed, this almost hatred of women. Yet it is not covered because it's not a black person killing somebody or cutting somebody.

Good point.

Gangsta rap is so popular largely because the white-controlled media, which defines black America for its consumers, finds that image of black life easier to sell than the culture represented by those straight-A students from Rutgers or by Ryan Christopher Clark, the straight-A black student who was one of the first casualties of the Virginia Tech massacre. Predictably, Clark's heroic role was barely noticed by the media.

Having little access to old media power, African Americans don't have the influence to make any aspect of black culture mainstream. If they had, we'd hear about black scientists, inventors, philanthropists, in other words, a presentation of blacks in a variety of roles, the way that whites are viewed. We'd hear about yellow, red, and brown pathology, as well as that which exists among blacks. The white dysfunctional family would be exposed. So dysfunctional has the white family become that Andrew Hacker, who is always harping on blacks, concluded finally in the *New York Review of Books* that if Daniel Moynihan were around today he could write a book about "the tangle of pathologies" in the white family. Instead, the white family is portrayed, in David Brooks's words, as "people who want to escape vulgarity" and vote for George Bush, or as the group that delights Sam Roberts with its rising numbers in Manhattan and increasing birthrate. Roberts is the *Times* man who got into trouble for saying that blacks are "prone to violence."

Even though the black columnists at the *New York Daily News* and *New York Times* condemn the violent precincts of rap music, their position is in conflict with the policy of both newspapers' sales departments. In order to appeal to youthful demographics, both papers cover the music so extensively that they fill what amounts to a daily supplement devoted to gangsta rap. As I told hip-hop panelists who were on an average forty years younger than I, people your age might be creating the songs but people my age are making all of the money from them: white men.

Imus defender David Gregory responded weakly to Dyson's body blow. "I was asking whether the same level of commitment was made to standing up to hip-hop as was made in standing up to Imus." Of course, no one can really determine the degree of commitment of black individuals and institutions who challenge gangsta rappers, since there are no media present to cover it. As journalist Richard Prince wrote recently:

> Sharpton and Jackson have spoken out against offensive rap music for years. At James Brown's funeral on December 30, Sharpton recalled that Brown asked him, "What happened that we went from saying, I'm black and I'm proud to calling us niggers and hos and bitches. I sing people up and now they sing people down. Tell them we need to lift the music up to where children and grand-mothers could sit and listen to music together."

When C. DeLores Tucker—the anti–gangsta rap crusader who founded the National Congress of Black Women—died in 2005, Barry Saunders of the Raleigh *News & Observer* wrote:

> During the 1970s, while he still had a claim to moral leadership, the Rev. Jesse Jackson attacked sexually suggestive songs and urged

performers to clean them up. Singers reacted angrily then, too, accusing Jesse of self-promotion at their expense. None of the performers took the reverend's name in vain the way Tupac Shakur and others did Tucker's, although that may be because they couldn't think of an insulting sobriquet to rhyme with "Jesse."

On the National Association of Black Journalists (NABJ) e-mail list, one member said, "I think the real issue is not whether Jackson and Sharpton have criticized the negative aspects of hip hop culture, but that mainstream media were not particularly receptive to the conversation when it was happening primarily among African Americans."

During another panel, an African American woman tried to educate Gregory about the varieties of hip-hop, including the kind that is positive (I listen to gospel rap on XM Satellite radio channel 33 every day), but Gregory wasn't paying attention. He gave most of the panel over to Armstrong Williams, who launched into yet another lengthy tirade against Al Sharpton and Jesse Jackson. Following the MSNBC playbook, Williams tried to connect the firing of Imus to the Duke lacrosse rape case: apples and oranges. Seriously, does anybody believe that the prosecutorial misconduct in that case is the only sort that happens in North Carolina? Anybody want to review the cases of all the poor blacks and whites and Hispanics in North Carolina jails? Anybody? MSNBC? CBS? CNN? What would have happened if the students had been black and the strippers white, and one of the students threatened to penetrate the strippers with a broomstick? That act alone would have gotten the black students some serious time, forget about rape.

On April 13, when Gregory again substituted for Matthews, the reporter reached back to the nineteenth-century newspaper style that Chesnutt wrote about. He incited and merchandized the racial divide that's proved such a big moneymaker for the cable networks. Gregory pronounced that white people were for Imus and black people were against Imus, with no polling data to back up his incendiary comment. His assessment ignored the fact that the National Organization for Women, a largely white organization, cast its lot with the black protestors. Imus disciple Joe Scarborough echoed Gregory by dividing the controversy into "team white" and "team black." Meanwhile, over at CNN, Paula Zahn was busy stirring up white mobs against Korean Americans following the Virginia Tech massacre.

A poll by CNN Opinion Research appeared on April 14. It showed that the majority of whites (55 percent) and blacks (68 percent) agreed that Imus's remarks were "offensive." More whites than blacks found his remarks to be "inappropriate." Only 6 percent of whites and 7 percent of blacks felt his remarks were not offensive. Other polls show that most blacks and whites are ahead of the politicians—on health care, the Iraq war, and gun control—who use race as a wedge issue, and apparently ahead of newsmen like Gregory who seek to market what the media calls "a racial divide." On April 20, appearing on Air America, Senator Bernie Sanders cited a poll that had 66 percent of Americans agreeing that wealth should be redistributed.

Big-shot journalists like Tom Oliphant, who seemed to be calling for mob protest against Imus's firing, and David Gregory were just trying to start something as a way of besting their competitors, like those turn-of-the-(last) century editors Chesnutt wrote about. During "all-Imus" week, the true divide was between the pro-Imus commentators, reporters, and producers; those who booked guests friendly to the Imus talking points; the black and white media employees we don't see on camera; the black executives of the companies that sponsored Imus; and the thousands of black consumers and stockholders.

Imus boosters in the media panicked as their monopoly over American opinion was threatened. Still, on Saturday, April 14, Imus's friends at CNN awarded him a moral victory. In all-day programming, which included the stupidest comments about rap and hip-hop culture to date, Imus was presented as a victim of a double standard. Changing the subject back to hip-hop gave the cynical producers an opportunity to recycle hip-hop video footage in which young black women willingly subject themselves to cheap "hooker" choreography. Even so, one of Imus's prime sponsors was Nutrisystem, whose ads portray one bikini-clad, middle-aged white woman boasting about her "smoking hot body" and another referring to herself as her husband's "trophy wife."

It became the consensus of the white talking heads that the hip-hoppers should be punished alongside Imus, as though these children have even a fraction as much sway with the American establishment as Imus. Members of that establishment have confessed that Imus says publicly what they say in private. Imus even received some good reviews in that Friday and Saturday's *New York Times*. Instead of conducting a public soul-searching about why some of its top columnists cohabited with Imus's bigotry for years, the paper printed op-eds by two writers who seemed to be suffering from protest envy. Instead of joining the coalition that was standing up against Imus's attack on the Rutgers team, a gay writer in an April 13 op-ed suggested that blacks lacked the moral high ground to criticize Imus because of homophobic comments made by one African American television star, the kind of collective blame that's been aimed at this writer's group since the time of the Romans.

The other op-ed, appearing on April 14, painted a rosy picture of Muslims in America and took another cheap shot at Sharpton. The writer concluded that the real fault line in America is between Muslims and Americans, not blacks and whites. Apparently nobody has informed this man that there are hundreds of millions of Muslims, both here and abroad, with African ancestry. Moreover, since this writer is connected to the neocon New American Foundation, one could view his op-ed as another attempt by neocons and the far-right American Enterprise Institute to control the American Muslim point of view.

Another tactic that Imus's groupies used to distance themselves from his racism was to cite their favorite blacks. On April 18, Tom Friedman tried to weasel away from Imus by spending most of his column praising Barack Obama, a tactic also used by David Brooks and David Gregory. Gregory's favorite Negro is Jackie Robinson! Finally, in the last paragraph of his column, Friedman tried to couple Imus's power with that of the hip-hoppers. Imus, mind you, owns a $30 million home in Connecticut, a New York penthouse, and a four-thousand-acre ranch in New Mexico. One of his fans is George Bush I, who has been interviewed on his show.

If the media continues to award white men and women commentators hours at a time to referee a "national dialogue on race" in America, shouldn't they at least acquaint themselves with the cultural and political trends in the different communities? Shouldn't they read Hispanic, African American, Native American magazines and newspapers? I do. Why doesn't C-Span, which is as close as American television has come to a daily town meeting on the air, read from ethnic newspapers, such as *Indian Country Today* and *Amsterdam News* or *Asian Week*, as well as from the *Washington Post* and *Washington Times*?

I didn't see Michael Eric Dyson participating in the "national dialogue on race" after he challenged Gregory. Maybe the producers at MSNBC thought Dyson was impudent. It would be smart for MSNBC to give Dyson as much time as they do those blacks with whom they are comfortable. Dyson is one of the most powerful advocates of African American aspirations since Malcolm X and, yes, I knew Malcolm X. MSNBC execs are comfortable with their regulars: black Republican operatives like Amy Holmes, a former speechwriter for Senator Bill Frist, Joe Watkins, a former aide to Vice President Cheney, and former Republican congressman J. C. Watts. They are the kind of people former football great Jim Brown referred to as "good Negroes": people who are not likely to make the white members of their audience uncomfortable.

Instead of Dyson, they brought on their old reliable Armstrong Williams to participate in MSNBC's "national dialogue." By the end of the week, Williams had stepped up his attack on rap music, Sharpton, and Jackson. At one point, Williams, who shrilly opposed the firing of Imus, said that the free market should determine the flow of opinion. This is a man who was handed $240,000 to promote Bush's No Child Left Behind policy without revealing that he was being paid by the government. According to *USA Today* (October 17, 2005):

> Congressional auditors last month found that the $240,000 contract violated a ban on "covert propaganda" and said the Education Department should ask for some of the money back. The Education Department has acknowledged that it is working with the U.S. attorney's office in Washington to investigate the Bush administration's contract with commentator Armstrong Williams. That suggests civil or criminal charges could be filed, according to Sen. Frank Lautenberg, D-N.J.

Is it possible that Armstrong Williams took the money and didn't do the work? How do we know that denouncing Jackson and Sharpton wasn't part of another covert propaganda effort? And why didn't Williams object to Imus's gay baiting?

Al Sharpton and Jesse Jackson were risking their lives on behalf of the civil rights movement while Williams was running errands for segregationist Strom Thurmond. And when Imus's media collaborators ganged up on Sharpton, using the same tactics Chesnutt's editors used to get people lynched, Sharpton soon started receiving death threats. So did the Rutgers team.

While newsmen like Brian Williams groveled before Imus, Howard Kurtz returned from time to time to lap up abuse from Imus, who called Kurtz a "boner-nosed beanie-wearing Jewboy." Imus also called publisher Simon & Schuster "thieving Jews." Yet the publisher of Simon & Schuster, David Rosenthal, told the *Times* that "it would be a shame if Mr. Imus lost his job. I think he has been a fantastic forum for authors and for people with interesting ideas." Imus smeared his CBS bosses as "money-grubbing Jews."

On January 28, Kurtz denounced *Grey's Anatomy* star Isaiah Washington for his homophobic remark on *Reliable Sources,* the corporate media's idea of media criticism. But three days later on January 31, Bernard McGuirk used the word "faggot" on the Imus show and it didn't seem to bother Kurtz. In fact, he appeared on the show later that week fresh from criticizing Washington as a gay baiter. Isaiah Washington tried to redeem himself by appearing in a public service ad that denounced bigotry. No such pressure has been applied to McGuirk.

On April 15, 2007, following the lead of Imus and his media posse, Kurtz grumbled about Imus being a victim of a double standard. Using fellow collaborator Gregory's word, Kurtz complained that hip-hoppers were subject to the same "intense" standard as Imus. Once again, a guest had to remind an Imus defender that blacks have protested misogynistic rap lyrics for years, but CNN, Fox, and the gang were not there to cover it. Another guest, Anna Marie Cox, had to remind Kurtz that he was a regular visitor to the Imus show; she explained her own appearance on the show as a desire to run with the big boys. Obviously nervous, Kurtz at one point referred to his guest, Clarence Page, as Clarence Thomas!

Kurtz was less than candid when he said he didn't know what was going on during Imus's show. He lied again when he said that nobody ever asked him why he was a guest on the show in light of disparaging remarks the shock jock has made about different groups. According to TomPaine.com, journalist Phil Nobile has been asking Kurtz this question for years.

"For many moons I have urged Howard Kurtz to cover the recurring media scandal known as *Imus in the Morning* in his *Washington Post* column. Yet Kurtz has resisted every tip, scarcely hiding his contempt in icy telephone exchanges. The frost continued when we met on an Imus remote at the World Trade Center in Manhattan a

few days before the New York GOP primary last March. He was following John McCain, who was appearing once again on the show. I
was tracking McCain too, intending to inquire into his affinity with
a man who ridiculed people like his adopted Bangladeshi daughter
as 'dothead,' 'Gunga Din,' 'Sambo,' and 'Punjab.'

"Kurtz was standing in a restricted press section when I introduced myself across the rope. He seemed less than thrilled. I extended my hand. He shook it with the same enthusiasm that
Israeli prime ministers display in photo opportunities with Arab
heads of state. In a quick parting gesture, I gave him a photocopy
of my *Newsday* op-ed (February 22) ripping David Remnick, editor of the *New Yorker*, for slumming with the man who lam-
pooned Tina Brown's *Talk* as 'a magazine for liberal homosexuals.'
More than a glorified guest, Remnick was in Imus's pocket to the
tune of $50,000 as winner of the now defunct Imus American
Book Award. Though an ardent race writer and friend of Ralph
Ellison, Remnick was oddly silent about Imus's racist repertoire.

"'If you don't start covering this stuff,'" I said to Kurtz, referring to my *Newsday* essay, 'people will start thinking conflict of interest.' (According to *Newsweek*, Imus turned Kurtz's *Spin Cycle*
into a best seller in 1997.) But my jab affected neither Kurtz's
composure nor his column. Subsequently he ignored five weekly
'Imus Watches' posted on TomPaine.com between March 24 and
April 28.*"

When gays and lesbians complained about Imus's homophobia, Imus quipped, "Eat me." Relentless jokes were made about
Hillary Clinton's sexual proclivities, often in detail, even describing the odor they imagine occurs after lesbian sexual intercourse.

On Monday, April 9, 2007, Donald Trump, one of the many
giants of capitalism with whom Imus associated and to whom

---

*Philip Nobile, "Tompaine.com Spotlight on Howard Kurtz: Missing
in Action on Imus? Condoning, Excusing, and Pardoning Imus," Tom
Paine.com, May 7, 2004, www.tompaine.com/Archive/scontent/3254.html.

most rappers have little access, delivered a message from Clinton: "Hillary really wanted to get on your show. She has a lot of respect for you, but it doesn't seem to be reciprocal. She'd do your show gladly, but you don't seem to want her on." But Clinton's request was treated with disdain by Imus. She became just another powerful political player humiliated by the "I-Man." He responded by discussing Clinton's husband receiving a "blowjob" in the Oval Office. No rapper ever had that kind of influence!

The fact that some black public intellectuals and media figures were tricked by the white nationalist movement that Imus represents into acquiescing to his strategy of diverting attention from himself to hip-hop is a huge blunder and calls into question whether they can adequately counter the enemies of African American progress. This is why I encourage an army of street and off-campus intellectuals armed with cyberspace to do for African Americans what the Anti-Defamation League does for Jews (and for blacks since the organization keeps under their scrutiny far-right groups that mean harm to both Jews and blacks), academic and media blacks not being up to the job. Black feminists, who were accorded a generous amount of time in the media to embrace the Imus strategy of blaming misogyny on black male culture, should study the experience of Jewish feminists in Germany when a far-right government came to power. The Aryan feminists with whom they had forged an alliance disowned them; they went to the camps with the men.* They might also study how the French colonialists manipulated Algerian feminism in the manner that Imus and his white nationalist collaborators manipulated them.**

---

*Marion Kaplan, "Sisterhood Under Siege: Feminism and Anti-Semitism in Germany, 1904–38," in *The Jewish Response to German Culture: From the Enlightenment to the Second World War*, edited by Jehuda Reinharz and Walter Schatzberg (Hanover, NH: University Press of New England, 1985), 242–265.
**Marnia Lazreg, *The Eloquence of Silence: Algerian Women in Question* (New York: Routledge, 1994).

Finally, Maya Angelou, constantly mocked by McGuirk on a show where white authors promoted their books and blacks were cast as illiterate, may have the last word about Imus and his crew and the crude manner in which blacks and Africans continue to be depicted in newspapers, cable, and television networks. On Thursday, April 19, WFAN announced that McGuirk had also been fired; it's poetic justice. Angelou wrote in "Still I Rise":

> *You may shoot me with your words,*
> *You may cut me with your eyes,*
> *You may kill me with your hatefulness,*
> *But still, like air, I'll rise.*

MJ, Kobe, and Ota Benga

Continuing the U.S. War against Black Men

In its filing, the defense said the Colorado Bureau of Investigation gave the prosecution evidence suggesting Bryant's innocence, and that the accuser retracted some of her statements to investigators a month before Bryant's trial was scheduled to start. The defense did not detail the alleged retractions.

January 29, 2004, between 3:15 and 3:20 P.M., EST, CNN ran mug shots of George Clinton, Michael Jackson, James Brown, and showed R. Kelly in an orange prisoner's jumpsuit. When's the last time you saw a black male author on CNN and I don't mean a tough-love artist who preaches that the problems of blacks are internal, or a black man who wrote books as a way of financing his drug habit.

The American media no longer call for the extermination of Native Americans and black Americans as they did in the nineteenth century. They've settled for a policy of confinement, and so the same stereotypes are endlessly recycled. Among those are the athlete and the entertainer, two of the most prominent being Los Angeles Laker star Kobe Bryant and Michael Jackson, the "King of Pop."

African Americans had nothing to do with the promotion of Kobe Bryant or Michael Jackson. White men own the teams, award the endorsements, and monopolize sports journalism. They issue hypocritical and often racist lectures to black athletes or attempt to diminish their achievements. John Cherwa, an edi- ior at the Orlando *Sentinel and Tribune,* and sports coordinator, released the *2006 Racial and Gender Report Card of the Associated Press Sports Editors* at the editors convention in Las Vegas.

The primary author of the report, Richard Lapchick, said in the summary, "When 94.7 percent of the sports editors, 86.7 percent of the assistant sports editors, 89.9 percent of our columnists, 87.4 percent of our reporters and 89.7 percent of our copy editors/designers are white, and those same positions are 95, 87, 93, 90 and 87 percent male, we clearly do not have a group that reflects America's workforce." For Jon Saraceno of *USA Today,* Roy Jones Jr. is merely a "good boxer." Sid Rosenberg, sports broadcaster for *Imus in the Morning,* said that the Williams sisters should pose in *National Geographic,* nude.

The record companies for which Michael Jackson has made millions are owned by white and Japanese men who require their young hip-hop musicians to market themselves as pimps. (In comparison to other ethnic groups, Eastern Europeans and Asian Americans, who make millions from the skin trade, for example, blacks are just as incompetent in this area of crime as they are in all others. Nearly four hundred years on this continent and not a single Martha Stewart or Ken Lay.)

When, in the minds of the "public," these employers' creations mess up, entertainers, athletes, politicians, and so on, African Americans are required to defend them. Moreover, their offenses are used to signify on other black men. Who is surprised when Wendy Murphy—one among CNN's stable of feminists—slimes Kobe Bryant by dragging in O. J. and Jim Brown, both black. Though Brown has been accused of battery in the past, he hasn't been accused of rape or child molestation. His conviction in the spat with his wife was based on his damaging a car he'd paid for, not spousal abuse. O. J. Simpson was acquitted by a criminal jury and was only held liable for the deaths of Nicole Simpson and Ron Brown when an all-white civil jury was impaneled, after the Browns' lawyer Daniel Petrocelli challenged the seating of every potential black juror. When Murphy lumps the three men together, I am reminded of the old 1896 song, "All Coons Look Alike to Me," by Ernest Hogan. Kate Couric laced into Kobe's reputation with the aid of one of these activists, who have been used by the white phallocentric media to slime black men. Couric enthusiastically denounced the basketball player, while portraying the groupie who lured him into the honey trap, for money, as an innocent victim. In keeping with the media style book, to avoid seeming blatantly racist, they next brought in George Foreman to display his new grill. And there was Katie Couric, who an hour before had been blasting Kobe as she had O. J., cuddling up to and flirting with Foreman. (Couric's being chosen over Bryant Gumbel to interview O. J. was one of the reasons Bryant left the *Today Show*.)

Careless defamation of a black man's reputation means nothing to Murphy and other Kobe accusers, including Naomi Wolf and human icicle Nancy Grace, who has a well-known grudge against the brothers, convicting Ray Lewis, Kobe Bryant, O. J. Simpson (with unfounded rumors), and Michael Jackson before these cases were presented to a jury. Grace portrays herself as a crime victim, as a result of her fiancé being murdered in a "minority" neighborhood, a claim that has been disputed by the fiancé's family. True, Grace plays the prosecutor on CNN, but on the day Martha Stewart's guilty verdict came down, she rose to Stewart's defense. She's not the only media feminist who is harsh with the brothers and easy on her sisters, and white women aren't the only ones who practice this double standard. Both black and white feminists, whose agitation around the case aided in their being wrongly convicted, prejudged the young men who were wrongly convicted in the rape of a stockbroker in Central Park. None of these black and white feminists, among whom are some prominent names, has apologized to the young men, who spent their youth in jail for a crime they didn't commit. Those prominent feminists, who lent their names to the hysteria that got the young men convicted on flimsy evidence, refused to return the phone calls of Rivka Gewirtz Little, who wrote a stinging article about their shameful role in the *Village Voice* on October 16–22, 2002. One of those, Naomi Wolf, participated in the chastisement of Kobe Bryant.

Feminist Susan Brownmiller, who wrote a book proposing that Emmett Till got what was coming to him, still believes that the accused were guilty, despite the confession of the real perpetrator and the DNA evidence that exonerated them. This is proof, I believe, that she and other well-known feminists have an irrational hatred of black men but defer to the white men who are their employers. A survey about violence against women in American households—which suggests that violence committed by white men against women is disproportionate to their numbers in the population—reveals that white women were scared to talk about it, while black women were quite candid when discussing domestic violence in black households. "A new study of white, working-class women in relatively stable families has revealed what the researchers call a horrific picture of lives saturated with serious domestic violence.

"The findings are part of a larger study funded by a $500,000 grant from the Spencer Foundation. . . . The study was conducted by Lois Weis, professor of education at UB, and Michelle Fine, professor of social psychology in the Graduate Center, City University of New York.

"The researchers defined 'serious domestic violence' as battering intended to cause serious physical injury. Ninety-two percent of white female respondents said that such domestic violence was directed against them, their mothers and/or sisters, either in their birth households or in later relationships. By comparison, 62 percent of black female subjects reported similar levels of violence in their lives."

It's ironic that the white middle-class feminist movement has ignored this study, which I sent to NOW, NPR, and the Pacifica network, where feminists are always dogging the brothers. I printed excerpts from this study in my last book of essays, *Airing Dirty Laundry,* and still the response is silence. There seems to be a cognitive firewall on the part of public intellectuals, the black and white pundit elite, and the media in general to any idea of black life that is not stereotypical, yet the dark secrets of the white and yellow communities are kept as such. Susan Antilla, the author of *Tales from the Boom-Boom Room,* about sexual harassment on Wall Street, said that her women informants were scared to talk about white male misogyny for fear of losing their jobs. And why did Arnold Schwarzenegger receive the women's vote in California? Seemingly, the more information that came out about his groping activities, the higher he climbed in the polls among women. He even had the support of feminist Susan Estrich, who once wrote in *USA Today* that the incarceration of black men has more to do with behavior than racism in the criminal justice system: longer sentences for blacks than whites, prosecutorial misconduct, police misconduct, and so on.

On the night of Schwarzenegger's victory, he was joined onstage by feminist Tammy Bruce, whose statements about black men were so racist that she was expelled from the National Organization for Women and began her own NOW chapter, whose members share her opinions. Hollywood women said they feared losing their jobs, were they to charge Arnold Schwarzenegger with sexual harassment. Schwarzenegger promised to probe the women's accusations following his election but then decided that it wasn't important. In December 2004 he announced that he was dropping his plan to hire a private investigator to examine sexual harassment claims. There was very little point to the investigation and it was time to "move on." Where are the feminist picket lines that materialized before the Capitol demanding that the Senate hear

Anita Hill's testimony? The kind of women who gave Mike Tyson, Clarence Thomas, Jim Brown, and now Kobe and MJ such a hard time. Maybe this is why the feminist movement has singled out black men to take the brunt of criticism for misogyny. Black men have no economic power over these women. Black men can't do nothin' for them or against them. Can't give them jobs at CNN, NPR, and Pacifica. Another reason cited by Latina writer Anna Castillo is that some white middle-class feminists believe their treatment in the United States is worse than that accorded black men and women. Shirley Chisholm famously asserted that she'd encountered more problems in her career for being a woman than being an African American. Yet when it came to her presidential hopes, her early white feminist supporters like Gloria Steinem abandoned her as the party convention approached. Shirley Geoklin Lim writes of attending a white middle-class feminist gathering on the day Martin Luther King was assassinated and the event being ignored by those at the meeting. They felt that racism was a black male problem.

Sometimes this irrational hatred for the brothers leads feminists to adopt bizarre positions. Attorney Roy Black asked, in an exchange with critic Wendy Murphy, about the actions of Kobe Bryant's accuser on the night of the alleged rape. "Why did she go up to his hotel room at or around midnight? Obviously, how long was she there and what happened?" Wendy Murphy answered that she didn't care whether she was up there "butt naked." But Wendy Murphy knew what she was up to when she made these outrageous attention-grabbing statements about Kobe Bryant. Similarly Dominick Dunne, a broken-down has-been hack movie writer and tabloid sensationalist, was used by the media as the point man in the sliming of O. J. Simpson. Apparently Wendy Murphy was designated as an auxiliary prosecutor by the *New York Times* and other media to denigrate Kobe's defense team. And so when Kobe Bryant's defense team scored a victory on March 2, 2004, by getting the judge in the case to open up questioning of Kobe Bryant's accuser's sexual history and turning over her underwear to them, the *New York Times* (on March 3) recorded Wendy Murphy's sarcastic remarks about the defense strategy: "They're doing this to go over the head of the court to communicate with would-be jurors who will say to themselves, 'Oh, poor Kobe.'"

The men who run the neoconservative *Newsweek* magazine brought in writer Allison Samuels to write the book on Kobe in its October 13, 2003 issue. She quoted an ex-girlfriend who described Bryant as selfish. (The article leaned heavily on the testimony of Bryant's ex-girlfriend, Jocelyn Ebron.) Among other accusations from the author of this padded article was that he "refused to hang out with his fellow Lakers after a game," and that he had a "big ego." She quoted another author who claimed that Bryant was "spoiled by his mother," which was typical of the kind of speculation and pop psychology floated in the article. The article mainly charged Kobe with being a loner (while the sister who takes orders from the men at *Sports Illustrated* criticizes black athletes for being gregarious). However, the claim that Bryant was a loner was refuted by his high school coach, Greg Downer, during an appearance on the *Larry King Show*. *Sports Illustrated* made a contribution to the media campaign against Kobe Bryant in the form of a hypocritical article entitled "When You're Asked About the Kobe Bryant Case," by Jackson Katz. It was just another example of white male media owners allying themselves with feminists, dumping all of women's hatred onto the shoulders of black men. The Katz article was a one-sided thrashing of Kobe Bryant disguised as scientific analysis. Junk science. For example, he said "false reports of rape are rare." Not when the suspect is a black male and the alleged victim is a white woman. Attorney Barry Scheck says that in 50 percent of the cases, white women who claim to have been raped by black men are lying. This can be proven through DNA, he said, "regardless of what Eldridge Cleaver said." Moreover, Jonna M. Spilbor, in her article "What If Kobe Bryant Has Been Falsely Accused? Why the Law of Acquaintance and Date Rape Should Seriously

Penalize False Reports," disputes the claim that false reports of rape are rare.

"Bryant's case has raised a firestorm of issues, but one in particular is at center court: Has this good guy been falsely accused? Even at this early stage, the majority of those asked say yes. To many fans, this case just feels false.

"If Bryant has been falsely accused, it won't be the first time that a false report has been filed in an 'acquaintance rape' case. In part, that's because the law fails to meaningfully penalize false reports, or to give those who have been falsely accused any justice. . . .

"The statistics on false rape reports in the U.S. are widely divergent, and often too outdated to be meaningful. Not surprisingly, the numbers also depend on whom you ask. Organizations that tout a feminist agenda claim the number of false rape reports to be nearly non-existent—about two percent. But other organizations, taking the side of men, claim that false reports are actually very common—citing numbers ranging from forty-one to sixty percent."

And why would *Sports Illustrated*, behaving like the proverbial fox guarding the feminist hen house, all of a sudden don an estrogen veneer when it comes to a black man? It has long had a reputation for sexism—largely because of its swimsuit issue—and among feminists it's known as "Sexism Illustrated." Over at the *Times,* where the feminists, black and white, are so hateful of black men that they even dragged their obsessions into Calvin Hernton's obituary, Selena Roberts said that Kobe should sit out the season. How is he doing? He was chosen to play on the 2004 All-Star Team. On March 16 Bryant tied a franchise record by scoring thirty-eight out of thirty-nine points after halftime in a game against the Orlando Magic. Of particular satisfaction to Bryant was the game-winning basket against the Denver Nuggets after the Denver fans, behaving like your typical lynch mob, booed him every time he handled the ball.

And the other *New York Times* gofer and twofer ended the year with a vicious assault on the character of black men. This time, black athletes. So did Katha Pollitt of *The Nation*, which has been as hard on black men as those owners of the corporate media. Notice no black men are ever invited to speak on these cruises *The Nation* is always sponsoring. Not even Cornel West, who is always in their ads for participating in the socialist events they regularly sponsor. *The Nation* even startled its readers by supporting a book that expressed sympathy for the police who beat up Rodney King in a review of *Official Negligence* written by Lou Cannon. The reviewer agreed with Cannon that the beating of King was justified. This is what happens to black men when a liberal publication hires a feminist editor. The author of the piece was Peter Schrag, who is allied with the right-wing Free Press, publisher of John McWhorter, the latest black hit man for the New York intellectuals (an oxymoron). He said that he and his friends never had an unpleasant experience with the police and termed my problems with the police "fabricated," in a hit job on me published by *Commentary*, a magazine that endorsed Charles Murray's *The Bell Curve*, which relied on Nazi research for its conclusions about black intellectual inferiority. Ironic, huh? McWhorter also made an emotional defense of John C. Calhoun on NPR. He is the intellectual stepson of Stephan and Abigail Thernstrom, who are responsible for his being a fellow in the far-right Manhattan Institute.

McWhorter's job is to ridicule black intellectuals on behalf of the second-generation übermenschen at the institute. Once he abandons his orders from his sponsors, the far right and the neocons, he will receive the same humiliation feminists and Naomi Wolf received when they turned their wrath from black men to white men. The feminists once complained to Victor Navasky, their publisher, because they weren't invited to contribute to a special travel issue. The name of Katrina vanden Heuvel was missing from the complaint in a letter they signed to Navasky, who responded by telling them in so many words to buzz off. None of them resigned.

Vanden Heuvel, who plays a progressive on TV, reserves all of her criticism for black men even though some black men are listed on the masthead of the magazine. Randall Kennedy, for example, who, like John McWhorter, advocates "sensible profiling." (Do we get to wear stars or triangles?) Roger Wilkins is also listed as a contributor. Maybe they don't read the magazine and maybe they aren't aware that black male–hating feminists like Katha Pollitt staff *The Nation*.

Appearing on Amy Goodman's *Democracy Now* show at the end of the year, the only example of sexism that Pollitt could cite for the year 2003 was the *Globe* newspaper's outing of Kobe Bryant's accuser, who was called "the victim" by CNN's all-white media jury, omitting the adjective "alleged." Basketball star Charles Barkley had to remind Nancy Grace of this when she referred to this groupie for athletes as a "victim." That's all Pollitt could come up with? This was a year when a white man confessed to the murder of forty-eight women. The Green River Killer. A white male nurse murdered a number of patients, many of them women. A white male–dominated government invaded Iraq, resulting in the murder and wounding of thousands of Pollitt's Iraqi brown sisters as well as her black and brown servicewomen sisters. Three women cadets at the Air Force Academy and half of the women in the army said they'd been subject to sexual harassment. And all Pollitt could come up with was the outing of Kobe's publicity-hungry accuser as the number one sexist outrage of 2003! She said this on progressive Pacifica radio where women broadcasters carry around in their heads the same stereotypes about black men as the American Nazi Party. They even have the kids on their Saturday *Youth Radio* program on their Berkeley affiliate KPFA issue angry accusations against black men. Black male haters in training. On the Saturday after New Year's Day, a "spoken word poet" hit the brothers with a fusillade of invective even bringing Al Green into her firing range. This was followed by an opinion piece about a black father who wasn't paying child support. (The typical face of domestic abuse and crime and child abandonment on the KPFA morning show is black! In a country in which half of men who are obligated to pay child support don't, where the divorce rate is 1 out of 2, and where millions of white women are welfare recipients abandoned by their husbands, child abandonment is hardly a black male issue. Isn't there a media outfit operated by the white center, left, or right that doesn't spread stereotypes about black men?) Amy Goodman, on whose show Pollitt appeared, is a progressive, but in the case of black men she agrees with her corporate feminist sisters. Pacifica prides itself in being above the tabloid, but not in the case of Mike Tyson, O. J. Simpson, and Kobe Bryant. And so on March 25, 2004, the day after Bryant's accuser underwent a three and a half hour interrogation about her sexual history, Goodman broadcast a story about the interrogation that was sympathetic to the accuser. She said that revealing the accuser's sexual history would discourage other rape victims from coming forth. Goodman made no attempt to present the defense point of view. She also neglected to present the viewpoint of what the *New York Times* referred to as "most legal experts," who agreed that "the hearing was warranted." The defense, according to the *Times,* "claimed that the semen other than Mr. Bryant's was found in the panties the woman wore when examined—that meant they argued that other sexual partners could have caused or aggravated the vaginal abrasions she had when she was examined." Goodman and the accuser's mother, who claimed on March 25, 2004, that her daughter was suffering more than Bryant, had to realize that Bryant faced life in prison if convicted. But, ignoring the advice of *Times* feminist Selena Roberts, who wrote an article entitled, "Bryant Should Sit for the Good of the Team," Bryant remained focused on his game. On March 24, against the Sacramento Kings, Bryant scored thirty-six points, six rebounds, and six assists.

Not to be outdone, neoliberal and progressive feminists like Terry Gross and Laura Flanders of NPR hit the brothers by using the occasion of the anniversary of the March on Washington to vent their grievances against black men by asking guests about the exclusion of women from the leadership that made speeches from the platform. When they not hittin' live black men, they diggin' up some dead ones. Of course, a number of black women writers have made this observation and many would agree that the male domination of the march was unfortunate. A program that you will never hear from Flanders and Gross? How the privileged white middle-class women's movement has excluded black, Asian American, and Latino women. (See their complaints in *The Feminist Memoir Project*, edited by Rachel Blau DuPlessis and Ann Snitow.)

Gross is married to Frances Davis, a "jazz critic" whose idea of jazz criticism is to whine about how white jazz musicians haven't been given credit for their contributions to jazz. (But finally, in the *Village Voice*, December 2007, Davis announced triumphantly that white jazz musicians had triumphed over black musicians.) Nothing about the great innovations black musicians have made in chord, scale, and rhythm theory. He should be joyful about Nat Hentoff receiving a Jazz Masters Award. As far as I know, Hentoff doesn't play an instrument, nor does Jan Wenner, who was recently inducted into the bogus Rock and Roll Hall of Fame. Davis's articles appear in the Arts and Leisure section of the *Times,* which over the past decade has attempted to deliver forms created by black musicians to white artists. The Emineming of black culture predates the Al Jolson phenomenon (who surrounded himself with blacks in order to add a flavor of authenticity to his product). Of course, the *Times* criticism of Afro-American music continues to be a joke. Recently critic Jan Parales wrote that the blues is limited to some simple chords. He should take a look at Bird's "Blues for Alice."

Hip-hop of course is the latest black invention to make millions for white producers and artists like Eminem. Some of our

current hip-hoppers, who make Mantan and Stepin seem digni-
fied, could have been extras in the old Al Jolson movies. *Hollywood Homicide* is the latest installment of hip-hop minstrelsy, a
shoot-em-up coon-chasing number in which police brutality
complaints are trivialized and Johnnie Cochran and Robert
Shapiro are invoked by the comical bagged coon as a way of luring
laughs from the white suburban audience that this movie is meant
to entertain. The kind of audience that should join O. J. recovery.
This movie appears at a time when a cop was acquitted for bang-
ing the head of a black teenager on the hood of a car and the
shooting of unarmed black men continues to occur across the
United States. Why would Gladys Knight and Smokey Robinson
lend their names to this trash? The big scene in this sorry mess of
a flick occurs when the character played by Harrison Ford and his
partner participate in the chase of an SUV, a reference to O. J.,
who seems to be lodged in the unconscious and dreams of many
white Americans, maybe even some of those who say that blacks,
when they complain about all-white juries acquitting Negropho-
bic cops, should move on.

Like Hollywood, CNN has already created the script that will
generate the ratings and excite their target white power audience.
(Now that we know the hotel worker was white, CNN will be able
to draw even more prurient-minded viewers to its vile product.)
In this ugly, coarse, ratings-driven plot, Kobe Bryant will be the
uppity black celebrity up against this poor innocent hick cheer-
leader victim. The Wheaties-faced Colorado prosecutor will be
arrayed against Kobe's rich lawyers. Both the prosecutor and the
"victim" will be Rocky Balboa against Mr. T, Paul Newman against
James Mason in *The Verdict*. If anybody doubts that CNN decided
to market high-profile blacks involved in scandals, all they had to
do was tune in to the March 27, "People in the News" segment.
The two people on the news were Janet Jackson and Kobe Bryant.
Their lives were raked over by a white man who said he was Janet
Jackson's biographer and a writer from *Sports Illustrated*. At the

end of the show, the audience was promised a "People in the News" on Michael Jackson.

CNN's feminists are also silent when it comes to the crimes perpetrated against women by white men. Remember Phil Spector, who rescued Tina Turner from big bad black demon Ike Turner in the movie *What's Love Got to Do with It,* produced and directed by white men? The fact that Spector has been indicted for the murder of a white woman, a blonde no less, has all but disappeared from the news. And one of his former wives, a Ronnette, predicted this turn of events. She said in her book, which I bought from a Broadway book stand for fifty cents, that living with Tina's white savior was like living with a monster. When Turner died, the *New York Times* used the term "ogre" in his obituary. This defamation was based on Turner's character as portrayed in the movie *What's Love Got to Do with It,* written, produced, and directed by white men. Tina Turner said that the movie was "unfair" to Ike. Alice Walker said the same of Steven Spielberg's treatment of the character Mr. in the movie version of *The Color Purple.* Why do you suppose black men appear even more sinister in the movie versions of both films than in the books written by black women, sort of like *TIME* magazine blackening up O. J? In the words of Yahoo News, Turner's name became synonymous with domestic violence (Mike Tyson for date rape, Clarence Thomas for sexual harassment, etc.). Yet Paul McCartney, whose ex-wife claimed he beat her during their marriage, gets a knighthood and Starbucks.

And what about the air force rape scandal that's been consigned to the back pages of the media because there are white guys involved? Why no twenty-four-hour cable news panels about that? And what did Miller, Wolf, and Grace do to come to the aid of Lieutenant Paula Coughlin who was drummed out of the air force after exposing the Tailhook scandal, which involved white airmen abusing and raping women in Las Vegas hotel rooms? She went down without hardly a peep from the black male haters at *Ms.* and NOW, an outfit where black men are always guilty. One out of five women,

19 percent at the Air Force Academy, have complained of sexual assault. On September 24, 2003, CNN finally reported a perpetrator of at least one sexual assault—a black former cadet. They apparently couldn't find a white cadet; given the enrollment of black cadets in comparison with that of white cadets, there must have been a large pool from which to sample. Or would uncovering the crimes of white male cadets alienate CNN's target audience: angry white males, the most spoiled, pampered, and subsidized group in the history of mankind. (What on earth do they have to be angry about?) In the Tailhook scandal, which included a number of white men, a black man was also offered up as a scapegoat; but he was acquitted of any responsibility in sexual assault. (And what became of those black soldiers who were accused of raping white women a few years ago? At least that's what the army interrogators tried to get them to say. The women told the press and the NAACP that the sexual acts they engaged in with these men were consensual. Are they still serving time? Or doesn't anyone care?) What do Miller and Wolf think about those cases? Or are they only summoned from the green room to beat up on the brothers? Well, maybe there's an exception. Wolf tried to call out powerful literary critic Harold Bloom for allegedly coming on to her twenty years ago. But that was only a one-hour story, and Camille Paglia and other feminist defenders of Bloom suggested that Wolf had it coming, because at Yale at the time she went around behaving like a flasher, exhibiting her "boobs" and carrying on. She found it easier to bring down Bryant, a black man, than Harold Bloom.

Even before Bryant's defense team reached all-white juries in Eagle, Colorado, and Santa Maria, California, they had to face the 24/7 cable news all-white jury and the Aunt Jemima white feminists. And if these juries don't convict them, they'll do a double jeopardy number on them like they did O. J. Because whatever transpires in the courtroom and no matter how skillful his attorneys, the media of white men, women, and their loyal black auxiliary will constitute a prosecutorial force less bungling than that Colorado one that is no match for Kobe's team. They will smear and distort the defense claims around the clock. Thus when Jermaine Jackson said his brother was being subjected to "a modern-day lynching," his point was ridiculed by Court TV's Catherine Crier. She said she was weary of African Americans complaining about a lynching every time they get into trouble. The lone black panelist, Attorney Flo Anthony, tried to clarify Jermaine's remarks (he didn't mention African Americans) but was heatedly rebuffed by the rest of the panel. One member of the panel, columnist Ted Casablancas, reduced her to tears when he rudely told her to shut up.

Does the media freak show surrounding the Jackson and Bryant cases resemble the kind of atmosphere associated with lynchings? Well, there are some similar features. District attorney Thomas W. Sneddon's press conference included the kind of celebration and mirth that occurred at the lynchings. These were festive occasions that whole families attended, and photos of these macabre affairs show grinning mobs having a good old time. The district attorney in Bryant's Colorado case ordered T-shirts that showed pictures of Bryant hanging but then lied about it. This diabolical incident, recalling the post-Reconstruction era when newly freed blacks were put back in their place through intimidation and terror, was reported by Howard Pankratz and Steve Lipsher of the *Denver Post:* "Judge wants names of seekers of anti-Kobe items EAGLE–Attorneys in the Kobe Bryant sexual-assault case traded accusations of malfeasance in court Friday, reducing the matter to peripheral issues of leaks to the media and tasteless souvenir T-shirts.

"One of the most sensational aspects of the routine motions hearing was Judge Terry Ruckriegle being told that employees of the district attorney's and sheriff's offices, including district attorney Mark Hurlbert and assistant district attorney Gregg Crittenden— who are prosecuting the case against the basketball star—had ordered T-shirts depicting a stick figure being hanged and derogatory statements toward the basketball star."

"This shows the bias of the investigators and prosecutors toward my client," said defense attorney Pamela Mackey. "Two members of this prosecution team had these T-shirts. . . . Mr. Hurlbert had one, and destroyed it sometime in October. And Mr. Crittenden held on to his until (Thursday)."

Not to be outdone, during a January game with the Utah Jazz, with Bryant present, an "entertainment" was broadcast over the speakers. Someone imitating Karl Malone's voice complained about his move to Los Angeles and his desire to return to Utah. After these complaints the voice said, "But at least my situation isn't as bad as Kobe's," to the delight of the crowd. Malone complained bitterly about this sketch, saying that it showed the Utah Jazz lacked class. This kind of jocular mood also pervades the media coverage of Michael Jackson. The same lame jokes about Jackson's appearance are made by commentators who've gone through considerable expense to alter theirs. Catherine Crier, Diane Diamond, and other Jackson critics conceal their faces behind chemical burkahs. Gloria Allred is so made up that she resembles one of Dracula's brides. She was characterized on MSNBC (March 19) as a "longtime Jackson critic." She's also a longtime O. J. critic, calling for his execution and the removal of his children from his home, which she also advocated for Jackson's children. She is also a longtime Mike Tyson critic, traveling all the way to Las Vegas to demand that his license be revoked. Yet when Clinton got into trouble with Monica Lewinsky, she defended him.

The district attorney apologized for his demeanor, but tabloid reporter Diane Diamond, who might be called a Jackson stalker, said she saw nothing wrong with the press conference. Footage of that press conference will show Diamond among the amused celebrants. This is the kind of journalism that Mary A. Fisher must have had in mind when she wrote about the laziness of the media regarding the Jackson case in 1994. "It is a story of greed, ambition, misconceptions on part of police and prosecutors, a lazy and sensation-seeking media and the use of a powerful, hypnotic drug. It may also be a story about how a case was simply invented."

Fisher claims that the first case arose from the ambitions of the thirteen-year-old accuser's stepfather, Evan Chandler, who exploited Jackson's friendship with his son. At one point, he asked Jackson to build him a house. Fisher said that the child denied being abused by Jackson until he was administered the drug sodium amytal, which is known to induce false memory. Chandler refused to be interviewed for the article and refused to appear on the *Today Show*, where Fisher repeated her charges before a nationwide audience. She said that the whole scheme was concocted by the child's stepfather to destroy the superstar. Since the current media humiliation of Jackson is based on the 1993 case, one would think that the media would present Fisher's findings. Instead, the 1993 accuser's uncle was permitted to engage in wild speculation and hearsay on the Larry King show followed by a sanctimonious discussion about whether the uncle's charges would influence a Jackson jury.

As long as there are profits to be made and products to be sold, a torrent of ugly speculation will continue to slime Jackson and Kobe. The media have turned into a carnivorous electronic predator that makes money by devouring reputations. This is damaging our justice system.

And so anybody who watches CNN during the day will discover its desperate attempt to boost ratings by exhibiting black men in an unfavorable light, as it searches for another O. J. to save the network as it vies with Fox, which has found the formula for dishing out red meat to its conservative audience. Heading toward extinction, CNN, which was saved by the O. J. trial, has decided that its profits lie in marketing black male scandal to a sick, miserable segment of the white public that gets off from such displays. This is why it's Michael Jackson, Kobe Bryant, and O. J. forever.

Though CNN is equipped with the newest snazzy techno shock-and-awe techniques, exhibiting and humiliating black men for profit dates back to the slave trade, when war criminals like Jefferson Davis and Robert E. Lee wrote about their slaves as though they were products. (Though both claimed slavery wasn't the cause of the war, deprived of their human merchandise, they lived their postwar years in poverty.) Much of the heavy lifting will be done by white women who can't decide whether they want a career or the pedestal. On January 16, the day Jackson entered a plea of not guilty, the CNN men took over, spending a day trading jokes and sarcasm about Jackson, led by Miles O'Brien, whose hatred for the singer is palpable. Every gesture Jackson made was termed bizarre, weird, peculiar, or strange. O'Brien was one of those commentators who blamed the Katrina disaster on Mayor Ray Nagin, when the consensus among scientists and engineers was that the levee break was due to global warming and incompetence on the part of the Army Corps of Engineers.

Miles O'Brien is supposed to be CNN's science editor. Whatever class this cable network had was lost after Bernard Shaw and Leon Harris left. Their replacements all agreed that MJ was a one-man circus. Given the tacky looneytoon graphics and circus presentation of CNN and Fox, their screaming anchor people, they should recognize a circus when they see one.

Jackson's arriving twenty minutes late and "sauntering" into the courtroom and then standing on top of a car to greet his fans was criticized for hours. The nigger wasn't humble enough for them. They wanted him to arrive on a mule cart dressed in overalls and bow before the judge with his hands clasped behind his back, the way natives used to salute their colonial masters. Of course, later in the day, the CNN anchorwomen led by Nancy Grace and some other women, including some low-grade trashy tabloid types from something called Celebrity TV, came in to do clean-up duty on Jackson on *The Larry King Show.* This was another all-white media jury except for Christopher Darden, who was dragged out of merciful oblivion to get another shot at a powerful black man. He's their "legal consultant," and judging from his appearance on CNN has become sick over O. J. The white men were egging him on all day into some kind of Pat Juber with O. J. and he was dumb enough to accommodate them, comparing Jackson's arriving at court in a van to O. J. in a van being pursued by the police. Huh? Obviously Darden needs help! They also have Jeffrey Toobin, another legal expert, who once said in a book that blacks are incapable of rational thought. Given his Afro hair he'd probably run into discrimination in Israel. When Michael Jackson's lawyer caught him in an inconsistency during the week Jackson made his plea, he was reduced to stuttering and backing up.

Some would argue that Michael Jackson and Kobe are superstars and that their cases have nothing to do with race. They would agree with John McWhorter, the right's new black rubber mask, that the only remaining issue about which blacks have a grievance is police brutality, which he says black people "fabricate," another case of a person using a Ph.D. as a cover to commit intellectual larceny. But Lionel Tate is no superstar. This boy was sentenced to life for killing a girl by using moves he'd seen on wrestling shows.

They've run his story along with those about Kobe and Michael. Sometimes the stories of the three run in succession at the top of the news. Sometimes Scott Peterson is thrown in so that their baiting of blacks won't look so obvious. But why Tate? For the same reason the *New York Times* ran a front page story about the problems of Malcolm X's grandson. The argument beneath these stories is that blacks are genetically prone to violence. CNN did a favorable report about the Nazi-style "scientific" studies done by Diana Fishbein, who believes that blacks are genetically violent, overlooking the fact that people of European ancestry nearly exterminated the indigenous people of this hemisphere and held brutalized Africans for centuries. If blacks are genetically prone to violence, maybe these violent genes will mutate into more benign ones as they apparently have among the European population. They also gave James Q. Wilson a forum. He subscribes to the same theory about blacks as Fishbein and is the philosopher behind Giuliani's fascist stop-and-frisk policies and George W. Bush's cynical initiative to get black people married instead of creating job programs and restoring college opportunities for welfare recipients. The president is a man whose wife nearly left him over his drinking and whose two daughters have gotten into trouble over theirs. Family values, indeed.

Perhaps CNN is following the lead of Roger Ailes, president of Fox News, whose media strategies it wishes to imitate. He won an election by putting the rapist Willie Horton's black face before the electorate, scaring white men in the South so that the percentages for Bush I climbed by twenty points in a single week after the ad appeared. Yet, in an appearance on Tavis Smiley's show on NPR, Ailes said that it's CNN that appeals to the hard right.

This hard right apparently gets aroused when a sexy black athlete is caught up in some scandal, especially when it involves white women. (According to *Spy* magazine, Klan leader David Duke had one of the best porn collections in the South. His favorite is interracial combos.) David Shields in his book *Black Planet* says that when he makes love to his wife, he thinks of Gary Payton. When covering the O. J. trial, Entertainment TV reported a poll that found American women would rather watch the trial than have sex. Apparently for millions of Americans, Kobe Bryant and Michael Jackson are like a megadose of Viagra! Black men have been in this position before and if the recent coverage of black men in the media is any sign, their pillorying will become more intense.

During the week ending February 29, 2004, a listener called in to Howard Stern's radio show. Like Don Imus's sidekick Bernard McQuirk, Stern regularly broadcasts material offensive to black Americans. The caller asked Stern whether he had ever "made love to a nigger," and whether "it smelled like watermelon." On the same day newspapers reported, to the delight of their white readers, who can only achieve pedigree by bringing black men down, that Michael Tyson and Michael Jackson were broke. That night it was broadcast that Yao Ming, the Yellow Hope, had received the endorsement millions once belonging to Kobe. On Friday of that week it was open season on some black men in Colorado when a white woman said that she had left a bar with what CNN described as two "big" black men and awoke the next morning in a bed and bloody, the kind of accusation that used to lead to massacres. A black man who contributed his DNA was found innocent and his attorney described the rounding up of black men as racist.

During this week the Larry David HBO show, *Curb Your Enthusiasm,* was about the sexual prowess of black men. One of David's friends said he was dating a black woman but felt inadequate because black men are large. In one scene David and his friend surround a black man in a public toilet and examine his penis. Yet Bruce Weber, one of those people at the *Times* (Janet Maslin is another one) who writes about race without having a clue, believes that it takes "daring" to write harshly about blacks. Anybody who holds such a belief must reside on another planet. He was congratulating a conservative college for daring to stage a production in which a black actor appears as an ape. This is the same critic who thought it brave for Rebecca Gilman to write *Spinning into Butter,* a play that contains hateful speeches about blacks. The kind of speeches you find in novels by Saul Bellow and Philip Roth. Black actor Andre De Shields was described as "snorting and baying, scratching himself, occasionally beating his chest with absent-minded, simian hubris." He said he went to the zoo for research. The photo accompanying the story showed white actress Phyllis French holding the "ape" by the shoulder, the kind of illustration that regularly appears in American Nazi publications. De Shields said of his role in the play, *Prymate,* written by Mark Medoff, "no conscious adult can come to the play and not think of O. J. or Kobe Bryant or of any African American who has achieved trophy status."

The play was directed by Edwin Sherin, the original director of the television series *Law and Order.* It figures. In a 2003 episode of *Law and Order: Special Victims Unit,* it was proposed that black men possess a rape gene that is passed down from generation to generation. Tell that to the generations of black and Indian women who have been raped by European men since Columbus arrived in the Caribbean. But, of course, this is not the first time the *New York Times* entertained its white readers with an image of a black man as an ape. When Ota Benga, a pygmy, was displayed in the monkey house of the New York zoo in 1906, the *Times* wrote, on September 11, 1906:

> As for Benga himself, he is probably enjoying himself as well as he could anywhere in his country, and it is absurd to make moan over the imagined humiliation and degradation he is suffering. The pygmies are a fairly efficient people in their native forests with enough intelligence to be successful hunters and to secrete themselves from hostile—that is, other tribes, but they are very low on the human scale.

The public's reaction to this despicable scheme characterizes the media attitude toward black men to this day:

> There were 40,000 visitors to the park on Sunday. Nearly every man and woman and child of this crowd made for the monkey house to see the star attraction in the park—the wild man from Africa. They chased him about the grounds all day, howling, jeering, and yelling. Some of them poked him in the ribs, others tripped him up, all laughed at him. (*New York Times,* September 18, 1906)

Another black man who was ridiculed, humiliated, and beaten by his enemies was Frederick Douglass, but in those days before the high-tech lynchings of today, Douglass had the ability to fight back. When he found himself attacked by newspapers alleging that he was involved with John Brown's raid on Harper's Ferry (he was innocent), he was able to defend himself with a magnificent letter to the editor. In those days before the electronic media, the accused received as many column inches as his accusers. When one is attacked by a twenty-four-hour cable network, however, one has about as much chance as an ant against an elephant.

I took CNN's word that it welcomed feedback from viewers by passing Mary Fisher's information on to CNN's Anderson Cooper, who tries to promote his show by screaming louder than the competition. Though CNN pretends to welcome comment, none of the information was used. Also ignored, largely, has been the testimony of J. C. Penney's attorney. J. C. Penney was sued by Jackson's accuser and his mother: "J. C. Penney's psychiatric reports refer to the mom as severely depressed, quoting her as describing herself as "sad over being a nobody. . . . A sad housewife getting fat."

> The J. C. Penney case also involved allegations of sexual abuse. That's right; the Jackson case is not the first time this mom has cried sexual misconduct. J.C. Penney's attorneys claim the accuser's mom eventually expanded her allegations against store security, claiming she had been fondled inappropriately.
>
> The documents also hint at the possibility that the mom rehearsed her children to corroborate her story. That's an allegation that may come back to haunt her as she prepares to lead her son through another court battle. But this one is against the King of Pop.

Rather than go to trial, J. C. Penney eventually opted to settle the case, awarding the family more than $100,000. The company's attorney says he believes the mom was out to scam his client, just as he believes she's out to scam Jackson. And I'm not making this up but on March 23, 2004, between 4:55 and 5:00 PST, CNN ran a story about a gorilla escaping from a zoo and attacking a white woman, while underneath the visuals a crawler announced that Kobe Bryant's accuser was going to testify about her sexual history behind closed doors. Coincidence? Or doing the Ota Benga on Kobe Bryant?

"Even as embattled pop star Michael Jackson continues to offer words of appreciation for the support of his fans, *Celebrity Justice* has exclusively learned that the mother of the boy accusing Jackson of child molestation also went looking for support—but in a very different way." In 2000, when Jackson first met his accuser, an article appeared about the boy and his family in *Mid Valley News,* a community newspaper in the town of El Monte, just outside of Los Angeles. The story was an emotional appeal, detailing the boy's illness, the toll his treatment was taking on the family, and asking for readers' financial charity. "Our car has been repossessed" the mother was quoted as saying. "One chemotherapy injection costs more than $12,000."

> Now, Connie Keenan, the editor of *Mid Valley News,* speaking exclusively to *CJ,* has characterized the accuser's mother in a most uncharitable manner. "My gut level: she's a shark. She was after money," Keenan told us. "My readers were used. My staff was used. It's sickening."
>
> In 2000, Keenan told us, the boy's mother approached the *Mid Valley News* and pitched her story: "She pleaded her case that her son needed all sorts of medical care and they had no financial means to provide it."
>
> Keenan agreed to run the heartfelt story and invite readers to help but recalled that, almost from the get-go, there were red flags. According to Keenan, the mother 'wanted the money sent to her in her name, at her home address.'
>
> And that was just the beginning. Keenan assigned the story to reporter Christie Causer, who was so moved by what she heard that, on Thanksgiving Day, she brought food to the family. But, according to Keenan, 'The mother, instead of being grateful that this woman brought her a complete Thanksgiving dinner, said "I'd rather have the money. This is nice, but I'd rather have the money."

Keenan insisted that her paper would solicit funds only if the mother opened a trust account to receive them. Sources tell *CJ* that, nine days before the article ran, the boy's mother did open an account in her name for the benefit of the boy at a Washington Mutual bank on the Sunset Strip and deposited one cent—but it was not a trust account.

The article gave readers a road map to make donations: the name of the bank, the account number, even the routing number. We've learned that, within the first three weeks after the article ran, $965 was deposited—and $750 was promptly withdrawn. But Keenan told us that that absolutely wasn't enough for the mother: "She really wanted another story done on her son because they just didn't make enough money on the first article. And I told her— and I can be a crusty old broad—'we're not doing another story on your son.'"

The mother's response? "Well, I'll take it someplace else," Keenan recalled. "I said, Fine."

And as if all that wasn't enough, it turns out that the boy was being treated at Kaiser Permanente in Los Angeles, at absolutely no cost to the family. That's right, there were, in fact, no medical bills. All treatments were covered by insurance.

The boy's father was a teamster member who worked at a supermarket facility in the LA area. *CJ* spoke with Paul Kenny, head of a Teamster's union in LA, who confirmed that the Teamsters negotiated a sweet deal when it came to health care coverage. "They're covered 100 percent under HMOs," Kenny stated. "Including Kaiser, which is an HMO."

"There was no cost to [the boy's father] out of pocket, at all," Kenny added. "Everything should be covered 100 percent under his contract. Everything. There is no exceptions."

When we asked Keenan if it was her impression that the family had to shell out for treatment, she told us, "Of course it was."

Two years after the article ran, when Santa Barbara County DA Tom Sneddon filed child molestation charges against Jackson,

Keenan realized that the boy she wrote about was the accuser and made contact with Jackson's lawyer. "I just had this gut feeling that something was wrong here. So I sent a copy of the [*Mid Valley News*] to Mr. Geragos, who was representing Michael Jackson at the time,' Keenan told us. "Because maybe there's a grain of truth to what Michael Jackson is saying—'I didn't do it'—or maybe it's just to stop a shark."

Both Keenan and the article's writer tell *CJ* they have recently been contacted by Jackson's defense team.

A source close to the mother spoke with *CJ* and insists that none of the money collected was misspent but wouldn't say how the money was spent.

On September 1, 2004, cable television was left obsessing over Michael Jackson as a way of improving ratings. Kobe Bryant's criminal case was dismissed because his accuser, Kate Farber, chose not to testify. Some said it was because the judge allowed the introduction of her sexual history, which would have shown her having sexual intercourse with a man before and after her encounter with Bryant. The prosecutor's expert witness, Michael Baden, concluded that the slight injuries on her body could have resulted from consensual sex, dealing a blow to the prosecution. The prosecutors dropped the case after spending at least $200,000 to prepare for trial, and just days before opening statements were scheduled to begin.

"A person's life and liberty are at stake," the defense attorneys wrote. "The game of hide-the-ball, find-it-if-you-can discovery is intolerable. This court must vindicate Mr. Bryant's constitutional rights and impose meaningful sanctions against the prosecution."

After the end of Kobe Bryant's case, like a one-eyed monster, the media returned to Michael Jackson to feast on. Years earlier Martin Luther King Jr., who was repeatedly arrested because of unjust laws, was subjected to scurrilous rumor mongering from his enemies, including J. Edgar Hoover. Some say Hoover was jealous of

King's Nobel Peace Prize. Some of Jackson's fellow performers and members of the largely white critical fraternity have attempted to undermine his achievements with comments that are vicious and cruel. For example, a media firestorm occurred over alleged love letters written by Michael Jackson to his accuser. No such letters existed, even though Larry King devoted an hour to them on his show. Some of those who accuse Jackson are hypocrites. Bob Guccione Jr., the publisher of *Spin* magazine, was often brought in by the networks to criticize Jackson, only to face sexual harassment charges himself.

Jackson is an exciting performer but is limited by Hollywood's Steven Spielberg–Quincy Jones formula for manipulating audiences in a Pavlovian manner. This kind of sentimental, mawkish collaboration characterized *The Color Purple*, which was used to place the onus for American misogyny on the heads of black men. Jones's score for this movie was three-hankie slick and contrived to tug at the heartstrings. I considered the work of Jackson's late choreographer, Michael Peters, to be warmed over Jerome Robbins of *West Side Story*. (Peters performed in *West Side Story* while attending dance school.) And so Jackson is surrounded by mediocre, commercial-oriented talent, the safe, predictable scores of Quincy Jones, and kitschy choreography. Moreover, like Jones and Spielberg, he is so overwhelmed by special effects that it's difficult to detect a clear narrative line.

Maybe Jackson has been smothered and overindulged by his family and his handlers. Novelist Al Young talks about swimming in a pool of a Motown producer and being told by his maid that Michael Jackson once swam there. His mother requested that no one else swim lest Michael contact germs. And so this great talent has been smothered and reduced to a cliché. His work doesn't have the political punch of Curtis Mayfield or Marvin Gaye of the classic "What's Going On" or the historical consciousness of a Afrika Bambaataa or the always evolving and fresh performance of a Prince or the gritty funky naturalism of his mentor, James

Brown. I found "Billy Jean" and "Thriller" to be mean-spirited and downright nasty.

What would happen were he to take a sabbatical, as saxophonist Sonny Rollins did when he desired to rejuvenate his career? What would happen were his collaborators David Murray or Cecil Taylor or Ishmael Houston Jones or Garth Fagan? Can you imagine what would have happened had the Prince of Pop collaborated with Sun Ra? What would an album produced by Kip Hanrahan be?

But of course I am of a generation that fails to find much merit in the movie *Titanic,* and my hip-hop fans accuse me of being old and out of touch. I got screamed on at a hip-hop panel for criticizing Snoop Dogg as a bad role model. And since some hip-hoppers have said that hip-hop has replaced the civil rights movement, does that mean that Snoop is Martin Luther King Jr. and Little Bow Wow, Reverend Abernathy? And maybe Michael had the last word for geezers like me when he told the late Ed Bradley that his new record is number one except in the United States.

But it's in the United States where he has been tried. The *New York Times,* which ran a cruel and tasteless editorial on the occasion of Malcolm X's death, has had it in for the Nation of Islam for its anti-Semitism. This stems from the accusation that Minister Louis Farrakhan once called Judaism a "gutter religion." The minister denies he said such a thing, but in order to mollify the feelings of those who were offended, he practiced a Mendelssohn violin concerto for three years and performed it, accompanied by the Oakland Symphony, "to say in music what I could not say in words." This would be like Dick Army memorizing the complete works of Oscar Wilde in order to apologize for calling Barney Frank a fag. And so it came as no surprise that when Jackson was alleged to have an adviser from NOI, the *Times* would take interest. "Public records from Illinois indicate that Leonard Muhammad, son-in-law of Nation of Islam leader Louis Farrakhan who is reportedly running many of pop star Michael Jackson's affairs, has a history of failed businesses, fraud allegations and unpaid taxes;

his life and career described." The problem with this story was that it included a photo of the wrong man and had to run a correction on January 5, 2004: "A picture by The Associated Press in Arts & Ideas on Saturday with an article about the involvement of Leonard Farrakhan Muhammad, the chief of staff to the Nation of Islam leader Louis Farrakhan, in the business affairs of the pop star Michael Jackson was mislabeled by the news agency and published in error. (It also appeared in the News Summary.) It showed Ishmael Muhammad, a minister of the Nation of Islam and son of its former leader, Elijah Muhammad." One couldn't imagine the black press mistaking a photo of a rising young NOI star. While the corporate press, which includes about 11 percent minorities, seem to be leading the lynch mob against Jackson, Bryant, and O. J., all three have received support from the black press. *Ebony* magazine, the lingua franca of black America, ran articles supporting O. J. Simpson, and the *New York Amsterdam News* and *Final Call* have supported Michael Jackson. This is not the first time the white and black press have been at odds. J. Edgar Hoover persecuted the black press for disloyalty during World War II.

And it's not surprising that Michael Jackson would solicit help from the Nation of Islam, a group that is visible in black communities each day. Why wouldn't he reach out to a black self-defense organization to function as a barrier between Jackson and those who would do him harm, including the Aryan Nation and prison guards, were he to be incarcerated through the efforts of a district attorney seeking revenge because Jackson put his name in a song.

Like O. J. Simpson, Jackson had been congratulated for transcending race and crossing over to the world community, and like O. J., who also stirred intense antagonism among American whites (while receiving support from millions of whites abroad), came home to the hood when he was in trouble. Both were welcomed because blacks know that even though they may become rich and famous, in the eyes of millions of white Americans, they are still "niggers." Even though O. J. and Michael Jackson, with their white wives, are viewed as having abandoned the black community, their support among the black community remains strong. Are black millionaires and celebrities treated differently from the average black by the criminal justice system?

Blacks know that a double standard has been applied to whites and blacks since the first slave ship sailed into that Virginia port in 1619. Why, some blacks ask, was Jackson's home raided on the same day that his album *Number Ones* was released? Why has the Santa Barbara County sheriff threatened to press charges against Jackson for complaining about his treatment when turning himself in? Even some conservative lawyers have found such a move odd. And why would the district attorney hire a public relations firm to promote the prosecution's case, convincing foreign observers that the American legal system has lost its mind. (During the O. J. Simpson trial, Simpson's dreams were entered into evidence!) In the O. J. Simpson civil trial, which civil libertarian Nat Hentoff called double jeopardy, the prosecutor was assured a victory when the case was moved from Los Angeles to Santa Monica. The all-white jury did what was expected of it, holding Simpson liable for the death of his wife, Nicole Simpson. Will Jackson be given a change of venue from Santa Maria, whose black population is 2 percent?

Jesse Jackson said that Michael Jackson's arrest was "impeccably timed that it leads to even more suspicions. . . . it seems aimed to destroy this media mogul." African Americans also cite the $3 million bail set by the district attorney as an example of the difference between the way white and black celebrities are treated. The bail for rock and roll producer Phil Spector and actor Robert Blake, both of whom were accused of murder, was set at $1 million.

Is Jackson being lynched? He isn't literally swinging from a rope, but the current media frenzy surrounding the case has taken on the atmosphere of an old-fashioned lynching. The media coverage endlessly recycles the same lame jokes about Jackson's appearance. All about Jackson being a freak and living in a fantasy world. One can argue that the zeitgeist of contemporary America is characterized by freakishness and fantasy. The American establishment, instructed by its public intellectuals asserts that the United States is color-blind, a whopper of a fantasy. Jackson is characterized as a freak who is constantly transforming himself when the United States might be considered the Empire of Morphous where people spend billions on weight loss schemes and cosmetics and where even pets are overweight. Some of the media commentators who joke about Jackson's altered appearance have gone through much effort to alter theirs. California, where I live, is the Mecca of losing oneself, and becoming something different from what you began as. Out here a steroid pumped B actor who has rented his face to some elderly social Darwinists can become governor. Brooklyn-born men and women become swamis and adopt Buddhism as a hobby. Ordinary individuals from the Indian subcontinent migrate to the Golden State and award themselves a Brahmin upgrade. California's standard for white supremacy was established by Celtic Americans who came to the West Coast in the 1850s. They weren't considered white in the east. And the current president, born to a patrician New England family, who was AWOL from his National Guard duties, enjoys dressing up as Tom Mix or Chuck Yeager. Jackson isn't a freak; Jackson is an American.

Some of the anxiety Americans feel toward Jackson and other black male celebrities is based on the dread and fear that has settled across the land as a result of the 9/11 calamity. The roasting of people like Jackson, Kobe, and O. J. becomes a diversion from an unknown future in which they will find themselves in the minority. Both media and politicians play to these fears. Jackson, Kobe, and O. J. wouldn't be the first black celebrities to be used by many in the white population to vent their resentment against blacks in general. When the Irish mob rioted in New York in 1900, two highly successful entertainers, Bert Williams and George Walker, became targets of their wrath. Even Nat King Cole, a sort of gentle chocolate Barbie, was assaulted by racists in Alabama. Marion Barry was busted for smoking crack, when it was being used by members of the Washington establishment; Adam Clayton Powell Jr. was expelled from Congress for enjoying the same perks as his fellow congressmen and refusing to be servile and deferential to whites. By the time he was redeemed by the U.S. Supreme Court, the ordeal had taken its toll on his health.

According to the latest census, whites, more than any other group, are likely to live among themselves. Thirty-seven percent of the population classify themselves as blacks. There is also anxiety about the millions of Mexicans who are pouring into the country and settling across the nation. One right-winger is author of a book entitled *Mexifornia*. According to the U.S. Census Bureau, the country's foreign-born population in March 2002 was 32.5 million, about 11.5 percent of the total U.S. population, 52.2 percent of whom were born in Latin America. This compares to 19.7 million foreign-born residents in 1990, 14 million in 1980, and 9.5 million in 1970, according to Census Bureau records. In addition, between 8 million and 12 million illegal aliens are believed to be living in the United States, mostly Mexican nationals, with anywhere from 1 million to 3 million more expected this year, according to U.S. border enforcement officials. Conservatives claim that these immigrants are costing the American public billions in services and health care costs. The extent of the anti-immigration hysteria was felt when President George W. Bush announced a new policy for illegal immigrants, which some in his own party protested as a amnesty program in disguise.

On June 13, 2005, Michael Jackson was acquitted of all charges. Many said that he won. I disagree. I believe the prosecutor won.

Sneddon's Victory

In the 1840s, Senator Simon Cameron compared President James Polk to an "unruly negro" and said that "the only way to treat an ugly negro who was unruly, was to give him a d—d drubbing at the start, and he would learn to behave himself." Thomas Jefferson offered some opinions about the form the drubbing should take.

In 1805 Jefferson had trouble with a slave named James Hubbard, who was always running away. Jefferson's solution? "I had him severely flogged in the presence of his old companions."

Michael Jackson has gotten his drubbing and his ordeal has sent a message to other black men, his "companions," who might become "unruly." That is, engage in exhibitions of conspicuous wealth, criticize mega corporations like Sony records, and marry Elvis Presley's daughter.

Black men with high-profile names called me after the verdict to express their relief. But while my friends and Jackson's fans view Jackson as the victor, in my opinion, Thomas W. Sneddon Jr., the Santa Barbara district attorney, won.

He satisfied his resentment against Jackson by humiliating the pop star, sending seventy sheriffs to ransack Jackson's Neverland sanctuary and subjecting Jackson to a trial that took a toll on Jackson's health. At the beginning of the trial, Jackson was dancing on the top of an SUV. At the end, he seemed like an emaciated zombie.

No wonder. His name had been dragged through the slime and he faced the prospect of being incarcerated in a California prison. The personnel there, in some cases, according to investigations into these Devil's Islands, make those charged with human rights violations at Abu Ghraib seem like waiters in a five-star restaurant. As if this pressure were not enough, he had to pay an estimated $5 million for his defense.

Sneddon was aided by electronic talking heads who seemed more like models for makeup artists than genuine journalists. Bimbos and Ken Barbies. Most predicted that Jackson would be convicted. But when the predominantly white jury refused to go along with their and Sneddon's script, they began to put their spin on the trial: Jackson was acquitted because he was a celebrity, even though the jury foreman denied that this was the case. Given the fact that the accuser's mother was a liar, they said, she should not have been a witness for the prosecution. This ignores the history of her son's lies.

The jury concluded that the accuser had been manipulated by his mother. Realizing the weakness of this case, Sneddon, with the cooperation of Judge Rodney S. Melville, was able to include past accusations, the most important of which was the 1993 case.

Many, including the media's favorite juror, the man who says that Jackson must be a child molester, concluded that Jackson settled that case for $20 million because he was guilty. However, one theory holds that the settlement was made on the advice of the late Johnnie Cochran, who didn't want to face an all-white Santa Maria jury, stereotyped by a BBC reporter as "pro-prosecution and pro-law enforcement."

Neither print nor electronic media mentioned that the 1993 accuser denied that Jackson had molested him until he was administered sodium amytal, known to induce false memory. It took a real reporter, not someone who plays one on TV, Mary Fisher, of *GQ*, to come to that conclusion in an investigative report, printed in that magazine. Her article also indicated that the 1993 accuser's father had manipulated the boy for financial gain. She blamed the absence of hard reporting of the case on "lazy journalism," and the 1993 accuser's father refused to face Fisher on the *Today Show.*

Both Fisher's article and footage of her *Today Show* appearance can be googled, which shows that lazy journalism persists. For example, members of the TV media continue to portray Jackson as broke when *Forbes* magazine places his assets far above his liabilities. The media also made much of Jackson's decline as a marketable pop star, yet a *New York Times* article reported "the self-proclaimed King of Pop remains one of the only stars who defined their careers in 1980s pop who can still crack the Billboard charts." Jackson's last album, *Invincible,* outsold those by Madonna and Prince.

So Sneddon used millions of California taxpayer dollars to get his revenge for being sassed in a song by an "unruly" Negro or, as his media enablers put it, a black man who is used to being in control. To degrade the pop star even further, he wanted to display photos of his penis, which was even too much for the prosecution-friendly judge. Jackson is forever marked with the scarlet *P.* Even after the jury acquitted him, Fred Graham of Court TV continued to refer to him as a "pedophile." Air America, the "progressive" network, cast Jackson as a pedophile on the day of the verdict by airing offensive and tasteless songs which remixed some of Jackson's. Makes you long for the 1930s left, which would have seen through Sneddon's motives immediately.

Sneddon says he has taught Jackson and his "companions" a lesson. Although many law enforcement officials play by the book, others use their position to engage in personal vendettas against individuals, institutions, and classes of people. Maybe the Jackson case has been instructive to the public as well. It is preferable to try criminal cases in the courtrooms rather than on cable.

Hurrah for Jeff Davis?

American history textbooks show the Civil War ending with Lee's surrender at Appomattox. A very moving scene in which Grant, a badly dressed general reeking from the stench of cheap cigars, accepts the sword of an immaculately dressed, chivalrous General Robert E. Lee, who achieved sainthood through the efforts of his Virginia fan clubs. ("Early biographers and historians, North and South, criticized him for major blunders. Lee . . . was blamed for the loss at Gettysburg.") What they don't mention is that through terror and negotiation the Confederates got it all back. By 1887 Jefferson Davis, sounding more like the victor than the vanquished, was able to say, "There *is* no *New* South! No, it is the *Old* South rehabilitated, and revived by the energy and virtues of Southern men." One of those southern men was Tennessean Andrew Johnson.

During the Clinton impeachment scandal, Andrew Johnson, Lincoln's vice president and successor, was presented as a tragic hero. President James Polk and other contemporaries had a different view of the seventeenth president. Polk said of Johnson, "He is very vindictive and perverse in his temper and conduct."

Some of the TV historians and others hold that Johnson was impeached because he stuck to his principles. In reality, Johnson was a racist, drunken bum who, on the campaign trail, got into vulgar exchanges with his hecklers. He helped restore the Confederacy by extending amnesty to the Confederate killers. "Instead of hanging prominent rebels as he had promised, he handed out mass pardons, until every former Confederate was beyond the reach of the law. He ordered the return of seized lands to the pardoned rebels—halting efforts to provide homesteads to freedmen—and withdrew black troops from the South. At the same time, the Southern states began to pass 'black codes,' laws that virtually reenslaved African Americans though a combination of contract-labor requirements, vagrancy laws, and apprenticeship arrangements." White violence against blacks proliferated with the approval of the southern press. "If one had the power," said the *Memphis Daily Appeal*, "it would be a solemn duty for him to annihilate the race." Race riots broke out all over the South. In Memphis, for example, law enforcement agents actually led mobs into black neighborhoods where the carnage, looting, and raping occurred.

What kind of system, personalities, and symbols do supporters of the Confederacy vouch for when they praise a country whose economy was based on breeding human beings like animals and whose defenders referred to those who attempted to liberate them as "nigger thieves," the term the James brothers, Jesse James and Frank James, used as an excuse to execute the citizens of Lawrence, Kansas. "They killed. They shot every man and boy they saw. They pulled them out of cellars and attics, knocked them off horses, and executed them in front of their families. They clubbed them, knifed them, stole their money and valuables, burned their homes and businesses. Black and white, ministers, farmers, merchants, schoolboys, recruits: at least two hundred died in terror." After the vicious murderer Jesse James was assassinated, the mob celebrated the outlaw with the shout "Hurrah for Jeff Davis." When the Confederates were restored to power, thousands of blacks were murdered by the KKK, which the late Shelby Foote likened to the French Resistance. (Shelby Foote used the n-word during an interview with a San Francisco reporter, Noah Griffin. He didn't know that the reporter was black.)

Like the present occupant of the White House (George W. Bush), President James Polk used a pretext to invade a sovereign country. He ordered General Zachary Taylor to cook up something that would create hysteria to propel an invasion of Mexico. His administration offered to buy the Southwest, but the offer was turned down. After winning the war, the United States annexed 1,527,241 square kilometers of Mexican territory. This included Texas, New Mexico, and California. Jefferson Davis and his Mississippi Rifles participated in the slaughter of the ill-equipped Mexicans. Then as now, war fever was especially high in the South; to this day, the homicide rate among white males in the South is higher than that of white males in the North. Walt Whitman blessed the war and justified the conquest on the basis of "peopling the New World with a noble race." Sam Houston called it for what it was, land theft, but used white supremacy as the justification for stealing the Southwest. (They wanted to seize all of Mexico, but Polk had promised a short war.) Henry David Thoreau was jailed for protesting the war. Tells you something about a country that has built more monuments to Jefferson Davis, a ruthless and arrogant dictator who presided over atrocities and massacres, than to Henry David Thoreau, who represented the best of the American spirit. Of this infamous episode in American history, for which James Polk was censured, Senator Jefferson Davis said, "I hold that in a just war we conquered a larger portion of Mexico, and that to it we have a title which has been regarded as valued ever since man existed in a social condition." According to historian Douglas Brinkley, appearing on CNN (February 6, 2004), the idea was to pretend that Mexico was the aggressor, when in reality the United States was.

Davis had as much regard for Mexicans as he had for Africans, despite an attempt by his apologists to paint him as a compassionate conservative, someone who is even shown palling around with his slaves. How did his slaves feel about him? When the Union troops came upon his house, a slave pointed them to where "old

Jeff's" papers were stored, and a slave who worked in the household was a Union spy.

Under this compassionate conservative's government, a measure was passed ordering that blacks found fighting for the Union be put to death. In 1863 the "chivalrous" and "gallant" Confederate Army moved into Pennsylvania. "In the course of their raiding and foraging, these units searched for blacks, seized them, and sent them south into slavery." A newspaper, the *Franklin Repository,* reported, "Quite a number of negroes, free and slave—men, women, and children—were captured by Jenkins and started south to be sold into bondage. . . . Some of the men were bound with ropes, and the children were mounted in front or behind the rebels on their horses." According to the book *When War Passed This Way,* "no one can estimate the number of Negroes who suffered this fate, for the practice continued throughout the time Lee's army was in Pennsylvania." Does this information make Peter Applebome and Tony Horowitz, fans of the Confederacy, want to get up in the gray—Jefferson Davis's favorite color—and join a reenactment? Would the thousands of NASCAR fans who waved the Confederate battle flag to greet their neo-Confederate hero George W. Bush put these flags away if they were familiar with this history?

This wouldn't be the first time Jefferson Davis and his colleagues enslaved people who had no way of defending themselves, whether they were slave or free or whether they were Mexican or Native American. Those Pennsylvania blacks got off easy. On other occasions, soldiers under Davis or serving in campaigns with Davis murdered people after they surrendered. This policy of Davis's Confederacy led to what some have called the greatest atrocity of the war. On April 12, 1864, at Fort Pillow, located fifty miles from Memphis, Tennessee, Confederate troops under the command of General Nathan Forrest slaughtered black and white troops after they begged for mercy:

The slaughter was awful—words cannot describe the scene. The poor deluded Negroes would run up to our men, fall upon their knees, and with uplifted hands scream for mercy, but they were ordered to their feet and then shot down. The white men fared little better. Their fort turned out to be a great slaughter pen—blood, human blood stood about in pools and brains could have been gathered up in any quantity. I with several others tried to stop the butchery and at one time had partially succeeded, but Gen. Forrest ordered them shot down like dogs and the carnage continued. Finally our men became sick of blood and the firing ceased.

This description came from an eyewitness, a Confederate soldier. Confederate apologist Winston Grooms, author of *Forrest Gump,* a postmodern reading of the Lost Cause myth, merely describes General Forrest's actions as "controversial." As an example of the hatred and spite directed at blacks—a hatred and resentment that led to the glorification of Davis and Lee—the white citizens of Memphis, in a vindictive slap at black advancement, erected a statue to this monster in the 1950s. Maybe Confederate sympathizer Ted Turner will finance a movie that will enshrine Nathan Forrest's deeds.

But instead of the opprobrium cast on foreign dictators like Stalin and Hitler for heading regimes that engaged in genocide, Nathan Forrest, Jefferson Davis, Robert E. Lee, and their colleagues (who, Ken Burns said in a candid moment, were responsible for more loyal American deaths than Tojo or Hitler) have been honored, as a result of one of the greatest propaganda campaigns in history. Not only has the rebel terrorist regime headed by Jefferson Davis been whitewashed by generations of apologists and historians, but by the American textbook industry and Hollywood in such films as *Birth of a Nation, Gone with the Wind,* and *Shane,* as well as numerous films that celebrate the nefarious activities of the James and Younger brothers who are shown as Robin Hoods.

Though film historians refer to Leni Riefenstahl's *Triumph of the Will* as the greatest propaganda film of all time, I'd choose Victor Fleming's *Gone with the Wind*. It was such an ingenious propaganda film that critics don't even see it as such. Besides, unlike *Triumph of the Will*, it was in Technicolor. Ken Burns's *Civil War*, which is the nonfiction redo of *Gone with the Wind*, has also contributed to a sort of springtime for the Confederacy, showing beleaguered and courageous southerners defending their homeland against the invading Yankees. This was the reading of the series by historian Leo Litwack. The Sons of the Confederacy showed Burns some love by making him a member of their organization.

Even General Stonewall Jackson was cleaned up in a neo-Confederate play, Jonathan Reynold's *Stonewall Jackson's House*, which argues that blacks were better off in slavery. As a sign of the times, Jack Kroll, the late *Newsweek* drama critic, recommended it for a Pulitzer Prize and Robert Hurwitt of the *San Francisco Chronicle* commended the playwright for having the guts to pen such a play, as though shoving ugly racist projects into the faces of blacks in the 1990s required some kind of courage. Because of the often bizarre punishments meted out to his own men, Jackson was much hated by those under his command, and though southern apologists and even a segment of National Public Radio saluted this killer, he was probably fragged by one of his own men, though the history books call it friendly fire. Stonewall Jackson was an early believer that faith-based institutions would civilize the blacks. He sent a contribution to a black Sunday school, a fact that his defenders point to as an example of this slaveholder's enlightened attitude toward blacks, and if television were around in those days, he'd have probably used black children as props as President Bush does.

Davis and his fellow war criminals are venerated by monuments erected on the basis of fraudulent claims. They are listed by James W. Loewen in his book, *Lies Across America*. Many of them were erected by the Daughters of the Confederacy, even though Davis nearly ordered Robert E. Lee, another Confederate with an inflated reputation, to fire on hungry Richmond women who were demonstrating for bread, confirming Sam Houston's description of Davis as "cold-blooded as a lizard." It shows again that some white women are the last Aunt Jemimas, the last ones to vote for those who would deny them choice. They praise men like Jefferson Davis, who was five minutes away from massacring their great-grandmothers in Richmond. They vote for California groper in chief, Arnold Schwarzenegger. Can you imagine blacks honoring someone who engaged such a hostile act against them, or Native Americans building monuments throughout the West honoring Zachary Taylor or Andrew Jackson? At least some southern women didn't share the enthusiasm of the Daughters of the Confederacy. In 1864 Richmond women were criticized for partying while men in gray were dying on the battlefield. In the same year Augusta Jane Evans published an attack on her countrywomen in the *Mobile Register*: "Can mirth and reckless revelry hold high carnival in social circles while every passing breeze chants the requiem of dying heroes. . . . Shame, Shame," she wrote, "upon your degeneracy."

Peter Applebome, who writes about race for the *New York Times*, glorifies the Confederacy in his book *Dixie Rising: How the South Is Shaping American Values, Politics, and Culture*. He says, "When the Supreme Court is acting as if Jefferson Davis were chief justice; when country music has become white America's music of choice and even stock car racing has become a $2 billion juggernaut; when evangelical Christians have transformed American politics; when unions are on the run across the nation much as they always have been in the South; when whites nationwide are giving up on public education just as so many Southerners did after integration—in times such as these, to understand America, you have to understand the South." Of course this wouldn't be the first time a northerner like Peter Applebome swooned over southern values. Frederick Douglass, the first great African American leader, noticed a similar trend in the 1890s, at a time when white terrorists had successfully destroyed Reconstruction by lynching and even massacring blacks who sought to exercise their rights. In a speech made in 1894 at Rochester's Mt. Hope Cemetery he criticized those who sought to romanticize the vanquished foe through "battlefield reunions, in popular fiction, inscribed on war memorials . . . and novels by Southern writers Joel Chandler Harris, John Easton Cooke, Thomas Nelson Page and Sara Pryor flooded the nation's mass-circulation fiction market with local-color stories depicting the ante-bellum South's refinement and civilization."

So successful has the second redemption of the Confederacy been that former members of the president's cabinet joined the tribute. John Ashcroft and Gail Norton had fond feelings for the land ruled by Jefferson Davis. "Secretary Norton went so far as to describe the South's struggle as honorable and unfortunately sullied by pundits crying slavery as 'bad facts.' Mr. Ashcroft, in the now infamous Southern Partisan article, argued that as good Americans we must defend the honor and principle of the great southern patriots Robert E. Lee, Jefferson Davis, and so forth. These men, after all, fought for so much more than 'some perverted agenda' as critics of the Confederacy claim," he said.

South Carolina was the first state to secede from the Union, and in keeping with the Confederate theme, George W. Bush often behaves as if he is the president of South Carolina in his appeal to religious fundamentalism and the homophobia associated with this faith. It was South Carolina that gave us the Civil War and Bush II. When he ran for president he pretended to remain neutral about flying the Confederate flag over the capitol building but slyly used his wife, Laura, to express his views. She said of the flag, "It's not a symbol of racism to me. I grew up in the South. Like everyone else here in Texas. And it's just a symbol of the time in our history we can't erase, really. The Civil War and, you know. There's just—that's the symbol of the Civil War."

Bush should have a painting of Jefferson Davis above his desk because they had similar careers. Both were unelected. Like Bush, Davis was a fraternity cut-up. Both participated in an unprovoked attack on an adversary who did not have the equipment to make it an even fight. Jefferson Davis participated in the Black Hawk War against Indians who were attempting to defend their land against a takeover by white settlers. Black Hawk, the Sauk leader, described the final battle in his autobiography. Like the black soldiers at Fort Pillow, the Sauk were murdered after they gave up.

> Early in the morning a party of whites, being in advance of the army, came upon our people, who were attempting to cross the Mississippi. They tried to give themselves up—the whites paid no attention to their entreaties—but commenced slaughtering them! In a little while the whole army arrived. Our braves, but few in number, finding that the enemy paid no regard to age or sex, and seeing that they were murdering helpless women and little children, determined to fight until they were killed. As many women as could, commenced swimming the Mississippi, with their children on their backs. A number of them were drowned, and some shot, before they could reach the opposite shore.

Besides Jefferson, another participant in this shameful conflict with the blame-the-victim title Black Hawk War was Captain Abraham Lincoln.

Just as some of Bush's advisers convinced him that invading Iraq would be a "cakewalk," Davis led his followers to believe that the Civil War would not be fought on southern soil. Like Bush, Davis lied about the reasons his nation entered the war. No mention is made of slavery in his inaugural address and to this day, some southerners and even historians, weighed down by the Lost Cause delusion, insist that the war was fought over states' rights and other ideals when both Davis and Lee would have been broke had it not been for land and slaves. Lee married rich; his father, Henry (Light-Horse Harry) Lee, served time in debtor's prison. "Save for some three thousand dollars he had received from his mother's small estate, he had no inheritance." He survived by marrying well. In 1831 he married a slaveholding woman, a distant cousin, Mary Custis, the daughter of George Washington's adopted son, George Washington Parke Custis. Jefferson Davis also married up, to Zachary Taylor's daughter. Deprived of his slaves after the war, he struggled constantly to make ends meet.

Indeed Robert E. Lee, depicted by his apologists as a compassionate conservative, was caught red-handed, participating in the very system that his apologists pretend repulsed him. On July 8, 1858, he wrote:

> I have made arrangements to send down the three men on Monday. . . . The man who is to carry them, is now undetermined whether to go by the mail boat, via Fredericksburg, or by Gordonsville. . . . He will have orders to deliver them to you at Richmond or in the event of not meeting you, to lodge them in jail in that City subject to your order . . . I may wish to send at the same time three women, one about 35 years old, one 22, and the other 17—They have been accustomed to house work, The eldest a good washer & ironer—But I Cannot recommend them for honesty—

Lee believed that "the painful discipline they are undergoing, is necessary for their instruction as a race, & I hope will prepare & lead them to a better things." Painful discipline seems to express the Bush administration's attitude toward the poor. Destroying the safety net for the poor will somehow make them stronger.

Both Bush and Davis designated duties to others, Bush to his vice president and staff, and Davis because of illness to his wife, Varina, and at other times to Judah Benjamin, his secretary of war, leading General Joseph E. Johnston to complain, "If that miserable little Jew is retained in his place our country will never be able to defend itself."

One difference is that Davis sometimes would appear on the battlefield, as at Manassas, raising the morale of his troops. In contrast, George W. Bush confines his military involvement to posturing, imitating a fighter pilot, and using soldiers and fake turkeys as photo ops before his admiring, uncritical press. (Southern newspapers were withering in their criticism of Davis and one described him as treating the people of the South like "white Negroes.")

Like Bush, Davis was an exponent of globalization, desiring to extend a system of cheap labor to other states and Cuba, just as the president is doing for multinationals on the hunt for wage slaves around the world. Like Bush, Jefferson Davis was known for a hot head, an attitude Bush has kept private. Davis once challenged Zachary Taylor, his future father-in-law, to a duel while Bush, under the influence of alcohol, is rumored to have challenged his father to a fight.

Bush seems to acknowledge his connection to Davis. "Last Memorial Day," reports Andrew Sullivan, "for the second year in a row, Bush's White House sent a floral wreath to the Confederate Memorial in Arlington National Cemetery. Six days later, as the United Daughters of the Confederacy celebrated Jefferson Davis's birthday there, Washington chapter president Vicki Heilig offered a "word of gratitude to George W. Bush" for "honoring" the Old South's dead. And why not? In 2004, Jeff Davis is hip. As Peter Applebome said, "Like Elvis, Jefferson Davis had never been better." Even Davis's arguments about race are also current. Instead of weasel-worded arguments hiding behind questionable graphs and statistics, and op-ed columns of pompous rhetoric or hiding behind black faces for hire, Davis was upfront with his opinions. He simply believed that black people are inferior to white people. "We recognize the negro as God and God's Book and God's Laws, in nature, tell us to recognize him—our inferior, fitted expressly for servitude . . . the innate stamp of inferiority is beyond the reach of change. . . . You cannot transform the negro into anything one-tenth as useful or as good as what slavery enables him to be."

Charles Murray's *Bell Curve,* which says the same thing, but in a pseudoscientific manner, not only received praise from the Irish American *National Review* and *Commentary* (published by Jewish Americans), but from the *New York Times* and Nina Totenberg of NPR, who gave the book Olympian praise, and from attack-queer journalist Andrew Sullivan. Richard Bernstein of the *Times* even asked that some thought be given to a theory that blacks excel at basketball because of genetic differences. (But now Bryant Gumbel has done a show about Eastern Europeans dominating the NBA; do you suppose those players received a genetic transplant from blacks?)

Jefferson Davis was ahead of his time, which might account for his popularity in the strangest of places. When contemporary southerners and northerners praise characters like Davis and Lee, are they also endorsing the policies of the system these men represented, or do they separate the men from their deeds and the consequences of their ideas? Is the Confederate battle flag a symbol of this system or merely an object revered by art-loving southerners? One can excuse Laura Bush. Her biographer reveals that she has led the life of the typical southern belle, a sort of stateside Saudi princess, isolated from blacks until she attended college and even then not knowing the significance of Martin Luther King Jr.'s visit to her Austin campus. Otherwise, how would someone as literate as she praise a flag representing a system that led to the destruction of millions of human beings and the forced separation of families? These family members were sent to death and enslavement camps called plantations, the subject of Harriet Beecher Stowe's great novel, *Uncle Tom's Cabin.* African women were sexually exploited to such a degree that, according to Joel Williamson and Chester Himes, a new race emerged in the United States. Although the contemporary press casts Thomas Jefferson and Strom Thurmond as the lone perpetrators of what a contemporary writer and ex-slave William Wells Brown called a "decadent" practice, the practice was widespread. Mary Chesnutt, the Martha Mitchell of the Confederacy and a friend of the Davises, said that every woman was aware of other women's husbands carrying on with African American women—but not their own, of course.

And what part of Confederate history are its champions celebrating. The part where they fought against the Union? Or the postwar part where ex-Confederates fought against granting rights to the former African captives. Eric Foner, in *Reconstruction: America's Unfinished Revolution, 1863–1877,* reports a massacre committed by the same ex–Confederates who are depicted in films like *Gone with the Wind* as the cream of knighthood. When blacks met to reconvene a constitutional convention, they were met by the city police force, which was made up of Confederate veterans.

> Fighting broke out in the streets, police converged on the area, and the scene quickly degenerated into what Gen. Philip H. Sheridan later called "an absolute massacre," with blacks assaulted indiscriminately and the delegates and their supporters besieged in the convention hall and shot down when they fled, despite hoisting white flags of surrender . . . The son of former Vice President Hannibal Hamlin, a veteran of the Civil War, wrote that "the wholesale slaughter and the little regard paid to human life I witnessed here" surpassed anything he had seen on the battlefield.

Jefferson Davis might not have been the "Lucifer" that Sam Houston said he was, but certainly the "country" over which he presided was a hell.

Back to the '30s?

Shortly after I began teaching at San Jose State University as an occupant of the endowed Lurie Chair, I started to receive e-mails from representatives of the International Union of Hotel Workers requesting that I cancel a speech I'd been scheduled to make before a convention held by the California Association of Teachers of English. They were boycotting the Westin Santa Clara, owned by Starwood, a multinational corporation. They charged the Westin with forcing its San Francisco and Los Angeles workers to pay more for health care, take on heavier workloads, and accept low wages. Starwood hotels in Los Angeles were accused of intimidating and harassing workers of color.

The e-mails were followed up by a visit to my campus office by a diminutive white woman. I told her I was busy and didn't have time to talk to her. The following week, she came to my class and passed out flyers, encouraging the class to urge me to withdraw from the engagement. "Other keynote speakers have decided to take a stand for justice and not enter the hotel. Why won't Professor Reed do the same?" the flyer read.

I was annoyed. The pressure continued when the woman came to my office accompanied by a woman pastor. We had some words, which must have startled my office mate and anyone within hearing range. I told them I didn't like their tactics and felt harassed by them. Finally, when I told them I was going to use the honorarium received from the speaking engagement to pay some Nigerian women authors whose anthology I was going to publish, we agreed on a compromise. I would make a short statement in support of the union before beginning my presentation.

Even though it was the Hospital Workers Union 1199 that helped an aspiring writer from Buffalo get a job in New York City, securing me an income while I was writing, my view of unions soured during the 1960s when white workers began to drift toward the candidacy of George Wallace.

Coincidentally, four of the books that I had chosen to use in a course called Special Topics, dealt with labor and unions: Chester Himes's *Lonely Crusade,* William Kennedy's *Ironweed,* Jack Conroy's *The Disinherited,* and Frank Chin's *Donald Duk,* which covers an 1867 strike waged by two thousand Chinese railroad workers in the High Sierras. Besides teaching books whose characters were union organizers and workers, I was taking the Greyhound bus from Oakland to San Jose each week. To go Greyhound is to be thrust into the America of the 1930s, but instead of Kennedy's white hobos, Steinbeck's dustbowl refugees, and Conroy's coal miners, whose position in society Conroy likened to that of mules, the passengers are Mexican families carrying their belongings in cardboard boxes and poor black people who live on food from the company's vending machines. Also on board are representatives of the white underclass.

The day came for me to speak.

I had planned to spend only a couple of seconds acknowledging the hotel union's boycott, but then found myself ruminating about what the fate of my parents' generation would have been without the union. The books, the boycott, my observations about Greyhound's America, and my family's history all seem to jell during remarks that lasted more than a couple of seconds.

My stepfather spent thirty years working for Chevrolet. His widow, my mother, is receiving a pension and health benefits from General Motors, which paid for three expensive heart surgeries. She's eighty-eight this June and has published her memoir, *Black Girl from Tannery Flats,* which she began writing at seventy-four. General Motors is the largest health provider in the country as a result of struggles waged by the United Auto Workers Union, one of the first unions to organize African American workers.

She was spared the fate of Larry Donovan's mother, who had to take in laundry to support her children after her husband died. Donovan, the lead character in *The Disinherited,* says, "I never found one of those Western Union canned greetings that fitted my mother—I never saw one that I could send her in remembrance of the nights she sweated over the irons or the days she spent bent over the steaming wash tub." In those days there were no survivor's benefits, unemployment insurance, welfare, or social security.

The elderly, like the character Bun Grady, had to keep working until some committed suicide, their bodies found near the railroad tracks. The women were old at thirty.

Throughout the novel, men are maimed by industrial accidents, but in the absence of disability insurance, they had to work as best they could with whatever body parts remained.

The setting for *The Disinherited* is the United States from the period preceding World War I until the Depression, and the characters in *Ironweed,* who live from hand to mouth, reside in 1938. Both novels show the state of white poverty before the safety net programs were ushered in during the Roosevelt era.

When Conroy lost his power struggle with the New York aesthetes, the era of the worker writer ended, according to Douglas Wixson in his introduction the 1991 edition of Conroy's novel. It was replaced by a writing that was characterized by "the eternal verities, textual difficulty, and personal confession," which, in Wixson's opinion, was "safe from FBI scrutiny."

This is the kind of writing that dominates college and university curriculums, no matter what the right-wing propagandists assert about radicals with tenure dominating college life. All one has to do is inspect the courses listed in the catalogs of ten American colleges or universities, selected at random, to discover that Euro-centrism still reigns.

So where would those young men who showed up at a town meeting shouting "social security must go" to find out about the sacrifices made by men and women like Lee Gordon, the union organizer in *Lonely Crusade*, who, in the face of police violence, picks up the fallen union banner? Or Kennedy's Francis Phelan, whose life is ruined after he accidentally kills a strikebreaker during an Albany trolley car strike? Or . . . the father, in Elzabeth Nunez's splendid novel *Under the Limbo Silence*, who has to compromise his position as a defender of the rights of Trinidadian workers in exchange for a polio vaccine his daughter needs. Certainly, not to cable television, which carries a number of business shows, but not one devoted to Labor or newspapers, which don't assign reporters to cover the labor beat. As a result, how many of our current students have ever heard of Walter Reuther, who, as strike leader for the UAW, during the 1930s, survived two assassination attempts? Indeed, according to Professors Philip Taft and Philip Ross, 'The United States has had the bloodiest and most violent labor history of any industrial nation in the world.'"

Both Conroy's and Hime's novels were subjected to hostile, ideologically driven reviews when they were published, but have managed to hobble along through small press reprints.

Conroy may have the last word, however, as the robber barons and the politicians they lease seem stunned by the initial backlash to their efforts to privatize social security. That's because they go first class and not Greyhound. Ending his 1991 introduction comparing Ronald Reagan with Herbert Hoover, he asks, "Is it possible that some of those who now lose their pride and stoop low may rise up angry?"

The Patriot Act of the
Eighteenth Century

Nations sometimes lose their bearings when confronted by an enemy. In a state of crisis or even panic, they implement measures that are later viewed as regrettable. From 1798 to 1800, the French were considered terrorists, pirating ships and making things uncomfortable for the fledgling American republic. The Federalist Party led a backlash against the French, and Thomas Jefferson and his Republican Party were seen as Francophiles. The XYZ Affair—a scandal centering on the fact that some French officials demanded bribes from American diplomats—brought relations between France and the United States to the breaking point. The Federalist administration of President John Adams considered such solicitations to be grave insults. There were cultural differences as well. In the view of Abigail Adams, Frenchwomen were risqué at best.

The reaction to the threat from France came in the form of the Alien and Sedition Acts, which were championed by the Federalists, passed by Congress, and signed by Adams in 1798. The Alien Act required immigrants to reside in the United States for fourteen years (instead of five) to qualify for citizenship. The act also gave the president the legal right to expel those the government considered dangerous. The Sedition Act punished "false, scandalous and malicious" writings against the government with fines and imprisonment. Most of those arrested under the Sedition Act were Republican editors, and instead of sending boatloads of aliens back to France, it resulted in no one's deportation. In a foreshadowing of the climate that inspired today's USA Patriot Act, at the turn of the century two hundred years ago, it was common practice to question the patriotism of citizens, immigrants, and the political opposition.

Jefferson, who was vice president at the time, drafted his position in secret and wrote it into the Kentucky Resolutions of 1798. James Madison, in collaboration with Jefferson, subsequently authored the Virginia Resolutions. In the second and fourth of the Kentucky Resolutions, Jefferson cited the Tenth Amendment, which gives the states powers not delegated to the government by the Constitution, to declare the Alien and Sedition Acts unconstitutional. Jefferson feared that a strong central government might put an end to slavery. Jefferson's fight against the Alien and Sedition Acts is often placed in the context of free speech, but it had unintended consequences beyond that. The Kentucky Resolutions were among the first to defend states' rights, and Jefferson had even threatened secession. Similar ideas helped spark the Civil War.

After Jefferson defeated Adams and was elected president in 1800, the Alien and Sedition Acts were allowed to expire. Adams, looking to distance himself from the mess, blamed the whole idea on Alexander Hamilton—who by then had been murdered by Aaron Burr.

The expiration of the acts did not end challenges to the First Amendment or the tendency on the part of some presidents to behave like monarchs, sometimes with the cooperation of Congress. The Espionage Act of 1917 prohibited "false statements" that might "impede military success." During World War II, FBI Director J. Edgar Hoover and President Franklin Roosevelt wanted to use sedition charges to suppress black newspapers, claiming they undermined the war effort with reports of racial dissension and demands for civil rights. It took Chief Justice Earl Warren's Supreme Court on March 9, 1964, in *The New York Times Co. v. Sullivan,* to finally declare as unconstitutional the Sedition Act of the Adams administration. Though the act had expired during Jefferson's administration, the court's action buried that particular threat to free speech once and for all—or so people hoped. Writing for the majority, Justice William Brennan held that L. B. Sullivan, an Alabama official, had not been libeled in a *New York Times* ad that had been paid for by civil rights proponents. Brennan supported his arguments by citing Jefferson.

Mom's Book

When I called my mother from New York in 1966, excited because Doubleday had signed to publish my first novel, she responded that she was going to write a book, too. Since she was burdened by a load of family responsibilities, I didn't take her seriously.

After my younger brothers and sister left home, my mother's responsibilities lightened. My grandmother, for whom she had cared for many years, died, and my mother and stepfather sold their home and rented a senior citizens apartment. In 1993 my stepfather died and then his mother, an Alzheimer's patient, also died.

My mother settled into a comfortable apartment in a building owned by my youngest brother and in 1998 began her book, *Black Girl from Tannery Flats*, filling composition books with notes written in an elegant penmanship that is no longer required of school students. I also encouraged her to make audiotapes because her storytelling talent was more oral than literary. Folklorist Cecil Brown, who provided a blurb for the book, recognized it as a style of black storytelling that was disappearing with my mother's generation. She was born in 1917. These notebooks and tapes were edited by author Carla Blank, my partner, who spent many hours transferring them to the page.

The memoir covers my mother's life from her birth in Chattanooga until the 1990s. Her mother, a busy caterer, worked in

wealthy homes on Lookout and Signal mountains in Chattanooga. Sometimes she joined her mother at work. She remembers the generosity of these employers and one, Mrs. Clifford
Grote, apparently took an interest in me. She nicknamed me
G. W., since I was born on Washington's birthday. Some still call
me that. My mother spent most of her time with her grandmother, whose mother, Lucy Hardiman, was among the last generation born a slave. Lucy Hardiman was apparently whipped a lot
because my mother records that her grandmother, Mary Coleman, cried when she mentioned the welts on her mother's back.
Mary operated a diner that catered to white foundry workers. She
insisted on being addressed as Mrs. Coleman.

Thelma V. Reed's story is also that of a teenager whose father
was murdered and whose mother suffered from schizophrenia.
Thelma was raped and bore the rapist's child. A single mother
who left Tennessee for Buffalo, New York, during 1940s, when single mothers were the objects of scorn and ostracism. But her story
is not unusual for black women in the South, seen as available by
white men and often oppressed by black men and white women.

It's the story of two young people, Thelma V. Reed and
Bennie S. Reed, who rose from poverty to the middle class in a era
when it was still possible to move up. When labor unions were
strong, housing inexpensive, and the American Dream for the first
time within the grasp of large numbers of citizens.

Her book is important to me also because it explains some
questions I had about my family's history. I'd taped my mother
and her late cousin about the "mean" Irish American ancestor, but
according to my grandmother, whom I interviewed when she was
in her eighties, there were Irish American men on her side of the
family as well as on her husband's, Mack Hopkin.

My mother's father was murdered by a Greek restaurant owner,
according to the family's oral history, after he had knocked on the
wrong door. I obtained a copy of the death certificate which includes the comment "stabbed by some man," written by hand. My

mother recounts her visit to Chattanooga's Erlanger Hospital where her father, his clothes soaked in blood, lay neglected on a cot in the hall. The doctor had told the nurses, "Let that nigger die." My mother, being a Christian, has forgiven his murderer.

I suspect that her longevity (she's ninety-one) can be attributed to her qualities of compassion, her ability to set aside grudges, and her inexhaustible optimism and faith. Hers is the African Jesus, one who isn't remote but present in everyday life, always at hand, a savior as well as a friend. For her, ancestors communicate through dreams.

Her book also illuminated my understanding of one of those aspects of family history that bothered me. I always wondered why my mother and grandmother maintained close ties with their white employers even after relocating to the North. I was a product of the 1960s and viewed these people as their oppressors.

Black Girl from Tannery Flats cleared up this question. During the crises in my mother's and grandmother's lives, their "white folks" were there to lend a hand. My mother's boyfriend, a dashing, handsome lad, always complained about the white women at the Reed House, a Chattanooga hotel, making sexual overtures to him. One day he was caught with one of them. It was one of her employers, Herbert Spencer, who enabled him to escape.

The Grotes assisted our family when my grandmother was committed to an institution for two years. Another employer insisted that a bus company compensate my mother for injuries she sustained during a bus riot that erupted when whites demanded that blacks yield their seats at the rear of an overcrowded Knoxville bus. In pre-Montgomery bus boycott days, blacks rode in the rear of the bus, whites in the front.

"You'd do it for me," she told the executives of the bus company. They paid.

Being a single mother, my mother had difficulty finding housing in Chattanooga. Mrs. Grote persuaded the authorities to bend the rules, enabling her to obtain public housing for her family, which included my grandmother and me. Before the civil rights revolution, some blacks, like my mother, survived through a combination of pluck, cunning, and help from benevolent white folks.

One would hope that books such as my mother's would inspire others of our elders to provide a different witness to history than that offered by our educational institutions. A history written by men who blame the slave trade on "African chieftains," exclusively. Purveyors of feel-good lies that diminish the contributions of African Americans, Asian Americans, Hispanics, and white ethnics to American civilization. How many students know about the working-class white southerners who lived in regions that refused to go along with secession, that in at least one southern state there occurred a secession within the secession. How many know that before demagogues arose, warning of "Negro domination," blacks and whites voted together or that populist Tom Watson was able to summon two thousand white farmers to prevent the lynching of a black populist.

My mother said that when the first copy of her book arrived, she commenced to do a holiness dance of celebration. She received calls from people all over the country, including former schoolmates and childhood friends. She made the cover of the local newspaper, the *Buffalo Challenger*. One woman says that she carries my mother's book wherever she goes. People are calling and asking her to recommend Bible verses to help them through crises in their lives. I have suggested that she get a 900 number and charge them. She says that would be un-Christian.

One of my mother's honors came from the Every Other Thursday Book Club, one of many that have sprung up across the country as black consumers spend hundreds of millions of dollars on books. A black writer can sell more books at venues like Margaret Troupe's Manhattan Salon than at chain bookstores.

Carla, Tennessee, and I flew to Buffalo for the book party. I had prepared a speech for the gathering, but the hostess told me to make it short because they didn't have time for me to read it; they wanted to hear from their honored guest.

My mother discussed her book before a rapt audience of black women and then delivered messages to some of them. Messages from their dead relatives. Nobody saw anything unusual about this and I don't doubt that my mother, like many African and Native Americans, may be in contact with another dimension, in this day when astrophysicists speak of string theory and wormholes.

Respect for such gifted people is widespread among people of the South. In fact, my mother (who began her book at seventy-four and finished at eighty-four) has delivered a new book. She said that a few years ago the deceased who had been visiting her since childhood had stopped coming. They'd been replaced by spirits bringing verses to her. In the old days, she would have been considered a prophet.

Miracle at Ein Raz

I am not the only writer who sometimes feels I am being stalked by a genie. That your wishes will come true.

In February 1992, I got so annoyed with the haughty attitude of some of the French questioners at a Paris press conference held in conjunction with a meeting of writers and academics at the Sorbonne, that I blurted out, "Paris isn't the center of the world's culture anymore. You can find artists and writers in Tokyo or Accra." A few years later, I was invited to visit both places and found plenty of artists and writers.

In 1993, the San Francisco Opera Company commissioned me to write a libretto based on the arrest of Jesus of Nazareth in the Garden of Gethsemane. The result was *Gethsemane Park*, with music by Carman Moore. It was performed in Berkeley, San Francisco, and New York. The libretto became controversial, and I was called up to the Union Theological Seminary to discuss it. Reverend Calvin Butts brought his congregation to the New York performance. He also had issues with the theology but said he was intrigued by the notion of Lazarus complaining about being brought back from the dead. Borrowing from the Gnostic heresy among other unconventional texts, Judas is the hero of my libretto; in my version, he's a recovering crack addict. A minister invited me to show a videotaped performance of the opera to an audience at a white Fundamentalist church in Hampton, Virginia, on Good

Friday. This was the kind of church that had photos of its former ministers and members on the wall. Some looked as though they had served in the Confederate Army. The members of the church didn't seem offended by the video and afterward we had cake and coffee in the church kitchen. The following Monday the minister phoned to tell me that he'd been fired for inviting me.

And so, in 2000, as a result of those coincidences that every writer knows, I was invited to visit Jerusalem and found myself and Carla Blank, my partner, walking through the Garden of Gethsemane, after having been just about kidnapped by an Arab Israeli cab driver. The embassy had warned us that such a trip was off-limits. As in the case of my trip to Accra and Tokyo, it was as though I had conjured the trip. But the 2000 trip wasn't merely about tourism. I found myself being questioned by Israeli writers about black anti-Semitism, since a *New York Times* op-ed had proposed that blacks were the country's only remaining anti-Semites (which was contradicted by an ADL report issued at about the same time which found that anti-Semitism among blacks was declining). This op-ed led to much media hand-wringing, talk show fodder, and lucrative book contracts. Michael Lerner and Cornel West shared a $100,000 book contact for the purpose of solving the whole thing.

One group consisting of black and Jewish intellectuals was funded by a foundation to solve the conflict between blacks and Jews (which some claimed had rent an alliance forged during the civil rights movement; this was incorrect; the black–Jewish alliance began around the 1900s when both were victims of brutality inflicted by the New York police, according to the book *Street Justice,* by Marilynn S. Johnson). This led to stays at five-star hotels and extravagant partying and dining. But because the group was composed of intellectuals, not a single game of golf was played.

Barry Glassner was right when he said that the issue was hyped, and it must have come as a surprise to Henry Louis Gates Jr., the original op-ed writer who started the whole controversy, when

CNN reported that during the 2004 presidential primary, Joseph Lieberman, a Jewish American, was the first choice among black voters before Al Sharpton entered the race for president. After Sharpton announced, the senator was second choice among black voters. And according to a poll conducted before the South Carolina primary, Lieberman was tied with Sharpton at 17 percent each. Apparently an asteroid had passed the earth making it no longer necessary for black families to recite the *Protocols of the Elders of Zion* at the breakfast table! In fairness to Gates, his op-ed was supposed to be followed by one addressing racial feelings among some Jews. The fact that it didn't appear demonstrates the one-sided nature of the Jewish–African American tensions. It's all the fault of blacks. It's all the fault of Reverend Louis Farrakhan, seems to be the editorial line of the media.

During my first visit to Jerusalem in 2000, I met a number of Israeli Jewish and Arab writers, including A. B. Yehoshua, with whom we met for coffee in Haifa. The second intifada had begun and the tourist sites were deserted, allowing Carla and me to take a leisurely stroll through the Garden of Gethsemane and other places I had read about so much when growing up that I could have conducted the tour myself.

In October 2003, I attended the International Poet's Festival in Jerusalem. It was held at Mishkenot Sha'ananim—the first area of Jewish settlement in Jerusalem outside the Old City walls, "the seed from which grew the new city of Jerusalem." The travel brochure says of Mishkenot Sha'ananim, "With its crenellated facade, somewhat reminiscent of that of the Old City walls themselves, the building gave the appearance of a fortress, as if to suggest that it was capable of defending its inhabitants, like the wall opposite. A covered balcony running the length of the building, supported by iron pillars and decorated by wrought iron arches, blending harmoniously with the grillwork of the doors and windows, added a touch of grace to the building without marring its austere simplicity."

We stayed at the Inbal Hotel located nearby, at 3 Liberty Bell Park, Jabotinsky Street. The hotel literature says that "the Inbal Jerusalem hotel is a modern, elegantly styled Five Star Deluxe hotel, reflecting the Jerusalem experience through the use of Jerusalem natural stone as an integral part of the interior decor. The hotel is located in the center of Jerusalem, adjacent to the Liberty Bell Park, within a short walking distance from Jerusalem's commercial center as well as the Old City, religious and archeological sites." It has the best breakfast buffet in the world and marked the beginning of the generous hospitality that our hosts had planned for us. They even tolerated my clumsy jazz piano playing. During our visit, *New Yorker* contributor Noga Tarvopolsky took us to lunch at the American Colony, called "the most beautiful hotel in Jerusalem."

The hotel, which has survived Ottoman, British, and Jordanian rule, is operated by Valentine Vester, a feisty, outspoken ninety-three-year-old. Of the security wall that has been erected, some of which encloses land belonging to Palestinians, she says, "It's hideous. And the West Bank is like nothing now, all checkpoints and barriers and fences." Of the Arabs she says, "The Arabs blame everything on the occupation." She admired the late Edward Said, who taught at Columbia University: "He was very hot on the Arabs standing on their own two feet and standing up for themselves."

During this second visit no one asked about black–Jewish relations. Instead of painting African Americans as bigots so as to entertain their white subscribers, the media had moved on to Michael Jackson and was using him to cast collective blame on blacks, for the same reason. Ratings. The Israelis were now concerned about suicide bombers. Natan Zach, the poet who'd organized the conference, during one of the most brilliant stand-up routines I'd ever witnessed, full of zinging one-liners, expressed his concerns. He said he was afraid that another suicide bombing would happen, causing the conference to be canceled.

Noga said she'd heard the explosion resulting from a suicide bombing that destroyed a café located a few blocks from her home. The bombing had occurred a few weeks before our arrival. A waiter, an Arab Israeli in his early twenties, was killed. She said that she attended his memorial and that his relatives were condemning their fellow Arabs for his murder. But in 2000, during my first visit, I'd heard other horror stories from Arab Israeli writers who live in Nazareth. About how their land had been seized after the 1947 partition and how they had to live on charity until they could recover economically. The Jewish Virtual Library acknowledges this: "Many Israelis, like many Americans, find the promise of equality is not always matched by the reality. Arabs in Israel have suffered economic and social discrimination. By virtually any measure—health, education, welfare—Jews are better off. One reason is that government spending has historically been significantly higher in Jewish municipalities than Arab ones. In addition, Arabs have a far more difficult time getting university educations or jobs." Israeli Army radio and other journalists asked whether I had come to support Israel. My attitude is to remain neutral. My friend Dr. Ibrahim S. Fawal, author of *The Hills of God*, a novel, will never recover from his family being uprooted from their home in Ramallah.

But I will never know the feeling of being hunted down and put in an oven. The Jews' enemies persecuted them before the Europeans ever set foot in Africa, but ironically it was some Muslim countries that offered them refuge from European persecution. While Israelis might regard their enemies as Arabs or Minister Louis Farrakhan, the record shows that Europeans and white Americans have caused them the most problems. It was a white American who blew up the Federal building in Oklahoma, inspired by an anti-black and anti-Semitic book, *The Turner Diaries*. It's usually white Americans who are involved in physical assaults on Jews. Europeans were the ones who actively sought to exterminate Jews, as well as the ones who aided and abetted the plan. Just as many American Jews believe the United States is the Jewish promised land, Jews in Germany believed the same thing. Thought they were assimilated. Thought that they were over. Some even fought in Hitler's army.

The threat from terrorism was addressed during the opening night of the conference. One Israeli speaker spoke of "a permanent threat that hangs over our heads." Another thanked those of us who came from abroad for ignoring the "fear mongerers." It was no problem for me. My neighborhood had been under siege by some young men whose form of recreation is blasting an eardrum-shattering bass from speakers embedded in their car trunks. The sound shakes the houses on our block. If an earthquake were to come, how would we know?

During the second week of December 2006, there was a full-scale shootout in my neighborhood, leaving forty-five slugs all over the street. During my stay in Israel, Americans were advised not to visit there. But given the situation in my neighborhood, this was the most peaceful week I'd had in a year.

Israeli poet Natan Zach spoke of his efforts to raise money for the conference and held up a sheet, which he said listed the millionaires who put up money for the conference. The sheet of paper was blank. During his speech opening the conference, he said that poetry is the custodian of the human condition, of tradition, while novels are relatively new. Over the next few days, a number of poets representing many countries read their work. Mark Rudman and I represented the United States. One poet, a member of the Israeli parliament, described as a left-winger, read about an Arab shepherd who was murdered by an Israeli soldier because he didn't stop when ordered to freeze. That would be like a U.S. congressman getting up and reading a poem about the numerous police shootings of unarmed blacks in the United States.

Though some Arab Israeli intellectuals complain of their second-class status, Israel in some respects is more democratic than the United States, where only millionaires can run for office and efforts continue to deny blacks the right to vote. In the nineteenth century it was the Democrats who set up obstacles to prevent them from voting. During this period it has been the Republicans. If the Florida secretary of state and the governor hadn't connived to prevent blacks from voting in the 2000 election, Al Gore would have been elected president and the war in the Middle East, the biggest foreign policy blunder in American history, likely would have been avoided. Israelis would not tolerate an imperial presidency either. No American president would tolerate the kind of heckling and cat-calls that I watched then Prime Minster Sharon receive when making a speech before the Knesset.

During our stay Carla, author of the then recently published *Rediscovering America*, participated in a panel about multicultur-alism at the home of Michael Richards, who was working as an officer in the American consulate. I had met Michael when I visited Nigeria in 1999.

I told her that during this trip I wouldn't board a bus. The next morning, after our arrival, I found myself on a bus. Our tour guide, an admirer of King Herod ("because if he hadn't built these walls, I wouldn't have a job") took us to the familiar sights. The promenade, with a view of the Temple Mount, the City of David, and the place, according to legend, where Jesus of Nazareth dined for the last time with his disciples. And then to the Old City where we walked over five thousand or so years of history. I took pictures of the Wailing Wall. The next day, I was corrected. It should be called the Western Wall because "Wailing" was the term used to mock the lamentations of the Jews who were permitted to visit the wall once a year by Byzantine authorities.

The man who corrected me was Moshe Dann. He is a history Ph.D., 1978, CUNY Graduate Center. He taught in the CUNY system, the New School, and, via John Jay College, a program at Rikers Island. He is the author of *The Black Press: Black Newspapers in Nineteenth Century*. He is a writer whose latest short story appeared in the *Ontario Review* (Fall 2006) and a journalist. His articles have also appeared in newspapers and magazines in North America and Israel and in the *Jerusalem Post*.

We were about to take a taxi for a second visit to the Garden of Gethsemane when he approached us in the doorway of the Inbal Hotel and asked, "What are you doing today?" I said we were going to visit the Garden of Gethsemane. He said it was probably not located where the tourist's map showed it to be because they'd found a Jewish cemetery there, including some of the graves from the First Temple, and that Jews buried their dead outside of the city and Gethsemane would have been located inside the city. What about the Church of the Holy Sepulcher? He assured us that this site might be authentic. He offered to take us to Hebron where Ishmael and Abraham are buried. We didn't have time for that and so he took us to Gush Etzion where, according to the documentation on display at the museum, several generations of Zionist settlers were martyred. The Gush Etzion Judaica Center provided background information about this site:

> Known as the southern gateway to Jerusalem, this strategic area comprises the block of communities that defended the southern approach to Jerusalem against the invading armies in the 1948 Israel War of Independence. Historically, the area is replete with Biblical scenes and stories of heroism and bravery starting with the time of our forefathers. It was here that Abraham and Isaac passed through on their sojourn from Hebron to Mount Moriah, in its pastoral landscape Ruth gathered the sheaves from the fields of Bethlehem, upon its hilltops David shepherded his father's sheep and then went on to proclaim his kingdom, and in its deep caves the Maccabees and the Jewish fighters of Bar Kochba sought shelter.
>
> Four brave attempts were made in the last century to populate the area, until finally on the fourth, after the 1967 Six Day War, the Jewish people were successful in settling the area permanently. The first attempt was in 1927, but harsh physical conditions forced

the settlers to abandon the settlement they had established, Migdal Eder. The second attempt was made by Shmuel Holtzman in 1935, who established the village of Kfar Etzion and after whom Gush Etzion is named (Holtz = tree = etz). Repeated Arab attacks drove the pioneers away. The third attempt was in 1943, when different affiliated groups established four settlements, the rebirth of Kfar Etzion, Masuot Yitzchak, Ein Tzurim, and Revadim, for a total population of 450 adults. In 1948, all four settlements were totally destroyed. The Arabs murdered 240 men and women, with another 260 being taken into captivity. Prime Minister Ben-Gurion in 1948 eulogized the defenders of Gush Etzion and their heroic stand against the Jordanian Legion as such. "I can think of no battle in the annals of the Israel Defense Forces which was more magnificent, more tragic or more heroic than the struggle for Gush Etzion. . . . If there exists a Jewish Jerusalem, our foremost thanks go to the defenders of Gush Etzion."

On the way to Gush Etzion, located in the West Bank, Moshe instructed us to look at one side of the street, to what was formerly Jordan. The British checkpoint still stands. Then we traveled across a bridge where autos were fired on so much by Arab shooters that a barrier had been built. Moshe told us that the settlers who were living in what he called "occupied Palestine" had to equip their homes with bulletproof glass because women had been shot while hanging laundry. Instead of the drab barracks associated with the kibbutzim I'd seen on television, these were modern villages whose architecture reminded me of the Moorish style found in Santa Fe, New Mexico. They were bathed in the same dramatic light. Also, unlike the dreary squalid refugee camps I'd seen in Amman, Jordan, the homes occupied by the Palestinians, located on the other side of the bridge, were also modern appearing and seemed to be built from the same materials. Moshe insists on a biblical Israel and pointed to some scenes along the way of biblical import. A valley, for example, where David fought Goliath.

Moshe criticized former Prime Minister Barak for giving the Temple Mount to the Arabs, because, according to him, ruins from the first temple that was destroyed by Nebuchadnezzar remain there. He accused the Arabs of carting off these ruins so that Israelis could not make a case for their existence. He said that the Muslims had no claims on Jerusalem because Muhammad never set foot in the so-called Holy Land. Muslim holy shrines are located in Saudi Arabia, he said. He did admire the late Yasser Arafat because Arafat, according to him, was a revolutionary. Arafat wanted to drive the Jews out of Israel, and Moshe pointed to two provisions in the Palestinian National Covenant. Article 9 of the document reads:

> Armed struggle is the only way to liberate Palestine. Thus it is the overall strategy, not merely a tactical phase. The Palestinian Arab people assert their absolute determination and firm resolution to continue their armed struggle and to work for an armed popular revolution for the liberation of their country and their return to it. They also assert their right to self-determination and sovereignty over it.

Moshe also admired Malcolm X, and when we returned from a visit to Ein Raz, we found the speeches of Malcolm X, a recording, underneath the door of our hotel room. On the way back to Jerusalem, after a telephone conversation in Hebrew, we stopped at a West Bank community called Efrat, where he picked up his daughter, Tehilla, who had ended her high school day and wanted to make the trip to Jerusalem. Standing guard in front of a grocery store were men armed with machine guns. Seems that Arab attackers had entered the store a few weeks before and stabbed some shoppers. Carla and Tehilla had a conversation in the backseat of the car. She was fiercely anti-Arab and told Carla about friends and parents of friends who had been seriously injured while going about everyday duties, driving their children to school, going to work, and so on. She wanted all of the Arabs killed. Carla thought it odd that this beautiful young woman all decked out in pastels would be saying such bloodthirsty things. She supported the Orthodox restraints on women. Tehilla said her older sister had not served in the military because she had married and become pregnant, which she said was a common happening to young women following their way of practicing Judaism. Tehilla said she wanted to be a singer but her religious training holds that it is inappropriate to stand before people and sing.

Simon Lichman and his friend Gabriel Levin said that Moshe's views reflect those of about 2 percent of the population and that most settlers would willingly move to Jerusalem if compensated. American and Russian immigrants seem to be among the most extreme of Israelis. I was told that some of the Russian immigrants had faked their Jewish heritage and were responsible for bringing drugs and prostitution into Tel Aviv. They said that the majority of Israelis were held hostage by a minority of people who are smitten with ideology. The same could be said about the political situation in the United States.

Before leaving the States, I'd received an e-mail from Simon, one of the Israeli poets I'd published on my zine, *Konch,* inviting me to a meeting between Israeli and Palestinian students. He lectures in the departments of English Literature and Folklore at the Hebrew University of Jerusalem. He was born in London in 1951 and has lived in Israel since 1971. A member of PEN International, he has chaired the Israel Association of Writers in English, editing a number of issues of its journal, *Arc.* His poetry has been published in journals such as *Konch, Modern Poetry in Translation, Tri-Quarterly, Stand, Jerusalem Review,* and *Tikkun,* as well as in his own collection, *Snatched Days.* His most recent work includes *Entertaining Angels,* a manuscript of poetry after paintings of biblical scenes, *Perhaps the Bear Behind,* which explores family life and local landscapes, and *Traditional Creativity Through School-Communities–General.* He founded and directs the Centre for Creativity in Education and

Cultural Heritage. Located in Jerusalem, the center runs education programs using folklore to bring Israeli and Palestinian school communities together. The Center for Creativity in Education and Cultural Heritage (CCECH) was founded in 1991 and began running the program between a pair of Jewish and Arab school communities in Ramle (near the airport). He sent me some materials about the program:

> Over the years we have worked in 6 pairs of Arab and Jewish communities (representing 13 schools) in Ramle, Jaffa, Abu Gosh and the Jerusalem area. We have worked with both Arab citizens of Israel and Palestinian communities on the other side of the Green Line (in and around Jerusalem). We have also run workshops, enrichment sessions and training courses for Jewish and Arab, Israeli and Palestinian teachers and student teachers, based on the use of folklore in "co-existence" education. . . . Our staff comprises of full-time, part-time, freelance and volunteer Jewish and Arab Program Facilitators and Coordinators, as well as an Internal Evaluator.
>
> We usually begin working with pairs of 5th grade classes (10–11 year olds) who will be together in the program for a period of at least 2 years. The school-communities, however, will continue working together, so that every new school year we carry on with the participating 5th graders (now 6th graders) while adding the new 5th grade classes. Teachers, parents and grandparents carry on meeting after specific children have graduated from the program. Therefore, we see it as a "total community program," with the parents reinforcing their children's positive experience of each other, working together as a team in the Joint Activities helping their children get the best out of the opportunities the program offers, as well as developing relationships of their own. Our goal is to build and help maintain long-term partnerships between the paired Jewish and Arab school-communities, which include as many classes in the

schools as possible. The longest partnership to date is between the Nisui/Ein Rafa-Nequba Schools in the Jerusalem area (which you visited) which have worked together now for 14 years. On-going, long-term programs offer communities the opportunity of developing a relaxed relationship of trust, which often leads to participants taking the initiative to create activities of their own outside of formal meetings between the paired classes. These have included children visiting each other's homes, community picnics and cooking groups. As you know, the extent of the work, (i.e., how many pairs of schools we work with and the number of classes in each school) depends on funding.

The program is funded largely by New Israel, an organization made up of, as Simon described it, "Young Jews who don't identify with established Jewish organizations. There's also a program in which elderly Jews and Arabs plant vegetable gardens and cook together."

On the Friday of our departure from Tel Aviv airport, Gabriel Levin, Simon's friend and translator of the poetry of Tahe Muhammad Ali *(So What: Selected Poems)*, picked up Carla and me at the hotel and we drove to Ein Rafa, an Arab Israeli town located outside of Jerusalem. We could see that the infrastructure of the town had not been given the attention received by Jerusalem. Simon had told us to meet him at the top of a hill near a mosque. We got the wrong mosque and while we were waiting, some Arab grocery store owners brought us orange juice. I bought a bottle of water. Noga warned us that some travelers, not realizing that Jerusalem is located in a desert, suffered from dehydration. We finally found the right location. Arab children were waiting for the bus bringing the Jewish students to the site. It arrived about ten minutes after us. The Israeli kids got off the bus and the Arab students greeted them. One Israeli kid was wearing a sweatshirt with Washington, D.C., printed on it. They'd met before. Under the program, the students meet two or three times per year. Simon is popular among the Palestinians in this town and was greeted warmly everywhere we went. After we watched the Jewish and Muslim students interact, we had lunch at a Lebanese restaurant located in the village. The restaurant's furnishings and equipment, down to the last burnished copper pot, looked as though they were on loan from a museum. If civilization were measured by the quality of goods one found in a flea market, the Middle East would win out over America hands down.

As we left the restaurant, Simon was recognized by an Arab family. The son had graduated from the program, and the family greeted Simon warmly. The son has since become a dancer. During sessions with the children he asks challenging questions about the stereotypes that are passed down, most likely from their parents. To the Arab children who express joy when a bus in Tel Aviv or Jerusalem is blown up, he asks whether they would be glad if he were on the bus. They like Simon, and so this gives them something to think about. To Israelis who say the land belongs to Israel, Simon asks which is more important, the Land or the Law. One of Simon's friends is the local imam, who opened his mosque to the children even though it was a Muslim holiday.

The Israeli government pays both rabbis and imams. The imam explained some aspects of Islam to the Israeli students. After he explained that followers of Islam are required to pray five times a day, an Israeli kid told him that an Arab friend of his prays only four times a day because he doesn't want to get out of bed. The Imam explained that Satan is probably behind the Arab kid's wanting to remain in bed. Everyone laughed.

After the session the students adjourned to a school where the Jewish kids explained some aspects of Judaism to the Arab kids. In the school's kitchen, we sampled food brought by Arab and Jewish Israeli parents. I remember date cakes and a dish made of sesame seeds. Afterward, I took pictures of the Palestinian and Israeli kids playing together. This is a picture that one rarely sees on American television, perhaps because it is not exciting enough to affect ratings. I was told about a nearby village, Neve Shalom, established twenty years ago by Bruno Hussar, a priest who believed that Arabs and Jews can live in peace, as they had done hundreds of years before partition. The town is multicultural and bilingual. One of the speakers at the session was an Armenian parent whose family came to Israel as a result of the genocide against the Armenians by the Turks. One sees postings reminding tourists of that genocide on the walls inside the Old City. After the lectures, the kids played together. Though it was a Muslim holiday, about fifteen Arab kids showed up.

The boys played soccer and the girls chatted. After the session, Simon had to pack his car and so Carla and I were left with the Palestinian kids. They were very eager to know about life in America. They were acquainted with pizza, spaghetti, burgers, and Michael Jackson. A couple asked me to take them back to the United States. Another child wanted me to come to his house and meet his parents. They performed a ring dance for us as I took video pictures. Finally the Palestinian kids disappeared down a hill with their teacher. The Jewish kids had returned to their homes. These kids, Palestinian and Jewish, obviously enjoyed each other's company. But gloom from the conference could be heard even in this peaceful setting. Varla Schimmel, a photographer and writer, said that suicide bombers presented such danger that friends were advising friends not to go shopping, even for groceries, unless absolutely necessary. Simon was constantly on the phone discussing whether his son should choose to go to jail because he didn't want to be a member of the internal affairs division of the Israeli army. He had just begun his mandatory military service. I talked to a couple who were present at the school. She was Jewish and he was Palestinian. I asked him how he got along in Jerusalem. He said that he had no problems. She said that his relatives, however, were afraid to walk through the streets.

For this book, I asked Dr. Lichman to provide an update about the program:

Since your visit we have increased our sphere of activities (although I can't say that the funding has increased by very much!). In the School Pairing Programs for the current school year (2006/7) we are working with approximately 520 children and 1500 family members (on average, three family members per child).

The Nisui/Ein Rafa-Nequba Program has recently moved from a 2 to 3 year program and has thus expanded by one third. The schools' staff rooms have also begun to participate in a series of activities (which we designed) in order to deepen the contact and knowledge between the schools on the institutional level.

The first group of children graduated from the second school-community pairing program in June 2006. The program is currently in its third year, and has expanded from 52 to 160 children and their families.

The program itself began as the result of a parent-initiative in response to a Jewish child realizing that he knew no Arab children despite the close proximity of Jewish and Arab neighborhoods in Jerusalem. The Palestinian schools were also anxious that their children meet ordinary Israeli Jewish children and families.

The CCECH's programs create safe, enjoyable and stimulating environments in which Israeli and Palestinian, Jewish, Moslem and Christian communities (children, parents, grandparents and teachers), may juxtapose their often shocking reality with direct, informative, warm and personal experience of each other.

For the last three years the CCECH has also been running a program for Bedouin and Jewish student-teachers in the Coexistence Project of Kaye Academic College, Beersheva.

In December I asked both Moshe and Simon to give me an assessment of the political situation in Israel since the Lebanon invasion. I also asked Moshe about his daughter, whom he introduced to us. He replied:

My daughter is going to school to make up for what she didn't do in HS so that she can go to college; she is married; her husband is in the army. She composes amazing songs. So does my older daughter, who lived on a hilltop in Shomron with her husband and my 2 little grandsons. The government kicked them out (to get ready to destroy yet more Jewish communities) so now they live near Afula.

The mood here today is that despite being threatened with extinction by Iranian nuclear weapons (supported actively by Russia and passively by the rest of the world), bombarded daily with small rockets from Gaza, threatened by Hizbullah with renewed missiles from Lebanon, constant terrorist attacks intercepted from Judea and Samaria ("the West Bank"), condemned by nearly the entire UN, a corrupt local political leadership that has no public confidence—we exist by the grace of God—a miracle. We still have faith that we can and will not only survive but prevail, that the world will come to its senses and its moral obligations that Jew hatred will turn into understanding and acceptance—a world filled with peace.

Warmest, Moshe

Above I mentioned Ibrahim Fawal, who has painful memories of his family's expulsion from Ramallah. I met Abe, as he is called, while attending the Birmingham Writers Conference in the 1970s. Abe and his late wife held a reception for me at their home. I wrote a review of Abe's book, *The Hills of God*, for the *Washington Post*. He has struggled to get his very fine book into mass circulation, which is unfortunate because Abe, who has a degree from Oxford, has a great deal to contribute to the issues in the Middle East. As a sign of the insularity of U.S. policymaking centers, not one Arab American scholar was asked to serve on the Iraq Study Group. Dumb. After both Moshe and Simon's answers to my questions arrived, by coincidence, I was invited to a holiday gathering at the home of John Diaz, editorial page director of the *San Francisco Chronicle*. Abe as well as his daughter Gina Jabar, a magazine writer, and her husband would be there. Also among the guests was Professor George Bisharat of Hastings College of Law. I asked Abe and George to adjourn to another room where I got the two Palestinian Americans to answer the comments sent in by Moshe and Simon.

Transcript of Ishmael Reed's Interview with Dr. Ibrahim S. Fawal ("Abe") and Professor George Bisharat, Hastings College of Law (December 19, 2006)

I asked Dr. Fawal and Bisharat to respond first to Moshe's remarks.

BISHARAT: Yes, my response is that it contains a lot of misapprehensions and misunderstandings and gross misperceptions of the realities of the world, particularly the relationship between Jews and Arabs in the Middle East.

REED: *How about you, Abe?*

FAWAL: He does not mention a thing about occupation. He doesn't say a thing about it. He ignores it. End the occupation and we can talk. And he ignores the support Israel gets from America. Hundreds of billions from America. And they use it to suppress us.

REED: *Do you find his position to be similar to the administration's position? Like stubborn. Like victory at all costs.*

FAWAL: I think he does. The last six years they wanted to get rid of Arafat. They got rid of Arafat. Even before they cut free of Arafat they wanted Abbas to be the prime minister. And for fifteen months not one word. No meetings. No solution. No discussion whatsoever. And then they had the fairest and the clearest election in Palestine. And then when Hamas won, they said, "No, we don't want them." So they wanted their people to win. If their people don't win, the elections are no good.

REED: *What do you think about his statement that all this is based on Jew hatred, that the whole world is against Israel?*

FAWAL: There has never been Jew hatred in the Arab world. A Jew started the Egyptian cinema. The Egyptian theater was by Jews. My mother's cousin, the son of a Greek and Orthodox priest, was married to a Jew. In my house there were two rooms under the balcony, there was a Muslim man from Gaza married to a Jewish girl from Jerusalem named Esther. They lived in Ramallah and worked in Ramallah. We never had that problem until World War II, 1947, 1948, and all that. They still live in Syria. They still live in Iran. There has never been a Jewish hatred. Excuse me, I never heard of the word "anti-Semitism" until I came to this country. Never.

BISHARAT: I think the fundamental misunderstanding in this statement is precisely that. Jews, Muslims, and Christians lived in peace for centuries until the Zionist movement, the political movement that was born in Europe and that was a reaction to anti-Semitism in Europe fixed on the idea of creating an exclusive Jewish state in Palestine, which was a majority Muslim and Christian country. So you know the conflict really has to do with the determination of a group of European Jews to establish an exclusively Jewish homeland in a state that belonged to another people.

REED: *Moshe is from New York.*

BISHARAT: That's particularly offensive. Jews in this country have a very well protected, very good life. And the fact that someone from New York could feel entitled to a country that belongs to another people, that a person because of his or her being Jewish has superior rights to people who have lived there for centuries, continuously, is an offensive notion.

REED: *When we toured with him he showed us where David fought Goliath and said there was a biblical mandate for Jews to have that part of the country. He said that Muhammad never set foot in Jerusalem.*

FAWAL: Do you know how many denominations there are in the Christian Church? Do you have any idea?

REED: *No.*

FAWAL: 554. And every one of them has the True Faith. So this interpretation is very subjective and very questionable. I go by deeds, wills, purchases. Ramallah, where I come from, was established in 1515. Okay? We used to think it was 1492. 1515. I don't know who was there first, in Palestine—Arabs or Jews. They were cousins and they were together for four, five thousand years. God knows how long. I know Ramallah; since 1515 we have been there. And you mean to tell me that a Russian Jew or Argentinian Jew or Polish Jew can come and claim Ramallah is his and not mine? No sir. I will never accept it. I live a privileged life here and I am happy. But I will never forget that Ramallah is my birthplace and I am entitled to Ramallah. Not the Russian Jew or the Polish Jew or the Argentinian Jew. On what basis? What basis? God gave it to them? You tell it to the Muslims. 1.3 billion people are wrong? Their Qu'ran is wrong? And now you are going to start when the Inquisition happened in Spain, and the Jews were expelled, where did they go? To England? To Germany? To Italy? The Netherlands? They went to the Arab world. To North Africa. And they lived for all these years in harmony.

I remember one professor at Oxford University said, "Everybody should read my book, should read this book. Read and learn from this book." I said, "What do you mean by that?" He said, "For all these centuries, Arabs and Jews lived in harmony in Palestine. Up to the 1920s. Muslim women and Jewish women were breast-feeding each other's children. Okay? We had no problems with them until the outsiders came."

I debated one medical doctor in Birmingham. He was from Hungary. I said, "You were born in Budapest?" He said yes. I said, "I was born in Ramallah. Ramallah belongs to you and not to me?" He said yes. I said, "Why?" He said, "God gave it to me."

Well that's it. I refuse to accept it. We either inherited it. Or we bought it. And we cultivated it and we plowed it, and we smelled it and we ate it. For hundreds of years. Not thousands of years, but five hundred years. It's theirs and it's not mine? I refuse to accept it. I will never accept it.

I then had Abe read Simon's statement:

> With regard to the present situation—once again we have found our-selves gripped within the inevitable impasse of war. We witnessed a bleaching out of hope in the eyes of people who were already worn down by never being able to take "normality" for granted.
>
> Governments and international aid agencies must be responsi-ble for rebuilding infrastructure and homes while our focus has been the task of helping to rebuild the psyche of participants in the programs and to look for the means to include as many new com-munities as possible.
>
> We will continue working tirelessly to educate children in the ways of hope, empathy and ethical understandings, so that they may live in the world as day-to-day proponents of peaceful, thought-provoking co-existence.

REED: *This is Simon Lichman, who works to educate Arab Israeli and Jewish Israeli kids about each other's histories and traditions. For example, he took the Jewish kids to a mosque where the imam explained Islam to them, and the Arab Israeli kids were talked to by a woman who is a Reform rabbi. This kind of exchange has been going on for a number of years, this program. Do you have a response to that?*

BISHARAT: I do. I think these kinds of efforts at dialogue are well meaning but misguided. They remind me of somebody who would sit down and ask the victim of rape to sit down with the rapist and have a conversation in which the two sides try to understand each other. You know a rapist has a perspective, certainly. Comes from a certain background, has reasons for his, usually, actions and the like. And I suppose there's a sense in which a rape victim could learn and understand from all that. But fundamentally what's going on is that one of these parties is systematically plundering, oppressing, dominating, and exploiting the other. And until that relationship of domination, exploitation, oppression, and the like stops, there's no real reason for dialogue. After that, after that process stops, there may be need for this kind of reconciliation, this kind of dialogue. Until that happens, however, this kind of program, it seems to me, is a way of helping the victimizer feel better—the elements of the sort of liberal conscience to be satisfied to a certain extent—but to me it's completely out of place and inappropriate.

REED: *What about—we were with him when his son was trying to decide to enlist in the Israeli army, which he is required to do. And Simon was urging him not to, because essentially he is a pacifist.*

BISHARAT: I respect that. I respect that.

FAWAL: Individually a great guy. I respect many of the positions [taken by] writers, musicians, actors, and directors. We have no quarrel with the Jews or individuals. But we do have—I have major problems with organized political parties that think Palestine is theirs and not mine. There is a professor at Oxford. His book is

The Politics of Partition: King Abdullah, the Zionists, and Palestine, 1921–1951. His name is Avi Shlaim. He's Jewish. He gave me a copy, and he took a copy of my book. I started reading it. And we met. He said that around 1900 there were 500,000 Arabs in Palestine and 50,000 Jews. He said 90 percent Arabs owned 99 percent of the land. This is not Arafat speaking, this is not Abe speaking, or George, or Nasser, or what have you. A Jewish professor of international renown.

We owned 99 percent of the land. Arafat signed and gave them 78 percent provided we would get the 22 percent. They built the settlements, they built the network of highways connecting the settlements together, and they took small Jerusalem and they made a huge county. And they had a wall dividing the land. And Palestinians can't go to their schools, people can't go to their farms, people can't visit their friends. And what's left, what's left—Sharon wanted to give 40 percent of the 22 percent of what's left, minus all these deductions that would bring to 8 or 9 percent—and that means cities would not be connected with each other. Or tunnels or bridges or what have you. An insane person, a lunatic person would not accept that solution. If you give it to me, deed it to me, I would not sign. That is insane. I mean—they accepted the reality. I have never met a Palestinian or an Arab who has not accepted the reality of Israel. Have they accepted the reality of Palestine? No, they haven't.

Though the African American mainstream is decidedly pro-Israeli, with the Congressional Black Caucus having a voting record favorable to Israel, considerable support also exists for the Palestinian cause, especially among artists and intellectuals. While working on this chapter, I was interrupted by a request from the Third Family Booking Agency in Paris. I was asked to write two songs for a top jazz artist that would be used in a film about black families who became displaced after they were banished by mob violence from land they owned. Watching an unedited version of the film, I could find a parallel to the condition of these families and those Palestinian families who were ousted from their homes as a result of partition. According to the film *Banished*, between 1864 and 1930 dozens of American towns expelled black families through mob violence, terrorism that is rarely discussed in the American media and educational system. Black homes and churches were dynamited, livestock slaughtered, and occupants often lynched. Thousands of acres of land left behind by African Americans were occupied by whites without any compensation being paid to the original owners. In Forsyth County, Georgia, blacks were forced to flee the two thousand acres of land belonging to them.

In January 1987, when blacks and their allies sought to exercise the blacks' right of return, they were assaulted by white terrorists. The whites who stole millions of acres of land belonging to Native Americans and blacks also believed that they had a divine mandate that gave them ownership of the land, sentiments expressed in documents like those defining the doctrine of Manifest Destiny and Robert Frost's poem, "The Gift Outright."

After I turned off the tape recorder, I left the two men sitting in a comfortable sunken room next to the kitchen. I could understand why they would object to Moshe's intransigence, his zeal, but for me, Simon had gone the extra mile by learning Arabic and risking the contempt of Zionists like Moshe. I told the women in the kitchen of my disappointment at the reaction to Simon's position. A reaction, given the uprooting of one people for the sake of settling others, that I could understand.

The women were more supportive of Simon. Gina Jabar, Abe's daughter, a journalist, said that any move toward people understanding each other is a good thing.

I then thought about that last day in Israel. After the children Simon's group had brought together went their separate ways. The Jewish children boarding their bus. The Palestinian children heading back to their homes, escorted by their teacher. I decided that no cause, no ideology, no man-made idea was worth harm coming to those children.

Bubba from Another Planet

In February 2007, a controversy about who was the first to identify, in print, President Clinton's becoming a black president began on a site edited by Richard Prince of the Maynard Institute. Jack White claims that he was the first, writing in the March 1998 issue of TIME. *But nowhere in this piece does White refer to Clinton as a black president, specifically. My piece, "Bubba from Another Planet," in which I do, appeared on April 19, 1998. Both pieces appeared months before novelist Toni Morrison's comments appeared in the* New Yorker *in October 1998. I reprint the Bubba article here.*

Last month in New York, I had dinner with one of the nation's top black journalists. We began to talk about President Clinton's problems and he said that they stemmed from his being too close to blacks. A few weeks later, I attended a reception arranged by members of Hawaii's black community, and I heard the same from them: some whites are after Clinton because he is viewed as a [n-word] lover.

An African American comedian has observed that because Clinton receives a check from the government, cheats on his wife, and plays the saxophone, he's a stereotypical black man. As scurrilous as this it may sound, there is an element of truth in this quip. Indeed, Clinton may be the blackest president since Warren G. Harding, who, when confronted with rumors about his black ancestry, supposedly said, "Somebody may have jumped across the fence back there."

Though nobody may have jumped across the fence in Clinton's background, as far as we know, my friends say that Clinton's style is certainly black. Miles Davis's biographer, Quincy Troupe, asked me to notice Clinton's manner of walking, bouncing and bobbing his head, as evidence of his blackness. One of Clinton's detractors, who seem to be ubiquitous on television these days, criticized Clinton's late mother's morality. I interpreted this to mean that Clinton's hip mother used to take him to jazz clubs.

Ronald Reagan seemed to go to out of his way to avoid having his photograph taken with blacks. And George H. W. Bush only seemed comfortable with Clarence Thomas. But just last week, Clinton seemed genuinely pleased as he was photographed giving one of his saxophones to a black eighth grader at a White House event.

Meanwhile, if it is as Clinton adviser James Carville says, that if some of those who desire to rid the presidency of Clinton are white supremacists, then they must be annoyed by the appointment of blacks to cabinet posts.

Every time you look around, Clinton is naming a black person to an important post. Last year, Eric Holder was sworn in as deputy attorney general, making him the highest-ranking black law enforcement official in the nation's history. Recently Clinton named Dr. David Satcher to be surgeon general, and he chose William E. Kennard last year to be chairman of the Federal Communications Commission. On Tuesday, Franklin D. Raines, the man who helped Clinton close the 1997 balanced budget deal, resigned as White House budget director to become chairman and chief executive officer of the Federal National Mortgage Association.

For white supremacists, the Clinton administration must remind them of one of those maligned Reconstruction governments of the sort shown in D. W. Griffith's masterpiece of racist propaganda, *Birth of a Nation*.

I have been critical of the president and mentioned, on a radio panel shortly after the 1992 election, that Clinton's cynical behavior in criticizing Sister Souljah in an appearance before the Reverend Jesse L. Jackson's Operation PUSH was indicative of a character problem. My fellow panelists, devoted Clintonites who included Paul Robeson Jr. and writer Playthell Benjamin, told me that my observation showed no political acumen and recommended that that I stick to writing fiction.

Clinton has been very good for the African American middle class, but his welfare reform program put poor blacks in peril. Things are becoming so bad in my town (Oakland, California) that during a recent public meeting we were warned that hungry people might soon break into our homes to raid our refrigerators.

But given his accusers, I can understand why the strongest support to the president is coming from African Americans. One of Rupert Murdoch's right-wing TV hosts grilled Andrew Young about African American support for Clinton and compared it to black support for O. J. Simpson. (One newspaper even referred to Clinton as the "O. J. president.")

Clinton often seems to have a symbolic relationship with black people. When *60 Minutes* aired Kathleen Willey's account of an alleged Oval Office encounter with Clinton, the hour was shared with the type of feature that *60 Minutes* has found improves its ratings: black people messing up. This time *60 Minutes* used three Fresno State basketball players to promote the stereotype: black athletes as criminals.

Clinton's relationship with blacks doesn't end there. The sex sting was first tried out on Washington Mayor Marion S. Barry Jr. Commenting about the government's use of women to entrap a public official, William Safire said, "Never before has the government stooped so low."

While Clinton seems to be, if not black, a white soul brother, a bubba from another planet, the same can't be said of some of his critics. Some of Clinton's right-wing critics, including white women who seem to be even more ferocious than the men, have expressed sentiments that make blacks uncomfortable. This includes Lucianne Goldberg, the literary agent who encouraged Linda Tripp to tape Monica Lewinsky. Goldberg's clients include Mark Fuhrman, the former Los Angeles police detective whose racist comments punctuated the Simpson trial. Goldberg told CNN's Dan Abrams that "nobody has taken the time to try to understand" Fuhrman. (Dan Abrams moved to MSNBC, where he became the boss and supporter of shock jock Don Imus.)

Independent counsel Kenneth W. Starr wanted to place two black men, Vernon Jordan and Frank Carter, Monica Lewinsky's first lawyer, before a white grand jury in Virginia, rather than a black one in Washington, according to talk show host Geraldo Rivera. What was that all about?

The self-appointed U.S. virtue czar, William J. Bennett, has called for the president's impeachment, yet he shocked Jesse Jackson when, in an appearance with Jackson on a Sunday morning talk show, he just about endorsed Charles Murray's neo-Nazi research about black inferiority by saying that's "something that ought to be looked into."

Bennett is a member of a foundation whose sponsors include publisher Richard Mellon Scaife, a man who seems to be bankrolling the entire anti-Clinton enterprise. Scaife is also one of the sponsors of the American Enterprise Institute, the outfit that supports Dinesh D'Souza, whose book *The End of Racism* was deemed so insulting to blacks that even two black conservatives resigned from the institute in protest. One of them called D'Souza "the Mark Fuhrman of public policy." Scaife also put some money behind California's notorious Proposition 209, which promises to reduce the black and Hispanic enrollment in the University of California's system to zero.

One of Clinton's most boisterous critics is Don Imus of the *Imus in the Morning* radio show. Many establishment lapdog journals kiss up to Imus, even *Washington Post* media critic Howard

Kurtz, who casts himself as some sort of media ethicist. Imus and his colleagues often crack racist jokes. He recently said that Clinton got the idea for going to Africa from *National Geographic,* a remark followed by the appropriate yuks from the cretins who surround Imus on the show.

And what about that trip to Africa? I mean, if you were a white supremacist, wouldn't you be tearing out your hair as you watched those pictures of Clinton attired in kente cloth dancing with Africans and playing the drums?

Flash forward to January 2008. In the next chapter, "Ma and Pa Clinton Flog Uppity Black Man," I continue my Clinton watch.

Going Old South on Obama

Ma and Pa Clinton Flog Uppity Black Man

During Bill Clinton's first run for President, I appeared on a New York radio panel with some of his black supporters, including Paul Robeson Jr., son of the actor and singer. I said that Clinton had character problems. They dismissed my comments and said that I didn't know anything about politics and should stick to writing novels. (Clarence Page, who has a monopoly on the few column inches and airtime made available to black columnists by the corporate media, said the same thing about me. I should stick to creative writing and leave politics alone.)

These criticisms didn't deter me. Writing in the *Baltimore Sun*, I was the first to identify Clinton as a black president as a result of his mimicking a black style. (I said he was the second, since Warren G. Harding never denied the rumors about his black ancestry.) As a result of his ability to imitate the black preaching style, Clinton was able to seduce black audiences, who ignored some of his actions that were unfriendly, even hostile to blacks. His interrupting his campaign to get a mentally disabled black man, Ricky Ray Rector executed. (Did Mrs. Clinton tear up about this act?) His humiliation of Jesse Jackson. His humiliation of Jocelyn Elders and Lani Gunier. The welfare reform bill that has left thousands of women black, white, yellow, and brown destitute, prompting

Robert Scheer to write in the *San Francisco Chronicle*, "To his everlasting shame as president, Clinton supported and signed welfare legislation that shredded the federal safety net for the poor from which he personally had benefited." (Has Mrs. Clinton shed a tear for these women, or did she oppose her husband's endorsement of this legislation?) His administration saw a high rate of black incarceration as a result of Draconian drug laws that occurred during his regime. He advocated trade agreements that sent thousands of jobs overseas. (Did Mrs. Clinton, with misty eyes, beg him to assess how such trade deals would effect the livelihood of thousands of families, black, white, brown, red and yellow?) He refused to intervene to rescue thousands of Rwandans from genocide. (Did Mrs. Clinton tearfully beseech her husband to intervene on behalf of her African sisters; did Ms. Gloria Steinem, whose word is so influential among millions of white women that she can be credited by some for changing the outcome of a primary, and maybe an election, marshal these forces to place pressure upon Congress to rescue these black women and girls?)

Carl Bernstein, appearing on Air America Radio, January 9, described Clinton's New Hampshire attacks on Obama as "petulant." His behavior demonstrated that regardless of Bill Clinton's admiration for jazz, and black preaching, he and his spouse will go south on a black man whom they perceive as being audacious enough to sass Mrs. Clinton. In this respect, he falls in the tradition of the southern demagogue: grinning with and sharing pot liker and cornbread with black folks, while signifying about them before whites. Though his role models are Martin Luther King Jr. and John F. Kennedy, he has more in common with Georgia's Eugene Talmadge ("The Wild Man from Sugar Creek"), Louisiana's Huey Long, and his brother, Earl, Edwin Edwards, who even hinted that he had black ancestry to gain black votes, Alabama's George Wallace, Texas's Pa Ferguson, and "Kissing Jim" Folsom, who wrote, "You Are My Sunshine." He employs the colorful rhetoric of the southern demagogue, the rustic homilies ("till the last dog dies"), the whiff of corruption.

Having been educated at elite schools where studying the War of the Roses was more important than studying Reconstruction, the undereducated white male punditry and their token white women, failed to detect the racial code phrases that both Clintons and their surrogates sent out—codes that, judging from their responses, infuriated blacks caught immediately. Blacks have been deciphering these hidden messages for four hundred years. They had to, in order to survive.

Gloria Steinem perhaps attended the same schools. Her remark that black men received the vote "fifty years before women," in a *Times* op-ed (January 8, 2008) which some say contributed to Obama's defeat in New Hampshire, ignores the fact that black men were met by white terrorism, including massacres, and economic retaliation when attempting to exercise the franchise. She and her followers, who've spent thousands of hours in graduate school, must have gotten all of their information about Reconstruction from *Gone with the Wind*, where moviegoers are asked to sympathize with a proto-feminist, Scarlett O'Hara, who finally has to fend for herself after years of being doted upon by the unpaid household help. Booker T. Washington, an educator born into slavery, said that young white people had been waited on so that after the war they didn't know how to take care of themselves and Mary Chesnutt, author of *The Civil War Diaries*, and a friend of Confederate president Jefferson Davis's family, said that upper class southern white women were so slave dependent that they were "indolent." Steinem and her followers should read, *Redemption, The Last Battle of the Civil War*," by Nicholas Lemann, which tells the story about how "in 1875, an army of white terrorists in Mississippi led a campaign to 'redeem' their state—to abolish with violence and murder if need be, the newly won civil rights of freed slaves and blacks." Such violence and intimidation was practiced all over the South, sometimes resulting in massacres. One of worst massacres of black men occurred at Colfax, Louisiana, in 1873. Their crime? Attempting to exercise the voting rights awarded to them "fifty years," before white women received theirs. Lemann writes, "Burning Negroes" met "savage and hellish butchery."

> They were all killed, unarmed, at close range, while begging for mercy. Those who tried to escape, were overtaken, mustered in crowds, made to stand around, and, while in every attitude of humiliation and supplication, were shot down and their bodies mangled and hacked to hasten their death or to satiate the hellish malice of their heartless murderers, even after they were dead.
>
> White posses on horseback rode away from the town, looking for Negroes who had fled, so they could kill them.

Elsewhere in the South, during the Confederate Restoration, black politicians, who were given the right to vote, "fifty years before white women" were removed from office by force, many through violence. In Wilmington, North Carolina, black men, who "received the vote fifty years before white women," the subject of Charles Chesnutt's great novel, *The Marrow of Tradition*:

> On Thursday, November 10, 1898, Colonel Alfred Moore Waddell, a Democratic leader in Wilmington, North Carolina mustered a white mob to retaliate for a controversial editorial written by Alexander Manly, editor of the city's black newspaper, the Daily Record. The mob burned the newspaper's office and incited a bloody race riot in the city. By the end of the week, at least fourteen black citizens were dead, and much of the city's black leadership had been banished. This massacre further fueled an ongoing statewide disfranchisement campaign designed to crush black political power. Contemporary white chronicles of the event, such as those printed in the *Raleigh News and Observer* and Wilmington's the *Morning Star,* either blamed the African American community for the violence or justified white actions as necessary to keep the

peace. African American writers produced their own accounts—including fictional examinations—that countered these white supremacist claims and highlighted the heroic struggles of the black community against racist injustice.

Black congressmen, who, as a rule, were better educated than their white colleagues were expelled from Congress.

Either Gloria Steinem hasn't done her homework, or as an ideologue rejects evidence that's a Google away, and the patriarchal corporate old media, which has appointed her the spokesperson for feminism, permits her ignorance to run rampant over the e-mails and blogs of the nation and though this white Oprah might have inspired her followers to march lockstep behind her, a progressive like Cindy Sheehan wasn't convinced. She called Mrs. Clinton's crying act, "phony."

Moreover, some of the suffragettes that she and her followers hail as feminist pioneers were racists. Some even endorsed the lynching of black men. In an early clash between a black and white feminist, antilynching crusader Ida B. Wells opposed the views of Frances Willard, a suffragette pioneer, who advocated lynching.

As the president of one of America's foremost social reform organizations, Frances Willard called for the protection of the purity of white womanhood from threats to morality and safety. In her attempts to bring Southern women into the W.C.T.U., Frances Willard accepted the rape myth and publicly condoned lynching and the color line in the South. Wells argued that as a Christian reformer, Willard should be speaking out against lynching, but instead seemed to support the position of Southerners.

Ms. Willard's point of view is echoed by Susan Brownmiller's implying that Emmett Till got what he deserved, and the rush to judgment on the part of New York feminists whose pressure helped to convict the black and Hispanic kids accused of raping a stockbroker in Central Park. After DNA proved their innocence (the police promised them if they confessed, they could go home), a *Village Voice* reporter asked the response of these feminists to this news; only Susan Brownmiller responded. She said that regardless of the scientific evidence, she still believed that the children, who spent their youth in jail, on the basis of the hysteria generated by Donald Trump, the press, and leading New York feminists, were guilty.

Feminist hero, Elizabeth Cady Stanton, offended Frederick Douglass—an abolitionist woman attempted to prevent his daughter from gaining entrance to a girls' school—when she referred to black men as "sambos." She was an unabashed white supremacist. She said in 1867," [w]ith the black man we have no new element in government, but with the education and elevation of women, we have a power that is to develop the Saxon race into a higher and nobler life."

Steinem should read *Race, Rape, and Lynching* by Sandra Gunning, and Angela Davis's excellent *Women, Culture, & Politics*, which includes a probing examination of racism in the suffragette movement. The *Times* allowed only one black feminist to weigh in on Ms. Steinem's comments about Barack Obama, and how he appealed to white men because they perceive black males as more "masculine" than they, an offensive stereotype, and one that insults the intelligence of white men, and a comment which, with hope, doesn't reflect the depth of "progressive" women's thought.

Do you think that the *Times* would offer Steinem critics like Toni Morrison op-ed space to rebut her? Don't count on it. The criticism of white feminism by black women has been repressed for over one hundred years (*Black Women Abolitionists, A Study in Activism, 1828–1860*, by Shirley J. Yee).

I asked Jill Nelson, author of *Finding Martha's Vineyard, Volunteer Slavery*, and *Sexual Healing*, how she felt about Gloria Steinem's use of a hypothetical black woman to make a point against Obama. She wrote:

I was offended and frankly, surprised, by Gloria Steinem's use of a hypothetical Black woman in her essay supporting Hillary Clinton. I would have liked to think that after all these years struggling in the feminist vineyards, Black women have become more than a hypothetical to be used when white women want to make a point, and a weak one at that, on our backs. It's a device, a distraction, and disingenuous, and fails to hold Hillary Clinton—or for that matter, Barack Obama and the rest of the (male) candidates—responsible for their politics.

On the second day of a convention held at Seneca Falls, 1848, white suffragettes sought to prevent black abolitionist Sojourner Truth from speaking. The scene was described by Frances Dana Gage in Ms. Davis's book:

> "Don't let her speak!" gasped half a dozen in my ear. She moved slowly and solemnly to the front, laid her old bonnet at her feet, and turned her great speaking eyes to me. There was a hissing sound of disapprobation above and below. I rose and announced Sojourner Truth, and begged the audience to keep silence for a few moments.

Many minority feminists, Asian American, Hispanic, Native American and African American, contend that white middle and upper class feminists' insensitivity to the views and issues deemed important to them persists to this day.

Their proof might be Ms. Steinem's lack of concern about how Mrs. Clinton's war votes affect the lives of thousands of women and girls—her brown sisters—in Iraq and Iran. One hundred and fifty thousand Iraqi people have been killed since the American occupation was ordered by patriarchs in Washington, D.C., patriarchs who were responsible for the welfare reform act.

With this in mind, I recently asked Robin Morgan, who was editor of *Ms.* magazine, when I was called the worst misogynist in

America, whether she still held those views. I replied to this accusation that I should be accorded the same respect given to the
men who ran the magazine at the time, Lang Communications. It
was made by Barbara Smith, a black feminist whom I debated on
television and whose bitter comments about the white feminist
movement make mine seem timid. She also criticizes the white
Gay and Lesbian movements. She said that when she tried to join
the Gay and Lesbian March on Washington, the leaders told her to
get lost. That they weren't interested in black issues. That they
wanted to mainstream. About me, she wrote in the *New Republic*
magazine, edited by a Marty Peretz, a man who once said that
black women were "culturally deficient," that my black women
characters weren't positive enough. For running afoul of this feminist "blueprint" for writing that she tried to lay on me, her views
and those like hers were repudiated by Joyce Joyce, a black critic
who deviates from the party line.

I also reminded Ms. Morgan that the *Ms.* editorial staff re-
flected the old plantation model, even though its founder, Gloria
Steinem, said that she's concerned about the progress of black
women. White feminists had the juicy editorial Big House positions, while women of color were the editorial kitchen help as
contributing editors. A few months later, Ms. Morgan resigned as
editor and was replaced by a black woman, but not before taking
some potshots, not at misogynists belonging to her ethnic group,
whose abuse of women has been a guarded secret, according
to feminists belonging to that group, but at Mike Tyson and
Clarence Thomas (incidentally, when the white women who ran
for office as a result of Ms. Anita Hill's testimony against Clarence
Thomas arrived in Congress, they voted with the men).

Robin Morgan had her secretary respond to my recent letter
and from the letter I gather that Ms. Morgan hasn't changed her
mind. I'm a worse misogynist than the men in the Pentagon, and
those who passed Clinton's Welfare Reform bill. I guess that bell
hooks, another black feminist, who won't be invited by the men

who run the *Times* to respond to Ms. Steinem, was right when she wrote in her book, *Outlaw Culture*, that white feminists are harder on black men than white men, but like other black feminists, from the nineteenth century to the present day, her point has been ignored by the mainstream media, who, when they view feminism, and just about every other subject, all they can see is white! (Except when it's crime, athletics, and having babies out of wedlock!)

Feminists are harder on Ishmael Reed, Ralph Ellison (yes, him too), and even James Baldwin, that gentle soul, than on Phillip Roth and Saul Bellow. Harder on Barack Obama than on Bill Clinton, to whom Gloria Steinem, a harsh critic of Clarence Thomas, gave a free pass when he was charged with sexual indiscretions by various women. She said that Bubba was O.K. because when he placed Kathleen Wiley's hand on his penis and she said no, he withdrew it. That when other women said no, he also halted his sexual advances. A letter writer to the *Times* challenged Ms. Steinem's double standard for white and black men:

> Bob Herbert (column, Jan. 29) writes that Gloria Steinem said that even though Paula Jones has filed a sexual harassment suit against President Clinton, Ms. Jones has not claimed that the President had forced himself on her. "He takes no for an answer," Ms. Steinem intones.
>
> Lest we forget, Anita Hill said no to Clarence Thomas. And her accusations nearly derailed his appointment to the Supreme Court.
>
> Patricia Schroeder, the former Congresswoman, did not claim that "somebody may be overstating the case" when Ms. Hill accused Judge Thomas of sexual misconduct, but Ms. Schroeder claims that now in Mr. Herbert's column. Again the left inadvertently exposes its sliding scale of moral indignation.
>
> *RAYMOND BATZ*
> *San Rafael, Calif., Jan. 29, 1998*

Black feminists also charge that white feminists deserted them during the fight against Proposition 209, which ended racial and gender hiring in the state of California, even though Affirmative Action has benefited white women the most!

They charge that white women were missing in action during the fight against the welfare reform bill. It seems that the cheapest form of solidarity with which they can express toward their minority sisters is to join in on the attack on Mike Tyson, Kobe Bryant, and Clarence Thomas and Mr., a character in *The Color Purple*, who, for them, represents all black men.

Though Steinem accuses men of being mean to Mrs. Clinton, she expressed no outrage about surrogate Bill Shaheen painting Obama as a drug dealer, or the innuendo promoted by Senator Bob Kerrey. Senator Bob Kerrey, who, apparently having made up with the Clintons, was recruited to associate Obama with what the Right refers to as "Islamo fascists."

He said, "His name is Barack Hussein Obama, and his father was a Muslim and his paternal grandmother is a Muslim." He added that Obama "spent a little bit of time in a secular madressa."

You'd think that the New School of Social Research would have fired Kerrey when he admitted to committing atrocities in Vietnam. Now this.

All of these attacks must be what Hillary Clinton meant when she warned her opponents, "now the fun begins."

One of the charges made by some black feminists is that white women middle class movement figures embezzle their oppression.

In the *New York Times*, Gloria Steinem's using a hypothetical black woman to do a house cleaning on Obama was what these women must have had in mind. (Phillip Roth does the same thing; uses his black maid characters to denounce black history and black studies: "Missa Roth, dese Black Studies ain't doin' nothin' but worrying folks. Whew!) Her using a black woman as a prop must have annoyed Nobel Laureate Toni Morrison who made blistering comments about Ms.Steinem during an interview conducted by

novelist Cecil Brown and carried in the University of Massachusetts' *Review,* where Ms. Morrison made the harshest comments
about Alice Walker's novel, *The Color Purple,* to date, even harsher
than those made by black feminist Prof. Trudier Harris, who, as a
result of her essay, published in *African American Review,* faced
such a hostile backlash from white feminist scholars that she
stopped commenting about the novel, which has become a sacred
text among white feminists, who are silent about how women are
treated among their ethnic groups. Steinem said that had Obama
been a black woman, he would not have made as much progress as
a presidential candidate and added that white men would prefer
voting for a black man over a white woman because they perceived
black men as being more masculine than they.

I wrote a response to the *Times*:

Jan. 8, 2008
Dear *Times,*

Even Dr. Phil would probably snicker at the level of pop
psychology employed by Gloria Steinem to explain the attrac-
tion of many voters to Senator Barack Obama. For example,
she believes that the preference for a black male candidate over
a white woman by some white males is based upon their
admiration for the black male's "masculine" superiority. "Masculine superiority?" All four of the current heavyweight champions are white as well as last year's MVPs of the NBA were
white men.

Moreover, Ms. Steinem is a long time critic of black men as a
group. She said that the book, *The Color Purple,* in which one
black man commits incest, told "the truth" about black men,
the kind of collective blame that's been used against her ethnic
group since the time of the Romans. . . .

I also made a reference to her abandonment of a tearful Shirley
Chisholm's presidential candidacy after supporting it. If she's so

concerned about the political fate of a black woman's presidential bid, why did she desert Ms. Chisholm in favor of the man?

She also said that "Gender is probably the most restricting force in American life." The fact that when white women received the vote, they experienced little of the violence that accompanied black men being awarded the right to vote, fifty years earlier, suggests that some groups, black men, black women, Hispanics, Asian Americans and Native American Indians face more restrictions than white women, whose college enrollment is far higher even than that of white men. (Steinem said that women are never "Front Runners." How many white women senators are there? How many black?)

Cecil Brown, author of the bestselling *Hey, Dude Where's My Black Studies Department*, wrote:

> I grew up in North Carolina, where I often heard my mother and my aunts speak of the racism of white women against them. Their experience is that of millions of black women who were and are discriminated by white women.
>
> In the Bay Area, where I now live, a professor friend told me, recently, that a white female student told him that she found the use of the expression, "white woman" in his lectures offensive, and asked that he not use it.
>
> Like this student, Ms. Steinem avoids the phrase "white woman," because it historicizes their gender. While she lectures to us about black men, white men, and black women, she can only think of her white women as women.
>
> "It's time to take pride in breaking all the barriers," Ms. Steinem ends her remarks. We have to be able to say: "I'm supporting [Hillary] because she'll be a great president and because she is a woman." But do we dare say that we should support her because she is a white woman?

Our letters were not published, but one written by a black feminist exposed the divide between black and white feminists, one that is rarely aired since white feminists have more access to the media than black ones and in their books report, falsely, a solidarity between them and black women.

Among letter writer Karin Kimbrough's comments:

> As a black woman and a feminist, I find it depressing to see Gloria Steinem set up this tired, false debate as to whether a black man or a white woman is more disadvantaged in national politics.
>
> She cites as evidence that "black men were given the vote a half-century before women of any race were allowed to mark a ballot." So what?
>
> My parents (who are Ms. Steinem's age) vividly recall racism in the Deep South, including barriers to voting as well as the barriers to many other supposedly granted rights like eating in restaurants, staying in hotels and using public facilities. These were all rights white women actively enjoyed.

Camille Paglia also weighed in:

> Hillary's disdain for masculinity fits right into the classic feminazi package, which is why Hillary acts on Gloria Steinem like catnip. Steinem's fawning, gaseous *New York Times* op-ed about her pal Hillary this week speaks volumes about the snobby clubbiness and reactionary sentimentality of the fossilized feminist establishment, which has blessedly fallen off the cultural map in the 21st century. History will judge Steinem and company very severely for their ethically obtuse indifference to the stream of working-class women and female subordinates whom Bill Clinton sexually harassed and abused, enabled by look-the-other-way and trash-the-victims Hillary.

An example of the problems that Barack faces as a result of there being few blacks having jobs in the old media occurred during an appearance by a white woman reporter on *Washington Journal*, January 14. So pro-Hillary was this reporter, Beth Fouhy, that one woman called and said that she thought that this woman was a Hillary spokesperson, before noticing that she was from the Associated Press. Obviously the media have been infiltrated by Steinem's legions.

Scathing comments about the white feminist movement by black feminists are included in *The Feminist Memoir Project*, edited by Rachel Blau DuPlessis and Ann Snitow. *Times* person Maureen Dowd also challenged Steinem, who is hard on black guys, but once confessed in the *Times* that she becomes embarrassed when a male of her ethnic group becomes involved in a scandal. Challenging Steinem's argument that "she is supporting Hillary [because] she had no 'masculinity to prove.'" Dowd wrote, "Empirically speaking, her masculinity is precisely what Hillary has been out to prove in her bid for the White House. What else was voting to enable W. to invade Iraq without even reading the National Intelligence Estimate and backing the White House's bellicosity on Iran but proving her masculinity."

Desperate, when the campaign moved into New Hampshire, the Clintons launched the brass knuckles attack on Obama that commentator William Bennett predicted would happen after Mrs. Clinton was upset in Iowa.

His voice shaking with rage, a livid Bill Clinton said that Obama's positions on the war in Iraq was a "a fairy tale," and that nominating Obama was "a roll of the dice."*

Writing in the *Washington Post*, January 13, Marjorie Valbrun, voiced the reaction of many blacks to Clinton's performance:

> If anyone needed any proof that the mean Clinton machine is alive
> and well in this campaign, all they had to do was watch Bill Clinton

---

*During the week of March 17, 2008, Clinton denied using racist tactics. He said he'd been subjected to a "mugging."

deliver his angry diatribe against Obama in New Hampshire last week just before the primary. His red-faced anger was clear and a little scary, too. It wasn't what he said but how he said it. His tone was contemptuous of his wife's main challenger, whom he described as a political neophyte who for some reason was being granted a honeymoon with the national media.

This is the same Bill Clinton who took on Sister Souljah, a young and, at the time, controversial black rapper who made incendiary racial remarks after the Los Angeles race riots. Many people accused Clinton of using the rapper, and an appearance before Jesse Jackson's Rainbow Coalition, as an opportunity to distance himself from Jackson, the ultimate race man. The move helped reinforce his white moderate bona fides.

On January 13th, when Tim Russert interrogated Mrs. Clinton about whether the attacks on Obama by her, her husband, and her surrogates were racist, she filibustered and dismissed such concerns as the one made by Ms. Valbrum and other blacks in a patronizing manner. She falsely accused Obama of comparing himself with JFK and MLK. He didn't. He invoked their names to make a point about hope. How some hopes, considered false by cynics, can be fulfilled.

So offended by what he considered a black man getting "cocky" with his wife, Clinton blew his top. "Cocky" was the word that nuns educated Bob Herbert used to admonish Obama. Herbert, one of three blacks whom the *Times* views as unlikely to alienate their readership, pointed to an exchange between Obama and Mrs. Clinton. When Mrs. Clinton, during a debate, commented that voters found Obama more "likeable" than Mrs. Clinton, Obama said that Mrs. Clinton was "likeable enough." Obama's reply prompted an Ante Bellum white man, Karl Rove, to refer to Obama as "a smarmy, prissy little guy taking a slap at her." He said that this exchange threw the primary victory to Mrs. Clinton. Notwithstanding the irony of Karl Rove referring to someone as "smarmy," if a reply as mild and innocuous as Obama's leads to his being flogged by Clinton and reprimanded by one of the Establishment's Black tokens, Obama is going to be restricted in his ability to take on the political brawlers and hit persons aligned with Clinton, like Don Imus's buddy, James Carville, a man who sneers at people who live in trailer parks, and who practices a no-holds-barred political strategy.

Both CNN and Carl Bernstein said that Clinton, in the midst of giving this uppity black the required flogging (Clinton's a Jeffersonian. Flogging blacks was Jefferson's idea of recreation), had misrepresented Barack's record. Also, those who commented about Hillary Clinton's tearful breakdown missed the commentary that accompanied this calculated attempt at seeming human and personal, which occurred, as Jesse Jackson Jr. noted, in the *Daily News*, when her advisors told her that she had to appear to be more human. "Why didn't she cry for the victims of Katrina?" he added.

She said that she didn't want to see the country "go backwards," or "spin out of control," the kind of vision of black rule promoted by D.W. Griffith's *Birth of a Nation*, and Neo-Confederate novelist Tom Wolfe's "*A Man In Full*." (Unfortunately for Obama, this was during a week that saw postelection violence in Kenya where Barack's father was born.) Hers was the kind of rhetoric that was used by the Confederates whose rule was restored by Andrew Johnson. Give the black man governing powers and no white woman will be safe. This was Mrs. Clinton's Willie Horton moment.*

Bill Clinton's orchestrating his wife's being more personal was a brilliant stroke. One that might doom Obama's candidacy, but will doom the Democrats' chances to win the 2008 election as well. As a southern demagogue, Bill Clinton calculated that no black man can compete with a white woman's tears, a leftover from Old South thinking. Black men have been lynched as a result of the tears of

---

*The first. Before the Texas primary, she rolled out the old Confederate No-White-Woman-Will-Be-Safe ad, the notorious 3:00 A.M. ad.

white women. While Jesse Helms, another southern demagogue, used a black man's hand in an ad that criticized Affirmative Action, Feminist Bill Clinton, who exploited a young woman, who held him in awe, and cost Al Gore an election, used his wife's tears, so desperate was he to achieve a third term and redeem his being impeached. But judging from angry black callers into C-Span's *The Washington Journal*, the day after the New Hampshire primary, and the following day, and my own non-scientific survey, many blacks finally get it. That they have been snookered by the Clintons. One angry man said that blacks supported Clinton during his marital problems and this is what they get for it. Another man said that he was going to vote for McCain as a way of protesting the Clinton's treatment of Obama. On Jan. 11, an irate black woman called in and said that she had been devoted to the Clinton's since the 1990s, but after his attack on Obama, which she likened to " a knife in my chest," and which she described as "low down." She said that if Hillary were nominated, she'd either "vote Republican, or stay home." Calling into the Journal on Jan. 13, a black woman from Ohio said that many of her friends were upset with the "subliminally racist" campaign against Obama that the Clinton's were conducting. These callers expressed the disgust that thousands of blacks feel about the Clintons dirty tricks campaign against Obama, which included sending out mailers making false statements about his view about abortion, and deceptively attributing another mailer, critical of Obama, to John Edwards. This black backlash against the Clintons provides the Republican Party with a golden opportunity to recruit black voters for McCain, but I doubt whether they will seize upon it. After all, while Clinton might have an office in Harlem, McCain has a black daughter!

A black Ph.D. caller said that he found blacks in a barbershop to be more prescient than he. They said that once whites entered the voting booth, they'd vote for the white candidate no matter what they said to the pollster. Some commentators recalled treatment that Howard Gant and Tom Bradley received. Both were considered

shoo-ins by pollsters for Senator from North Carolina and Governor of California because whites misled pollsters about how they
really intended to vote.

Later in the day of Jan. 8, Larry Sabato of The University of Virginia, appearing on The Chris Matthews Show, commented about a
previous segment during which Dee Dee Meyers and Pat Buchanan
opposed Michael Eric Dyson's argument that white racism was
a factor in Obama's New Hampshire defeat. He said, "I think its
very naïve, given American history, to automatically dismiss the
racial voting theory before it's investigated. There is some evidence
that race is one of several factors involved in this upset." Chris
Matthews, who, apparently, has taken a new look at racism in the
United States, after the Imus debacle, and a couple of other white
commentators, including NBC News political director, Chuck
Todd, agreed with this sentiment that race was a factor. But most
white commentators agreed with Pat Buchanan, and Dee Dee
Meyers, former Clinton press secretary, who said that the difference
between the polling that showed Obama with a double digit lead
and the actual outcome had nothing to with white voters telling
pollsters one thing and voting the opposite. For people like Pat
Buchanan, nothing has to do with race, unless he can use race to stir
up votes in one of his campaigns.

Predictably, the *New York Times* also followed the line that the
racial attitudes of whites had nothing to do with Obama's narrow
defeat in New Hampshire, not surprising since the line of the
New York Times, on the opinion page and elsewhere, is that we
have entered a "post race" period.

Such is the rage of blacks against the Clintons after Iowa and
New Hampshire that if Hillary Clinton is nominated, she will not
be elected president. Obama and his "Joshua" generation will in-
herit a party that has lost its way. This would be a new development
for the progressive movement since, from the abolitionists to the
progressive movements of the twentieth century, black progressives
were the followers and not the leaders. When Frederick Douglass,

Richard Wright, and Ralph Ellison got out of line, the progressives replaced them with another more obedient black spokesperson. After he broke with his progressive sponsors, Richard Wright was assaulted (*The God That Failed* by Koestler, Silone, Wright).

An uninformed *Times* op-ed writer, a CMD, said that Obama had gotten farther toward the nomination than any other black. Not true. When Jesse Jackson won the Michigan primary, there was an eruption of panic among the party elite. Ben Wattenberg and others were brought in to smear Jackson with the charge of anti-Semitism and out of this emergency arose the white conservative wing of the party, the Democratic Leadership Council, whose founder, Al From, still brags about how he put black people in their place. Clinton was the DLC's candidate for president.

The reason for the 1960s rift between the Black Power people and the New Left was because when the black nationalists arrived at Freedom Summer, the northeastern liberals were giving orders, while the blacks were taking the risks. The black nationalists took control of the movement and dragged Stokely Carmichael, who was devoted to nonviolence, kicking and screaming into their ranks, and into their philosophy of armed self-defense, according to Askia Toure, whom Mary Snow in her book, *Freedom Summer*, accuses of purging the northern liberals from SNCC. The progressive white women left SNCC, but not before borrowing the SNCC manifesto and using it as it their own, according to Snow. They changed the pronouns and this became the beginning of the modern feminist movement. The reason that much of the feminist movement's fire is aimed at the brothers is because some of these women went away mad (*Going South* by Debra L. Schultz). Based upon Stokely Carmichael's remark that the position of women in SNCC was "prone," they accused the black men in SNCC of misogyny. According to black women, who were members of SNCC, the white feminists, led by Casey Hayden, took Carmichael's comments out of context. Their views about their clashes with white feminism are printed in *The Trouble Between Us* by Winifred

Breines, a book ignored by Mark Leibovich, writing in the *New York Times*, January 13, 2001. He repeated the charge about Carmichael made by white feminists without asking black feminists what they thought. Typical of a member of the Old Media, which takes its cues from those whom the patriarchy has appointed to lead the movement.

If Cynthia McKinney is nominated for president by the Green Party, a test for corporate feminists like Gloria Steinem, so concerned about the lack of opportunities for their black sisters, black voters will flock to McKinney by the thousands, which might tip the balance if the contest is close between Mrs. Clinton and her Republican opponent. Others will leave the line for president on the ballot, blank. This rage against the Clintons will go unnoticed by the segregated old corporate media, which has more information about the landscape of Mars than trends in the Black, Asian American and Hispanic communities. They rely upon their handful of colored mind doubles, who tell them what they want to hear.

Modern day Indian scouts. When they're not available, all white panels instruct each other about who is a racist and who is not, how black people feel, how they are going to vote, continuing what some blacks regard as the white intellectual occupation of the black experience, an attitude that dates all the way back to a letter written by Martin Delaney to Frederick Douglass, 1863, in which he complained about the favorable treatment Douglass gave to Harriet Beecher Stowe's book, *Uncle Tom's Cabin*, while ignoring his *Blake, or the Huts of America, 1859.* "She can not speak for us," he wrote.

Clinton will still receive some support from some black democratic loyalists, and celebrities, although some of them are beginning to distance themselves from the couple after Iowa and New Hampshire smears against Obama, but a large number of black people, who helped elect Clinton, twice, will defect.

Representative James E. Clyburn, a black Congressman from South Carolina, told the *New York Times* (January 11, 2008) that "he may abandon his neutral stance in his state's primary, based in part on comments by Senator Hillary Rodman Clinton about President Lyndon B. Johnson and the Rev. Dr. Martin Luther King, Jr." He and other blacks interpreted Hillary Clinton's remark about the two as implying that Johnson did more for the cause of Civil Rights than King, who, like Obama, made great speeches.

Also one wonders whether Henry Louis Gate's Jr., media appointed leader of the Talented Tenth (a phrase that W.E.B. DuBois used to appoint the black elite as the true leaders of the Negro masses, an insult to grassroots leaders like Fannie Lou Hammer), will follow suit. While smearing a number of black male writers as misogynists, in the *Times* and elsewhere, when Bill Clinton was caught with his pants down, Gates Jr. said. We will "go to the wall for this president."

Are the Clintons new in a South where husbands like George Wallace extended their power by getting their wives elected? Hardly. Take the Fergusons:

> In Texas there was a couple called the Fergusons, affectionately called "Ma and Pa Ferguson."
>
> Miriam Ferguson was a quiet, private person who preferred to stay home in her big house in Temple, Texas, and take care of her husband, raise her two daughters, and tend to her flower garden.
>
> But in 1923 she was elected governor of Texas, the first woman governor elected in the United States.
>
> Her husband, Jim Ferguson, served two terms as governor, but during his second term he was impeached, which meant he could not run again for public office. So Miriam agreed to run to clear his name and restore the family's honor.
>
> She served two terms as governor: from 1925 to 1927 and from 1933 to 1935. She and her husband became known as "Ma" and "Pa" Ferguson. Her campaign slogan was, "Two Governors for the Price of One."*

---

*www.tamu.edu/upress/BOOKS/2006/altermiriam.htm.

List of First Publications

"Assisted Homicide in Oakland." *Playboy*, December 2007.

"Back to the '30s?" *Playboy*, September 2005.

"Black Philanthropy." *Green Magazine*, April-May 2006.

"Bubba from Another Planet." The *Baltimore Sun,* April 19, 1998.

"Charles Chesnutt." *Harlem Moon,* 2005.

"Color-Blind Coverage?" The *San Francisco Chronicle*, September 9, 2005.

"The Colored Mind Doubles." *CounterPunch*, April 24, 2007.

"Jefferson Davis: Hurrah for Jeff Davis?" In *American Monsters: 44 Rats, Blackhats, and Plutocrats*. New York: Thunder's Mouth Press, 2004.

"I Was a Victim of Unfair Lending Practices." The *New York Times*, January, 16, 2003.

"Imus." *CounterPunch*, April 24, 2007.

"The Last Days of Black Harlem." *Matador,* Spring 2007.

"Ma and Pa Clinton Flog Uppity Black Man." *CounterPunch,* January 14, 2008.

"Miles Davis." In *The Show I'll Never Forget.* New York: Da Capo Press, 2007.

"MJ, Kobe, and Ota Benga." *Black Renaissance Magazine,* Spring-Summer 2004.

"The Patriot Act of the 18th Century." *Time,* July 5, 2004.

A Playwright of the Blues. New York: Theater Communications Group, 2007.

"Showing White Students Some Love." *Playboy,* December 2006.

"Sneddon's Victory." The *Oakland Tribune,* June 2005.

"Sonny Rollins." In *The Vibe Q: Raw and Uncut.* Kensington, 2007.